# THE HARD ROAD
## to the
# SOFTER SIDE

# THE HARD ROAD
## to the
# SOFTER SIDE

LESSONS FROM THE
TRANSFORMATION
OF SEARS

## Arthur C. Martinez

*with*

*Charles Madigan*

Crown Business
New York

Published by Crown Business, New York, New York.
Member of the Crown Publishing Group.

Random House, Inc. New York, Toronto, London, Sydney, Auckland
www.randomhouse.com

CROWN BUSINESS and colophon are trademarks of Random House, Inc.

Printed in the United States of America

*Design by Susan Maksuta*

Library of Congress Cataloging-in-Publication Data

Martinez, Arthur C., 1939–
The hard road to the softer side: lessons from the transformation of Sears / Arthur C. Martinez with Charles Madigan.—1st ed.
          p.     cm.
1. Sears, Roebuck and Company—Management.   2. Corporate turnarounds—United States—Case studies.   I. Madigan, Charles.   II. Title.
HF5467.S4 M37   2001
658.1'6—dc21
98-024237

ISBN 0-8129-2960-8

10 9 8 7 6 5 4 3 2 1

First Edition

*To Liz, Lauren, and Gregory*

# CONTENTS

Contents

# CHAPTER I

# Sears' History:
# The Bad and the Brilliant

In THE LIFE of every individual and in the life of every corporation there is a defining moment. The thinking, the abstraction of planning, melts away, the fog lifts, the air clarifies, and under a bright sun and fresh sky, what must be done takes on a stunning, undeniable shape. It is rare that an event of that nature would happen in the life of a corporation and in the life of an individual at the same time.

My moment, and Sears' moment, too, came on a company jet with a handful of Sears executives heading home from a trip to Mexico to review the company's business there. It was early December 1992. I had been on the Sears team for only three months. I had been brought in to revive the Sears retail business, its merchandising group, and potentially to run the whole company. (I'll tell you later about the unusual journey that carried me to Sears, a trip that led some to conclude I had lost my mind.)

My first weeks on the job had been real eye-openers.

I dove deep into this treasure of a company and found layer upon layer of trouble, a hemorrhaging of red ink, indecision about what to do, and an almost palpable anxiety.

My most formidable adversary, and ultimately my strongest ally, would be culture, a century of culture and the mammoth bureaucracy it had created. Bureaucracy was so deeply developed and planted at Sears that it seemed for all the world as though the place had been designed by one of those obsessive Soviet functionaries at mid-century. At the same time, a lot of it took on the earmarks of the classic Potemkin village, with fresh paint and flowers on the outside masking an operation that was close to collapse. The enemy, I knew from the outset, was us. The challenge would be to find what was solid, dependable, even brilliant inside of this company and use it to create an entirely new Sears.

That had been my message and my mantra since the day I arrived at Sears: Cultural transformation must always be at the top of the agenda at Sears. The reason for that was the same on the day I left as it was on the day I first walked in.

Sears was in love with its past and entrapped by it at the same time.

## Trapped in the Amber of Its Own History

These kinds of things happen to institutions all the time. They keep playing out yesterday's agenda without recognizing that the world has changed and that it continues to change every minute of every day. They ride their old horses onto a modern battlefield, then puzzle about why they are losing a war to an enemy who has tanks and machine guns.

The great irony was that Sears had been a model for change from the very beginning, from its huge catalog operation to its shift to retail stores, a wrenching struggle that transformed the nature of the company, and the nature of the American retailing industry at the same time. Even as I was leaving in the fall of 2000, Sears was embarking on another in its long string of adventures, this time moving onto the Internet, finding a new way to reach customers and meet their needs.

At the same time, the company I walked into in 1992 was becoming the poster child of the business stagnation movement. It was as though Sears had forgotten the strongest parts of its own history, the most important lessons it had learned in decades of serving the American consumer.

Sears' roots were more than a century deep. The company had earned a strong and important place in American history. It could not be viewed as just another big business slipping off track, or as an ailing dinosaur waiting for time to bleach it into whitened bones. If the company died, a big piece of history would die with it, along with the dreams of thousands upon thousands of customers, employees, and investors everywhere.

I was the outsider on that flight from Mexico, but I was beginning to know what had gone wrong, and I had a strong sense of where we had to go to fix it. It was going to be a tough, long march, a struggle to save the part of Sears history that was golden and shed the parts that were locking the company in a bad place. This would be a battle with a vast bureaucracy and a deep, troubled culture and everything that entails. I am not a shy man, but I knew the scope of the challenge I was facing. No one had ever revived a retailing business of this size—or, for that matter, just about any other business of this size.

## Resistance to Change

I didn't know then that I would have to face that challenge twice during my eight years at Sears, that the same demons that caused problems for Sears the first time around were waiting on the sidelines, even as we were racking up strong numbers and basking in the glory of a successful transformation.

The basking, I came to understand, was one of the problems at Sears. There was, and there remained, a strong institutional tendency to sit back and conclude that all the problems were solved, that the retailing heroes had fixed it once and for all.

That was never the case. Sears was an institution that needed to be pushed, prodded, or shaken at least once a day. The story was in the numbers.

In 1992, Sears had sales of more than $50 billion in some 800 stores and 2,000 other locations around the nation. It was an insurance company, a real estate company, a banker, an investment company. It wound up losing $3.9 billion in that awful year.

It was a humbling experience, but, apparently, not humbling enough. Even that level of loss was not enough to shake the company to its foundation and force it onto a different track.

Ed Brennan, chief executive officer at the time and a Searsman to his very soul, the last in a long line of Searsmen in his family, was on the jet, along with a few other Sears veterans and financial people who had been wrestling with the company's problems for years. Sears was lost in the sea of the marketplace, clinging to its remarkable history the way a shipwrecked sailor clings to the one piece of oak that keeps him from drowning. The customers who had made Sears a marketplace legend were abandoning us. The stores were in bad shape, capital starved and looking it.

Our competitors were coming from all sides. Home Depot and Wal-Mart were gobbling up market share. In malls all over America, many of them there because Sears put them there by deciding on its location a long time ago, competitors large and small were stealing our customers. They were offering state-of-the-art retailing to enlivened shoppers who had found so many new places to spend money that we simply weren't competing anymore.

We had made embarrassing mistakes. We were struggling with the fallout of an auto store fraud scandal on the West Coast. A whole decade of internal tinkering had failed to address the company's problems in the marketplace. The institution was turning almost completely inward, focusing on itself instead of its customers and its competition, a problem I would struggle with for eight years. My challenge was to take that declining retail business and revive it: to find out what was wrong, find a new customer, and strengthen what Sears had to sell to bring the place into the black again.

That flight from Mexico was all about the kinds of changes that had to happen if we were to save Sears from its competitors and, in a very real way, to save it from itself. That was one of the deepest problems at Sears, a culture that simply would not change, that kept looking to the past for solutions to problems that were brand new. As the outsider, I had very bad news to deliver. I had looked at the Sears universe from every conceivable angle, and what I had concluded was that there was trouble at its heart. We had to invent a new Sears that would compete with the best, that would draw back its customers, enliven its employees, and reward its shareholders once again.

But before we could do that, we had to fix what was broken at the heart of Sears. In Ed Brennan, I was facing a man whose very life was defined by this company, the embodiment of all those tall, handsome Searsmen who had built the institution over a century. I had to convince him that if we were to save Sears and bring it back to health, we had to kill the one part of Sears that almost everyone could identify.

The Sears catalog was a big part of the problem. It was 108 years old, employed 50,000 full- and part-time workers, and, along with its mall stores, was the most familiar part of Sears' history. On billions of dollars in annual revenue, it had lost $150 million in each of the past seven years.

I delivered the news.

Ed excused himself for a moment to go to the rest room. When he returned, it seemed to me as though there were tears in his eyes. But he knew we were right about this, that it took an outsider to make and carry out this kind of decision.

I had done my homework before I joined Sears. I knew these were honorable, hardworking people who had a strong measure of pride in the institution. But I was waiting for an important answer. It would determine whether I would have the freedom I needed to begin working on a vast transformation, a metamorphosis so important that it would determine the future of the company.

Ed gulped hard.

And then he agreed.

At that instant, a new Sears was born, not yet a healthy baby, but, I believed, a baby with a brilliant future. This was the decision that paved the way for one of the most remarkable turnarounds in American business history. All we had to do was mother it back into the marketplace, educate it, and transform it. We had to change its culture, change its way of doing business, change the very way it thought of itself.

I knew it was going to be hard.

I didn't know how hard.

I would be a fool to suggest that Sears is done with this process, that I walked away from the CEO's office leaving the Perfect American Corporation in my wake. The picture looks better now (we had the best year in our history in 2000), but if you were reading the headlines only a few years ago, you might have thought we were headed for a decline as deep as the one I found in 1992.

## A Revival That Was Widely Doubted

There was widespread doubt about the sticking power of the first turnaround. In 1997 and 1998, we were in deep trouble with the federal government (and state governments just about everywhere, too) because of the bankruptcy reaffirmation problems. We plummeted from the media heights, no longer viewed as the hottest story in retailing. We got into deep credit trouble when personal bankruptcy became the favorite pathway for solving debt problems in 1997 and 1998. We built a first-rate transformation team full of highly attractive executives, the kind of people outsiders are always eager to steal away, and steal them they did.

And we fell prey, once again, to Sears' old nemesis, that assumption that you only have to do it right once and that everything will be fixed and humming along forever after. Then we reached down and grabbed our bootstraps and started pulling hard, fixing the problems one at a time, just as we had between 1992 and 1996.

I could spend all of my time thinking about nothing but trouble, because handling trouble is one of the unavoidable realities of being in business today. In fact, I believe that every business is in trouble, but some know it and some don't. But to focus only on trouble, I would have to overlook that remarkable transformation the first time around, our successful climb back into healthy numbers the second time around, and the contributions of thousands and thousands of people, employees and customers alike.

# The Importance of "We"

"We" is the most significant word in this book.

Take Sears out of America and what is lost? A huge chapter in business history, a million wonderful stories, fortunes made, blown, and made again, a golden contract with generations of Americans who shopped there. Sears was the vehicle that an emerging middle class turned to for its belongings, for the material comforts that would define quality of life.

It was and is simply that important. Keeping Sears alive was as much of an obligation to history as it was an obligation to the marketplace. Because of that, it would be convenient to anoint myself America's double turnaround king and to spend a lot of time telling everyone exactly what I did to take what is undeniably the most important company in the nation's business history and bring it back to life.

But it didn't happen that way.

The credit must go first to the employees of Sears and second to the only collection of people who could possibly be more important to the fortunes of the company: its customers. It is not as though we forced them to come back. It would be more accurate to say that we invited them back into our stores by creating a good place for them to shop and by telling them how and why they were important to us. The loyalty and the interest and some of the trust Sears had earned across generations were still there.

Weld those two factors together—the loyalty of Sears' customers and the diligence of all of the Sears people who answered the call for transformation—and you have the keys to the Sears turnaround the first time, when we finally got marketplace traction in 1993 and 1994 and put the company $1 billion into the black ink again.

The second time around was harder.

If our victory in the first transformation was a victory over the Sears of the past, our challenge in the second turnaround was dealing with the present, with the Sears tendency to sit back, look at the landscape from the high ground of some good numbers, and conclude we had figured it all out.

In both cases, the same institutional forces were at work, the biggest one being the tendency to coast, to think yesterday's numbers dictate tomorrow's fortunes. In the modern retailing environment, that is just not true.

Today's numbers describe yesterday's success, and they have to be built every single day. If you are not thinking about how you are going to win tomorrow, you will most certainly lose. Our own transformation the first time around and the decline that followed it is strong evidence of that reality.

I am going to tell you in this book exactly how those revivals occurred, but you should know there are thousands of people, thousands of voices, behind the Sears story, from the sales staff who first approach you in our stores right up to the executives who reported to me at the company's headquarters in Hoffman Estates, Illinois.

Sears produced its own legend over a century in the marketplace and the object lessons it created during its transformation are equally significant. They are all about people, products, places, and strategy, along with everyone's need to have some sense of mission that carries them into battle every day.

## The Sears Lesson Book

The first and most important lesson is obvious to anyone who has followed Sears' modern history over the past nine years. It should be underlined in brilliant colors and displayed someplace where everyone in the world of business can see it and think about it all day long.

### The Customer Is Everything

Lose that connection and you lose your business. Cherish it and understand it and nurture it because it is motivation, ammunition, and sustenance all wrapped into one.

## Your Employees Are Golden

Reward them for brilliant performance. Work hard to keep them on track. Recognize that their education is not an expenditure but an investment. Listen to them because they are generally closest to the customer and her needs. Give them ownership of their business, of their own destiny.

## Know Your Enemy

It is not sufficient to know merely who that enemy is. Know how it thinks and operates and how it affects the market. Know its history and its strategy. Don't stop with an understanding of what it did yesterday. Work hard to know what it will be doing for an extended collection of tomorrows and wage your battles there. Assume that your competition is out to crush you and be sophisticated about returning that dark favor in kind.

## Know the History That Created Your Company

Understand it well enough to embrace what has great value and to replace what is shopworn, damaging, or out of date. Recognize the role that culture plays in the marketplace, too. If trust has been one of the legacies of long experience with customers, do everything to make it grow and shed anything that undermines it.

## Time Is Not Your Friend

In such a competitive, changing marketplace, time is not your friend. If transformation of a company is like a highway, it must be viewed as a construction project that will never end. The destination may well always be satisfied customers and shareholder value, but the direction it takes to get to those locations is constantly changing, and you must be open to that challenge if you are to reach your goal.

✦

I didn't just make all of this up.

These lessons, and many more that constantly presented themselves as Sears struggled to expand its influence in the marketplace, have been delivered by the tough experiences of the eight years that passed after I walked into Sears in 1992. But they are core subjects and very much at the heart of what has happened to everyone who worked so hard as Sears brought itself back into the world of the living, indeed, the thriving.

There is plenty of devil in the details that follow.

I will tell you about my mistakes, my small and not so small triumphs, and about the frustrations and glories of having your hands on the tiller of one of the greatest institutions in American business history.

But first I have to tell you how that great old ship got so close to the rocks and what we did to achieve the sharp change in course that saved Sears the first time around.

# How Sears Lost Its Customers

Customers don't generally just walk away unless they have someplace compelling to go to shop. When you are a company with a history, and with customer loyalty as strong as Sears', you have to help them leave. Failing to pay attention to them is one way. Ignoring your competitors is another. Focusing almost all of your energy on the construction of a magnificent, frustrating bureaucracy is the third.

It is rare that all three of those elements come together in one place. But that is what had happened at Sears, and very much what I found when I arrived in 1992. The company was not literally headed for the block, but that was one of the deep and abiding fears that began to form for me once I realized the depths of the company's problems and developed an awareness of how it got into such deep trouble.

What troubled me so deeply was my sense of what would be lost.

Think for a moment about what was at stake.

In the first part of the twentieth century, Sears delivered thousands of ready-to-build houses to construction sites all over the nation. How do you measure the value in that part of the American dream? Many of those homes still sit on their foundations, have been lovingly kept and restored, and are viewed as parts of our national treasure. People who had only been able to rent suddenly found themselves able to own their own solid piece of the American dream.

And that was just one part of the role it had played.

# Merchant to a Growing America

Sears could proudly and honestly say that it had whatever a growing America wanted and needed. Early in its century-long history, when it was still a catalog company, it sold civilization on the High Plains, sophistication to the working class, comforts to the farm wife, even treadmills so the family farm dog could be put to more productive use running a first-generation washing machine.

It struggled from the very beginning of the twentieth century with the issue of credit for its customers. How much risk should a company carry in its quest for new customers? How do you sell to one farmer who gets a check for wheat once a year and to another farmer who has regular income because he sells milk every day and gets a check once a month?

It found its solution. If the piano was to be an essential piece of musical furniture in every parlor, then Sears would sell pianos to its customers on terms: $5 a month, every month, for three years. From its catalog inception well into the first half of the twentieth century, it was putting pianos in parlors everywhere.

Consider the realities of life on the American plains in the 1890s.

Sears brought lace and bows and Sunday church hats into mundane lives, good suits and tools that would last forever, guitars, zithers, and toys that made Christmas dreams come true. Later on, it delivered baseball bats and gloves endorsed by Ted Williams.

It bonded with entire generations of buyers, simply by being there and being dependable, the biggest and best catalog of them all in the beginning and, when America shifted to wheels and started driving everywhere, the biggest and best retail stores.

Your town knew from World War II onward that it had finally arrived when Sears opened a store, a sign that a community had reached a mystical demographic maturity because serious retailing attention was being paid. These were not small decisions for Sears and represented marketing and survey sophistication long before those disciplines became central weapons in the retailing armory.

Still later, when downtowns yielded to suburban shopping centers, Sears was the seed corn.

Where Sears planted itself at mid-century, shopping malls grew.

And where shopping malls grew, Sears planted itself.

Its customers were everywhere.

As it expanded, it created its own marvelous marketplace culture. Sears buyers were legendary for their independence and creativity. Old Sears, the Sears that was triumphant in the explosive economy that followed World War II, was a model of marketplace democracy. Its people knew how to ignore orders from headquarters when they made no sense, and they had the confidence to take risks and reap huge rewards. Most important, they knew the people who shopped in their stores, they knew their communities, and what they wanted.

They were customer-centric long before that phrase worked its way into business school rhetoric.

Sears was in place to serve the needs of a mobile America because it recognized in the mid-1920s that the nation had changed, that it would someday be driving to shop.

The soldiers and sailors who came home from the war started families that would fuel the baby boom generation, and Sears became part of that culture, too. Every August, the ritual included a stop at Sears for polo shirts and slacks and skirts and blouses and book bags.

In the North, when snow threatened, customers came to Sears for shovels. In the South, it was lawn mowers and supplies for the perfect garden. People filled their homes with Sears furniture and cooked on Kenmore stoves.

Weekend craftsmen wanted Craftsman tools. How much of America has been constructed over the last six decades by Craftsman tools? How many mechanics opened their red tool boxes to display rack upon rack of well-kept, perfectly maintained wrenches and pliers and screwdrivers, all of them from Sears and all of them guaranteed for life?

If a customer needed it, Sears would be happy to sell it to them. It was a safe shopping assumption that the price would be right, the product would be solid, and the sales staff would be professional and ready to help. All of that made Sears a marketplace marvel and such a strong company that it was the envy of all other businesses at mid-century.

## Abandoning the Customer

What happened?

It is a complicated story with a simple summary: We forgot about our customers. Look at the 1970s and 1980s, and you can see the problem.

We became completely self-absorbed, a huge company that was much more interested in its own administration, on rule making and what was happening inside, than in what was happening in the marketplace. It was almost as though Sears had wrapped itself up in a blanket woven from its own history. Instead of looking intently out of the windows of its own businesses to see what was happening in the real world, it spent its time and energy looking into the mirror.

This problem was compounded as the numbers got worse and worse and the competition—competition focused almost totally on the marketplace and what it wanted—became more intense. The Kmarts, the Wal-Marts, the Home Depots, an entire spectrum of retail shopping spots swept in to fill the gap created by Sears' inability to focus on its customers.

We forgot that our customers needed us for themselves and for their families, for their clothing, appliances, tools, the thousands of other small and large things they wanted and for services to bring some comfort into their lives. We missed the fact that their lives and their families were changing, that they were making different kinds of decisions about money and how it is spent.

We forgot about watching how our competition was developing, too, about the way their stores looked and felt. We forgot that the American shopper had so many new options that the old formulas, the standards we had used to measure our success, the way we looked and felt in the marketplace, just weren't enough anymore. We forgot that the battle for their affections, their interests, and their money was constant and intense. That played out in loss of market share to a whole collection of challengers who were sleek, aggressive, and eager to turn change in the marketplace into an asset.

Imitation was the sincerest form of flattery at first. Wherever there was a Sears store in the 1970s, it seemed, a Kmart store slipped in. Later it would be a Wal-Mart store, or a Home Depot, or a Circuit City. Because we weren't watching the marketplace, they snatched up our disgruntled customers. It is a simple, painful lesson. If you don't move to meet the needs of your customers, someone else will. Thinking you are simply too big to have to deal with competition is a fatal assumption. It might not be able to bump you off overnight, but as time passes, you will bleed a bit, then a little more, then a little more, then die the death of a thousand cuts.

Business in America, any business, is a war fought every day over the loyalties of customers who are always eager to make decisions about where they will shop. There was a time when Sears was not only number one, but numbers two, three, four, and five, in retail sales, too, because its five marketing regions were so robust. That was in the 1950s, before our competitors moved so aggressively to win customers. Shoppers don't make their decisions and commitments over the long term. They vote each day whether you have done well, whether you have presented them with the abundance they demand, whether you have pleased and welcomed them. If you have slipped in any category, you have given them the only reason they need to take their business elsewhere.

Open your business history to any page in the book and you can find the same phenomenon playing out. Big Blue—IBM—was absolutely unbeatable until a whole field of competitors moved rapidly into the computer business. Apple was born in marketplace heroics and got so big so fast it stopped listening and became painfully vulnerable. General Motors was king of the hill when chrome-heavy behemoths reigned until astute, aggressive competitors from Japan presented better and more efficient imports. Pick your industry. Lose contact with what the customer wants and you lose your business to people who are paying closer attention at your expense.

That is Sears' story.

## A Monument to Bureaucracy

Instead of listening to those customers, we paid attention to ourselves and to the magnificent bureaucracy we had constructed. What more need anyone say about Sears than that, at the most critical point in its history, when its relationship with customers was fractured and about to shatter, it wasted its energy and its money constructing the world's largest office building, a second-place monument today to its own arrogance?

This building was constructed in downtown Chicago on the assumption that nothing else would ever change and that Sears would just keep on getting bigger and bigger and bigger. Sears was already starting its slide when the building was completed in 1973, the product of internal squabbling and empire building all over the company. By 1983, the idea that this huge black symbol would hold 13,000 headquarters employees by the turn of the century was already out of date. Whole floors allotted to computer operations were constructed on the assumption that computers would always be big, hot machines. The fact that they were shrinking every day left vast areas of empty space. Downsizing took care of the head count.

Many of the people who worked in the tower hated it because it so complicated their lives, adding an internal commute to their desks to the commute they were already making to get downtown. True, the old headquarters on Chicago's West Side had become a dangerous place and required an army of Sears police just to protect people coming to and from work. But at least in the old headquarters people could turn out their own lights. Computers did that kind of work in the new building. They provided an excellent, high-tech reason not to care about the place because the people who worked there played almost no role in its operation.

Most important, the tower stands today as a symbol of what went wrong. It was all about arrogance and empire, and not at all about customers. There was a hidden assumption behind the building that technology would some-how be able to manage Sears' future, that the company would march on because it had been marching for so long.

## The Price for Ignoring Competition

Relationships with customers are exceedingly fragile and precious, and that was a point the tower builders had missed. Home Depot was just being born in this era, and it would ultimately bite into Sears' market share the way a shark chomps on wounded prey. But no one was willing to recognize it at the time. It was one of the strongest contenders among the superstores when I arrived at Sears in 1992, but no one had anticipated what its birth and devel-opment would mean.

The belief was that Sears was just too big, too powerful, to fail. I have a list in my mind of other retail companies over time that succumbed to failure and consolidation. They are the modern era's business tombstones: Montgomery Ward, W. T. Grant, Gimbel Brothers, Polk Brothers, Zayre's, Madigan's, Alexander's. That list is bordered in black crepe. Right beside it is another list—R. H. Macy, Newmark & Lewis, Carter Hawley Hale, Saxon Home Centers, Best Products, Paul Harris, Garfinkel's—all of them in bankruptcy court. The list doesn't stop there. Steel companies, railroad companies, banks, airlines. Pick a business or an industry and there are many examples of what happens when an institution thinks it is too big to fail, when it forgets about the primacy of its customers in the business formula.

I can tell you now that this self-centered attitude had become such a seri-ous problem that, despite our size and our history, we were in danger of losing everything. You cannot know how much of a transformation this has been without recognizing that key point.

Sears was so far off course as the 1990s dawned that it was heading for a collapse. Look at its competition and look at its own position in the market-place. It had among the highest operating costs in retailing with a declining base of customers. All of the numbers on all of the charts were headed in the wrong direction. There was no plan to recoup the loss and build for the future.

It's easy to think that rebuilding a company is as simple as finding a strat-egy and putting it into place, hiring some new executives, sprucing up the stores, then sitting back and counting increased revenues. What we discov-ered, basically from looking at how we had gotten into such deep trouble in the first place, was that nothing will work for long that does not put the cus-tomer first.

Looking back, that is an amazingly simple formula for a company that amounts to a huge collection of shopkeepers and buyers. That is what Sears is, after all—shopkeepers and buyers.

Retailers.

We all have the same nightmare. Everything is in place, the sales staff is on the floor, the goods are well-displayed and competitively priced, the ad campaigns have run, and it's opening time on a bright Monday morning.

You throw open the doors and prepare for that onslaught of customers, with their scent of profits and success and promise, and no one shows up.

That was where Sears was headed a decade ago, and I can tell you now, after a lot of work, a lot of change, and a good deal of success, that I know why. It was because we had forgotten that our contract was with the people who only wanted to come and buy.

To get them back and bring the company back to good health, we had to seek out a mission, create an atmosphere of productive change for our employees, and send messages to the world of investment that we presented a stunning opportunity for shareholders.

But what we had when I arrived was a great history, a disappointing present, and the uncomfortable prospect of a short, dismal future.

# Rising from the Ashes

Given those conditions, it is not surprising to me that a figure from mythology presented itself. It would become a metaphor for what we would try to achieve. What was most amazing about the story of the Phoenix was that the mythical bird could only re-create itself from its own ashes after it had been consumed by fire.

It took 500 years.

It did not take long for the feeling to settle on me. We had an enormous job to do and we would not have 500 years to create our own Phoenix. We would not have 500 weeks. We would not have 500 days. In fact, we would not have much time at all in which to get the job done. Remember those lists of dead retailers and shopkeepers in bankruptcy?

Undoubtedly, they thought they had time.

The very idea of the Phoenix would play an important role in the Sears revivals. We reached out and took this bird from mythology as the symbol of what we wanted to become. I organized my management teams around the concept and gave them something graceful, significant, and almost mystical as a goal. It fit the theme perfectly.

We needed some fire and some magic to revive this great institution.

When I started working on September 1, 1992, all we seemed to have in abundance was ashes.

There were many surprises over eight years, trouble I didn't know existed when I came on board, a history that had been deeply hidden inside this huge company. There were some stunning good surprises, too, the best being the discovery of people who love this business. That is what helped create the "we" that saved Sears, that helped it rise like a Phoenix from its own ashes.

That may be the most important requirement of them all: You have to have passion for the business and its customers, for the numbers it creates every day, for the messages it sends and the value it represents. This business is full of frustration, sometimes frightening, and sometimes very rewarding,

19

but the passion for it is what carries the people who succeed at it. If that is missing, you are in the wrong business.

## Face to Face with Sears Culture

It took a while to find that passion inside of Sears.

It wasn't there on that first day when I came to meet the management team. Although it wasn't my first step into the culture of Sears management, this was my formal introduction, on August 11, 1992. I was coming in as chairman and chief executive officer of Sears Merchandise Group.

The company was already in the process of making decisions to spin off all of those interests acquired over the years that were not directly connected to retailing. That would be complicated and delicate, but it was under way before I arrived and I wasn't part of the discussion. Allstate and Sears had become like bread and butter in the mind of the consumer, but the spin-off was already planned. Those things were all about the past. I was all about what Sears was to become in the future. I don't think people realized at that point what that would mean.

I didn't, although I meant to find out as quickly as possible.

Brennan was to introduce me to the management team. They didn't really know me, although they knew that I had been vice chairman at Saks Fifth Avenue, the upscale, New York–based retailer. Who was this "Ax from Saks? Does anybody know where he is coming from? Does anybody know who he is?"

That is one measure of how isolated the place was. I don't want to paint myself as the most public character in the history of retail, but someone in the business would have to be pretty oblivious not to know who Arthur C. Martinez was and what he had done. This was a company where executives never ventured into industry-wide settings to know the leaders of their competition, more evidence of aloofness and self-absorption. It would not have been hard to find out about me at all. I had an established track record that was apparent to anyone who wanted to look at the businesses I had helped run.

But no one was even looking.

I didn't know most of the management team, either, although I realized that they were at the very top of a company that was in deep trouble and obviously had no idea what to do about it.

All of this must have been a little frightening for them.

## The Rule Book: 29,000 Pages and Growing!

Sears was a company built on the old military model. Follow the rules. Listen to and obey the commanders. There was even a rule book. It had 29,000 pages. I am not exaggerating. It told everyone how to do just about everything. They only had to read and follow accepted, defined procedure. They didn't even have to think. It was a formula that stripped personality out of the process, along with inventiveness and creativity. It turned people into perfectly interchangeable parts in a retailing assembly line.

The fact that it didn't work was immaterial.

Or so it seemed.

After all, it had brought them this far.

I realized that I wasn't just looking at a management team. I was looking at more than a century of Sears history and culture, the people who had moved to the top by following the rules and not taking chances. No wonder they had isolated themselves in a big black glass castle in downtown Chicago. What else would the commanders from an old retailing army do in such troubled times other than hide from a hostile marketplace? They were like the people trying to escape the plague, telling themselves all the old stories, looking to a very old testament for guidance, and waiting for the bad retail sales virus to go away.

And then, in came a new field general from a world they knew very little about, from that battlefield of retailing where the aggressor was first chipping and then biting and then gobbling away at their franchise. What they knew at that point was that their way didn't work anymore and that their board had become so worried about the situation that it reached outside for a solution.

I have a lasting impression of that meeting, of how they all seemed when I first walked in to introduce myself.

They looked like deer in the headlights.

It was a very short meeting, and Ed Brennan was his usual gracious self. I didn't have a lot to say, other than to announce that I wasn't coming to Sears with preordained answers. I was eager to get to know them, to listen to their ideas and collect their perspective on the issues. I told them that one of the things I was going to be fostering at Sears was a lot of two-way communications.

It makes sense, doesn't it?

Talk and listen, with the emphasis on listening.

I didn't know at that point how unusual that process would be for the people at Sears. They were all playing roles that had been cast long before I became something to worry about that had popped up on the institutional radar screen. They had their fiefdoms, their budgets, their responsibilities, all dictated long before I arrived.

They had their own world, almost completely separate from that other part of Sears, that "sellers and buyers" part that plays out every day in the stores. They thought that was enough. They showed up for work, in most cases tried hard, and were sincere team players, working every day to build the wrong institution to perform the wrong task in the wrong place and at the wrong time.

I knew that because I had done more than a little groundwork before I arrived. What I found still surprises me, but fits almost perfectly into the puzzle that shows what went wrong. I had an important advantage that day because I had spent some time—two days actually—with a senior team in the Sears Merchandise Group before I was introduced to the troops.

These were the top seven, eight, nine people on the merchandise side of the company. They were getting together to go through one of those strategy processes that are so popular in big corporations. I thought it was just the perfect time to jump in and see what people were talking about, to hear what was going on at one of the most important levels in the company.

I wasn't confused about the process at all, but I was a little stunned by what I heard.

Remember, I came in from Saks.

We did a lot of talking at Saks about our one clearly identified competitor, Neiman Marcus. Nordstrom was a comer in that formula, too, but they were a little further out on the bull's-eye for us. Every time we sat down to talk, it was the same set of questions: "What the hell is Neiman's doing? What is their real estate strategy? What is their advertising strategy? What product do they have that we don't have? How are they priced?"

It wasn't sufficient to pump out the simple answers to these questions. Knowing your competition isn't enough if you want to win the battle. You actually have to find a way to be your competition, to struggle to get inside your competition's head, to know its strategy and how it will play out. Reporting what they are doing, what they did, was one part of it. But the goal was to know what they were going to do and to create plans to steal market share. We took it very seriously.

I love visiting my competition. I want to see what's on the racks. I want to see how long it takes for a sales associate to approach a customer. Tickets on an item tell a story. I look at the computer codings on the price tags. When did this item reach the floor? How long has it been there? How fresh is the merchandise? If you know how and where to look, you can often tell. How well stocked are they? What is the pricing strategy? What are they moving, when, and why? Why are paint chips missing from the columns? Why are there cracks in the mirrors? That means they aren't paying due attention. Could they use the walls better for display? How accessible is everything?

What did I hear during that strategy session visit?

It was so predictive of what was to come that it still astounds me.

The conversation was absolutely insular. It was all about ourselves. It was about where we had come from to where we were today. It was about "the rate of improvement." It was a conversation about what was going on inside of the company. There was no real conversation about who was running what in the marketplace. No one was talking about who was the best competitor we had in the businesses we were running. No one was talking about what the competition was doing that was allowing them to win share, to take our customers away. No one was suggesting what we could do to emulate the competition, to use their best practices, to counteract them or somehow deal with the problem.

It was totally self-absorbed.

They were not talking about the dynamics of the marketplace, the external world of retailing. It went like this: here are *our* problems. Here is what *we* have done about them. Here is what *we* have come from. There was simply no outside context for anything we were doing. I was struck by that. Imagine the conversation: Here is what *we* did a year ago and now *we* are doing this! *We* have moved all the way from there to here!

So what?

Did we close a gap? Did we lose ground while we were changing? Did we go down a wrong path? It was a meeting that longed for a lot of very simple questions from the outside about the business we were in. But that was missing. It was almost as though Sears were its own island nation, that it could simply send out for customers if more were needed. There was no point of connection to the world outside of Sears.

This drove home a notion that would play an important part when it came time for us to create a new Sears. The place, it was apparent to me, was isolated from the customer, the competitive world, the marketplace, best practices, whatever label you wanted to apply to what was really happening in retail. The drawbridge was up, the fortress was sealed, and no outside thinking was allowed inside.

Because of that, the whole process had this ponderous quality to it.

It seemed fatal to me.

About the only advantage to the structure of that meeting was that Ed Brennan wasn't there, which meant no one had anyone to play up to. They were nice people, but they just weren't really focused on the context in which they were operating. Obviously, they were a little desperate.

The impression set during that preliminary two-day visit was still in my head when I went to meet the people who were running Sears. I told them I was looking forward to getting started with them. That was on the surface. Beneath the surface was my conclusion that this company had insulated itself from the marketplace. That thought was sitting just beside the price it was paying for that distance.

It is an important number, probably the best measure of all of what happens when a giant loses its way. Color it deep red, underline it, and recognize it for the disaster that it was. More than a century after it was born, decades after it won dominance in a growing America, millions upon millions upon millions of satisfied customers later, Sears, Roebuck and Company had lost $3.9 billion. There were reasons, of course. Allstate took a huge hit because of hurricane damages, and that pulled the numbers down. But there was no way anyone could look at the company's retail operation and call it aggressive and healthy.

This was a disaster that reached far beyond the management team I was facing. It stretched out into a vast collection of dingy, dark stores that had, for the most part, abandoned the proud history that helped create them. It touched more than a quarter of a million employees at every level who saw their failure measured out every day in terms of declining sales and rapidly eroding profits. It broke that mystical bond of confidence that motivates investors to buy stock.

But most important of all, in a marketplace that was full of heavy competition, where Sam Walton was creating a new legend with his Wal-Mart stores, where Home Depot was translating customer service and spectacular inventory into big numbers, where every Sears store in every mall faced long lists of aggressive competitors for almost everything it was selling, it was almost begging customers not to bother to come in.

It thought it was trying hard to be everything to everybody and in the process, it was becoming nothing to anyone.

Sears had among the highest operating costs in the entire business and it was so blind to reality that it thought its "everyday low-pricing" strategy would be the ideal solution. How can you turn nearly $4 billion in losses into a profit with low prices and very high operating costs?

It made no sense.

## Searching for My Own Answers

I recognized that my first and most important challenge would be to find out why everything had gone so far off track. But this bureaucracy wasn't going to present it to me on a platter in the form of a report from the Division of What Went Way Wrong.

I would have to find out by myself.

That may be one of the most valuable lessons for anyone in business. Finding out yourself is more than just taking in reports and analyzing numbers. You have to do all of that, but you have to talk and listen, too, at every imaginable level. A bureaucracy will present only what serves its own interests. I had a strong sense there had been more than enough of that at Sears.

I spent some time with Brennan in those early days, just to get his spin and his perspective on things. He is Sears' history come to life, a third-generation Searsman who had worked his way up, following a tightly structured company's pathway to the top. He knew his business, and his reflections were constructed on experience that had carried him all over the company. He could tell me all about how Sears had reacted to a problem in Buffalo in 1978, or how it handled its challenges when he was in Atlanta.

You don't write off experience like Ed's. But you also have to recognize how difficult it was for such an insider, in the best sense of the word, to deal with the kind of problems Sears was facing from the outside. I knew that some hard decisions were coming, that I would have to ask him for support to make the cuts that I believed were essential to the rescue of our company.

One of the elements people generally overlook in examinations of business culture is the impact that it has on those who are exposed to it for many years. I don't think it is an exaggeration to say that people fall in love with the history of their company and the role they played in helping to create it. But that means it becomes increasingly difficult to make decisions that seem to cut to the heart of the institution. It is an almost romantic relationship. There were some very tough moves on the horizon, and I knew they would be landing hard on the nerve endings of Brennan and the veteran Searsmen he had around him. They had already shed thousands of employees and were struggling to find a solution to Sears' problems.

But I knew that it would take an outsider to identify what was wrong and an outsider to execute the repair plan. I respected the history, but I was not personally beholden to it. I think that objectivity was of great value to Sears in my early days there, because it helped me construct not only an accurate synopsis of what was wrong, but a strategy that would get us past the surgery, into recovery, and well on the road to the future.

I had two direct reports when I got to work. Woody Haselton was in charge of retail and Al Goldstein was in charge of catalog and specialty retailing. Both of them were Sears veterans. I tried to spend some time with each of them to get to know them, let them express themselves. I wanted to see what they thought of the challenges we were facing. The immediate trend of the business was not good, and I wanted to get some insight into what was driving that trend.

I got a lot of cautious responses.

There was a real bunker mentality at work. In 1990, Ed Brennan had resumed command of retail. During that time, things were getting worse and worse and worse, so it really reinforced employees' desires to pull a lid over themselves and wait out the storm.

Whatever anybody thought was going to cause the storm to end was another question.

People were frightened and because of that they were very cautious.

The advice I was getting was to stay invisible: stay invisible to the media, stay invisible to the financial community, lay low, they are out to get you. There was a victim mentality running through Sears. People were telling me that everyone would want to come to talk to me, but that I just should not do that for the first four or five months until I got settled in and figured out what was going on.

How could I figure out what was going on without talking to people?

Of course, I didn't have any answers. Anybody who thought I would at that point would have to have been under the influence of some mind-altering drug. The idea of being invisible was so hostile to me that I just decided I would have nothing to do with it. It was just not the way I function. I told them I would be making myself available. I decided I would tell them what I didn't know and that I intended to establish lines of communication that would be in place whether the times were good or bad.

## My Own Sears Marathon

At its heart, what Sears was suffering from was a cover-up.

It wasn't a cover-up in the moral or legal sense of the word, not like a Watergate cover-up. But the company simply refused to be candid about its issues and its problems. That was what I had to attack first. And I wasn't going to be able to attack it in the black fortress downtown.

By the time I came to Sears, the company was in the final phase of construction of its new headquarters in Hoffman Estates. The tower simply didn't work for Sears. It made face-to-face communications virtually impossible. The new headquarters was long, low, and full of light and open spaces, just the kind of place you needed if you wanted people and the ideas and passions they carried with them to mix. I was told in September that it would take about five months to get the new headquarters completed, that I could stay in the tower until my new office was ready.

I didn't like the smell and the feel of what was going on in the tower.

I thought then, as I think now, that in some respects even moving to Hoffman Estates was not far enough from the shadow of the tower. It's a 40-minute ride west from downtown Chicago on a good day. The irony of the trip is that if you are headed downtown, at some points that tower sits right in the center of the windshield. It is what you see in the rearview mirror if you are headed west.

Could we ever be anything different as long as that tower still cast its long shadow? It bothered me, but it wasn't anything I was going to spend a lot of time thinking about. I had other work to do. Our future, for better or worse, was going to be built out in Hoffman Estates. It wasn't going to be built in any sense in the Sears Tower.

I told them to build me a temporary office at Hoffman Estates. I got myself a secretary and I went to work.

Even this early in the game, I had a method of operation in mind. There are a lot of ways a person at the top of an organization can get information. He can turn to his subordinates and ask and get their version. He can stack paper and statistics so high on his desk that he would have to use rock-climbing strategies just to escape. He could follow the advice of the people who created the problem, grab a shovel, and help dig an even deeper pit. He can sit back and pretend he is the great guru of retail sales, issuing religious edicts by the hour and waiting for the institution to respond.

Or, he can walk around.

That was my decision—to walk around. Perhaps it was a vestige of my years of running marathons in New York, a difficult but strangely rewarding way to find out all about the territory you have covered. No one can run a marathon for you, tell you what it was all about and transfer the true value of the experience. You have to do it yourself. I simply wasn't going to sit there and get everything filtered to me through Al Goldstein and Woody Haselton. I wanted to meet the next layer of management down in the organization. So I just created a map in my head and began my own Sears marathon. I walked out to sit down with the Sears Brand Central team. I walked out to visit the automotive folks, the apparel folks. I walked over to visit the marketing organization. I asked them to tell me what they were doing, what issues they were facing. What kind of objectives do you have for your business? What function do you perform and what are your goals?

It was surprising. It wasn't the same atmosphere I sensed when I met the board or spent those 48 hours with the senior team. These people were almost all very receptive. They were eager to demonstrate their knowledge. They wanted to show me that they had energy. Some of them were pretty closed about the process, but not very many. I ran into a few office politicians, and they were easy to spot. I quickly came to realize during these visits that just about everyone I was talking to was pretty goddamn frustrated. Some of them obviously had a lot of skill and a lot of energy, even passion for what they were doing.

What they wanted was some leadership. And they wanted someone to make some decisions about the future. The old way wouldn't work anymore. Everyone was too familiar with good ideas that made their way to the top of the company and then just disappeared into the ether.

Anyone who has been deep inside of a company knows the process. There is one version of the truth on the surface, the public face, the facade of Sears. But spend some time and develop some connections, and it doesn't take long to identify another reality that is playing out. You might have sensed this at some point in your own business, or you might have seen it among the people you work with. These are the conversations people have when they think no one is really listening. Maybe an edict comes along that everyone salutes on the surface, but when they get together after work, or when they go back to their offices and look into their cups of coffee and think about what they have heard or what they have read, that little voice says, "What a dumb thing to do." Other voices join in, and before long there is a chorus passing judgment in a very private, but very real, way. If you want to know what is really going on, you have to find that place and listen.

What were they telling me?

Where are we going? This company has been drifting for a long time. It is getting worse. The situation is in free fall. What is it going to take to get us out of this?

It was a cry for help from an organization. What did they know about me? Not much at all. But at least they were open to the sense of what was possible. They were willing to talk openly. I came away from those visits with a sense that there weren't too many hidden agendas swirling around Hoffman Estates. I'm not going to kid you. It was a massive brain dump. Not only was I listening to what people had to say, I was assessing them, measuring them against my standards, and trying to understand what role they were playing inside Sears.

## Building My Own Kitchen Cabinet

It didn't take me long to realize that this was not a situation we were going to change in little increments. We were not going to reengineer our way out of this debacle. The consulting companies were there early on with their offers—McKinsey; Booz, Allen; all the regulars. Someone said that Monitor Company had done a lot of work for Sears and we might just want to look at them.

I knew the process.

I told everyone I would be happy to listen, but right up front, I told them I wasn't interested in asking them to do any work for me. It wasn't a hard decision. Here is how it went.

First, I don't have the time and I know what their agenda would look like. There would be a two-month phase followed by a four-month phase followed by a three-month phase followed by a one-month phase, and it would then be a year later and nothing at all would have happened.

Second, it would be a learning experience for them, but not enough of a learning experience for me to give them that responsibility. I don't want and can't afford to take the time, anyway.

I was not interested in that.

31

Besides, I was starting to form my own kitchen cabinet. My assumption was that we would have to figure out all of this as best we could and, needless to say, as quickly as we could. I was looking for allies, and I was fortunate because I found two good ones very early on. I met Russ Davis just after I had arrived at Sears. He was going to become a very important person for me. He was in his mid-50s then and, like me, had come from the outside about two and a half years earlier. He was the chief financial officer of the merchandise group. He had come in from Federated Department Stores. He was a low-key, salt-of-the-earth, no bullshit, no pretenses, no artifice kind of guy. From the very beginning, he was talking to me about how the business really was, where the problems were.

I felt an immediate connection with this guy. He was honest, and it was clear that he was not out to advance any personal agenda. He just wanted to help things at Sears to get better. It took me a little bit of time to recognize just what he had walked into when he took that job. In a sense, he was in a little of the same situation I was in when I walked into Sears. But at least I was the guy in charge.

He walked in as the chief financial officer and wasn't the guy in charge. He was in a position to know by the numbers what had gone wrong, but not in a position to fix it. The words "trusted adviser" simply don't convey enough of a measure of the role he was playing for me. He told me these were good people, that most of them wanted to do the right thing, but that they were completely lost in the marketplace and didn't know what to do about that.

I found Jane Thompson in the corporate planning organization in the Sears Tower. Brainpower is the description that comes to mind. She was an ex-McKinsey consultant, the person you wanted to talk to at the Firm when you needed some conversation about retailing. She became my chief planner. She had only been at Sears for three or four years. She knew the numbers, she knew where the problems were, and she knew why they weren't being addressed.

Between Jane and Russ there was plenty of intellect and plenty of insight. They had not been co-opted or corrupted by the system. They still maintained their freshness of approach. I began going down an interesting path with them, one that was paved with analytical and financial information about where Sears was and how it had got there.

## A 100-Day Goal: Which Problems to Attack First

I sensed one of our biggest and toughest problems early on.

Obviously, there was trouble at the core, in retail, with its messy stores and bad apparel and bad attitude, but there was an immediate problem screaming even more loudly for a solution. It was the catalog division, and it was sucking money out of Sears at an alarming rate. The catalog alone, a centerpiece in this institution and, for decades, the customers' most familiar connection with the name Sears, was losing $150 million a year!

Thirty days into the job, it was all starting to add up.

It wasn't like a big, bright light went off that carried the label The Problem! The gravity of the situation began to dawn on me. I love numbers, and it was the numbers that told me the story—that, and the profound disconnect between the Sears organization and the real world. It still sounds like an oxymoron to me, but what we had invented was negative momentum. A vortex. A black hole. Things were always getting worse rather than better.

Because of that, the premium on speed and getting into action became more important.

In that quiet kind of way that you speak to yourself, I told myself that I had to decide what was going to happen at Sears and I had to make it happen real fast. That was my 100-day moment. I concluded a month into my new job that Sears could not afford for me to spend six months or nine months or a year figuring out what the problem was.

As it will once you have collected enough information, what business schools call "prioritization" happened. These were the big issues:

1. What are we going to do about the catalog?
2. What are we going to do about our store portfolio (how many have we got, and so on)?

3. Should we be in all of the businesses we are in?

4. How do we stop being a high-cost operator?

There was a fifth item, too, but that was only in my head at that point. It was the most simple question and the most complicated question at the same time: *Just what the hell was this company going to be when it grew up?*

Everyone was waiting to see what was going to happen. The people at Sears knew I had been walking and talking, that the Ax from Saks had been on a ramble. There were 350,000 of them top to bottom. They knew they were in deep trouble and they wanted to know exactly what I was going to do about it. They wanted to know what my leadership style was going to be, what kind of decisions I was going to be making.

I had a sense that the customers were waiting, too.

The strangest thing about the problem at Sears was that after all of that trouble—all of that insulation, all of those bad decisions, the feeling that everything had eroded—the customers were still out there, waiting to reconnect with an institution they had trusted for many, many years.

A lot of that became apparent a little later when we took a close look at the data we produced to help decide what we would be. Customers know all about erosion. They can sense when things are not right in the stores, when the sales associates aren't around, when the service is awful, when it takes so long to handle their complaints. The remarkable thing is that despite all of that trouble, they still wanted to trust us.

All we really had to do was show them we deserved it.

I had a talk with Ed Brennan.

I told him that I wanted to make all the big decisions at Sears about the things that were not going to be a part of our future and about the things that would survive and grow.

I told him I wanted to do that by the end of the year.

It was already October 1992.

The battle with history had begun.

There was one lesson I didn't want to forget along the way.

As bad as conditions had become by 1992, they were only the surface layers of a century-old story. It would have been unconscionable for me to push ahead without recognizing I was standing on the shoulders of some remarkable people who could trace their lineage back to a box of watches and a very smart clerk who wasn't satisfied with his job in a railroad backwater.

The only real way to understand what Sears could become was to have a clear understanding of what it had been, right back to the beginning.

# CHAPTER 3

# The Story of Sears: A Century of Selling

You can't walk into Sears headquarters at Hoffman Estates without sensing something that was around long before I arrived. It is history, one of Sears' most important creations, the one product no competitor can buy and the one reality no one inside of this company can afford to ignore.

If you want to know all about business in America in the modern era, where it came from and how it grew, then Sears is the perfect place to start. People are the products of their own experience, and corporations share that very same character trait. What went right and what went wrong over more than a century is all wrapped up in the Sears brand.

The message of Sears history is that it cannot rest on its laurels; what worked yesterday will definitely not work today or tomorrow.

This company spent far too many years reworking its old formulas and applying shopworn solutions to brand-new problems. I think Sears' history is more important than that because it gives us a colorful and powerful collection of object lessons on the value of change and on the role that people played in that process. When the company was functioning as it should have—and for many, many years it did—it was because Sears was able to anticipate important changes in the marketplace and take advantage of its position to turn them into profits and new ways of operating.

The early Sears story is all about adapting to conditions, an important message that I would revive after my arrival in 1992.

Sears was not afraid to abandon what didn't work. It was not afraid to bring completely new lines of merchandise and philosophy into its business. It was not afraid to give its employees control over their own destiny. Over more than a century, it found great value in paying close attention to its customers and what they wanted. Those are simple messages handed down to the people who work for Sears today. They are integral parts of the fabric of that history.

## Richard Sears Started Small

It is hard to believe that an institution that sells so much merchandise to so many people today began in North Redwood, Minnesota, with Richard Sears, a box of watches that no one seemed to want, and a thought that rural people might be interested in the accuracy and heft of a citified, gold-plated watch.

Trained as a telegrapher, the ambitious young Sears was rising in the ranks at the Minneapolis and St. Louis Railroad. He was working as an accountant at headquarters in the mid-1880s when he decided to create an opportunity for himself. He didn't like the idea of working for a salary. He suggested a transfer to the North Redwood railroad and express office. It was a backwater in this backwater of a railroad's little empire. But Sears realized he would have lots of time after he completed his railroad work to trade on the side. He also got a break on coal and wood prices from the railroad. He was buying whole-sale, which enhanced his opportunity when it came time to sell retail.

Richard Sears read trade magazines and catalogs as a hobby and paid par-ticular attention to the mail-order jewelry businesses. He was intrigued by the potential for profits in that kind of selling. Midway through 1886, as was the custom of the era, an East Coast watch company sent a box of pocket watches on spec to a local jewelry store, which refused them. These kinds of things happened all the time. Companies were not above creating fictitious customers to send merchandise to, or simply shipping off boxes of stuff on the assumption someone would eventually want it. Sears contacted the company. Of course it would be willing to sell the watches to him. He would have to pay $12 each.

In an augury of what was to come, Richard Sears then sent letters to his fellow telegraphers on down the line, remarking on the fine quality of the watches and offering each for sale at $14. From his knowledge of catalogs, Sears knew watches of similar quality were selling for $25 each. He knew the telegraphers could make quick money by reselling at a decent price the watches he sent them. He told the telegraphers they should send him no money unless they were pleased with the product, and that they could pocket whatever they made selling the watches to the retail customer.

This worked so well that he ordered more watches, this time with an important refinement. He made his own purchases, held the invoices himself, and shipped the new supply to his buddies in the telegraph business, COD. Telegraphers were bonded in those days, so his risk in the venture was slight. Working capital was born. The watch company didn't know it, but it was financing Sears's new business.

It took just six months for Richard Sears to make $5,000.

He abandoned railroading and moved to Minneapolis to found the R. W. Sears Watch Company. It took him less than a year to outgrow Minneapolis. Chicago, the rail hub of the central part of the United States, was the next address. It was 1887. Sears formed a brief partnership with watchmaker Alvah Curtis Roebuck, watches mutated into merchandise, letters became catalogs, and Sears, Roebuck and Company grew and grew and grew.

## Sears's Rapid Expansion: An Astounding Collection of Merchandise

Selling the watches also helped Sears find his voice, certainly a purple voice by today's standards but a brilliant, carnival barker kind of selling voice in its time. He was the master behind the rhetoric in the original Sears catalogs, and that hot sales pitch convinced a whole generation of rural Americans to spend money at Sears on everything from plows to patent medicines. In his 1897 catalog, Sears told his customers:

> Your patronage has been so very liberal that our business has grown beyond our most sanguine expectations; in fact, we honestly believe the remarkable growth of our business is without a parallel in the history of mercantile concerns. We can assure you that your trade has been greatly appreciated, and at no time have we been blind to the great responsibility taken in the endeavor to fill promptly the thousands of orders and answer the thousands of inquiries that reach us daily.

This was the heyday of catalog sales in America. Rural America—most of America was rural then—did almost all of its shopping by mail. That would be changing dramatically in a very short period of time, but Richard Sears's move to tap an eager, isolated customer base paid off magnificently. Right from the start, he seemed to recognize that this connection to customers paved the pathway to dependable fortune.

Ceres, the goddess of agriculture, was on the cover of that early catalog, along with a cornucopia that spilled forth a sampling of the amazing collection of merchandise available inside. On its first page, the big book announced: "Sears, Roebuck and Co., Inc., Cheapest Supply House on Earth. The Most Progressive Concern of its Kind In The World."

The competitive spirit and marketplace passion was there right from the beginning.

Sears policy was to supply its customers any product on which they could save money. No matter what it was that you might buy from a local business, Sears promised it could sell you the same or a better item at savings of 15 to 75%. "The unprecedented growth of our business proves that we have succeeded in supplying the wants of the people . . . ," a bold Sears wrote in the catalog.

This rhetoric went on page after page.

Sears offered an astounding collection of merchandise. There was "The

Princess Bust Developer and Bust Cream or Food" for $1.46: "If nature has not favored you with that greatest charm, bosom, full and perfect, send for the Princess Bust Developer and you will be pleased over the results of a few weeks use." The fact that the device looked like a chromium toilet plunger didn't dampen the sales pitch at all.

The catalog king had a remarkable passion for pickles. And not just one kind of pickle. Sears offered 24 varieties of pickles in barrels, all the way from the 30-gallon barrel of medium-sized pickles for $3.85 to the "Sweet Spiced Gherkins, finest article in the market," in 1-gallon buckets for $0.90. It might seem excessive until you think about it as an early example of abundance. If you wanted pickles, there was no need to order from anyone other than Sears.

It presented every imaginable kind of patent medicine.

"Injection No. 7, French Specific, . . . Having a great reputation abroad as a reliable cure for all troubles of the urinary organs in either male or female," sold for $1. The catalog rhetoric sent a hidden message about this purported cure for everything from "gleet" to gonorrhea. The customer could buy a $1.10 bottle of laudanum, or tincture of opium. Without reflecting the slightest hint of irony, a few pages later, the catalog suggested the Sears laboratory's own "Cure for the Opium and Morphia Habit," at $0.75 a bottle.

All of those items seem exotic and, of course, were not representative of what the catalog actually sold—nuts and bolts. Literally, every kind of nut and bolt you could imagine. It sold not just pianos, but a selection of pianos in a wide price range. It offered a vast collection of farm implements of every kind. It sold oak and other hardwood furniture. Anything anyone might want or need marched on page after page, all at prices guaranteed to undercut anyone, anywhere.

The company's growth as a catalog empire was so rapid that it was, indeed, the most remarkable business of its era. And on almost every one of those yellowing old pages, the message is the same: We recognize the value of customers and we will do everything we can to make them happy, even to the point of giving them their money back if they are not satisfied.

As well as it did as a business, I think Sears and his catalog played an even more important role in the evolution of the sense that this huge, young America was actually one nation. There has always been an argument that the movies were the seedbed of national culture, as though people had to learn from the silver screen how they should dress, what they should own, what pleasures they should seek in their lives.

I don't think so.

Farm people did not dress or romance like Rudolph Valentino. But they did long for the kind of style that was available to everyone in those old catalogs. A nation of immigrants was in need of a new national uniform, and Sears had everything they needed to outfit themselves as modern Americans of the era.

There is a strong argument to be made that it was the Sears catalog and the goods and fashions it was selling that taught practical, perhaps even fashionable, style to an eager and growing nation. It was the great gathering place for sensible stuff at reasonable prices. How else would someone in a lost corner of Kansas know what fashionable women were wearing in the Easter parade in New York?

In a nation that had very little of anything in the way of comforts, Sears inserted itself between people's dreams and their ability to pay, and filled that gap with an all but unimaginable collection of merchandise. Long before Wal-Mart thought it invented the idea, selling quality at low price was the mission for nineteenth-century Sears. The American farmer bought his first good cream separator from the Sears catalog, along with that first squeaky violin for his daughter ("Our Stradivarius!" Richard Sears pumped in the book; it cost a little under $2), the best dress his wife owned, and, a little later, the family's first encyclopedia.

Sears never found much of a customer among the big-city moneyed interests. From the very start, it was a people's business, selling common people's merchandise. Sears was not the place to look for expensive turn-of-the-century furniture, but it could and did bring indoor plumbing to the farm, which was a much more important measure of cultural progress. In the era before boys fell in love with cars, they fell in love with buggies. Sears was

41

there with a vast collection of horse-drawn vehicles and every imaginable harness, saddle, and piece of equipment connected to that trade.

Sears was so great at tapping that market that it included pages of testimonials from its customers right behind the buggy-and-cart section of the catalog. In virtually every case, the letters confirmed the wisdom of Sears early low-pricing strategy and remarked on the tremendous savings. It was as though Richard Sears had marketed directly to an appreciative nation of penny-pinching skinflints.

Mr. R. W. Sears,

Dear Sir. The vehicle you shipped me some time ago reached me in safety and has proven entirely satisfactory. I do not think you can be excelled anywhere in the line. I am well pleased with the surrey and think I got more than full value for the money. I feel that I have saved at least $50 by ordering this vehicle from you and in future, if I have or can get orders in this line, I will cheerfully place them with you. F.A. Schilling, Mobile, Ala.

Little American farm girls did not want delicate European china dolls to play with, so Sears came up with its own line of functional babies that were so durable they lasted long after children grew up and so realistic they could say "mama" and dampen their own little diapers. It was a business designed and dedicated to meeting the demands of everyday life. It changed its own inventories to meet that demand, and changed people's lives in the process. It was generally not on the cutting edge. Instead, it was astute at identifying what people were already buying, then selling it to them by mail at big discounts.

Whenever it got too fancy with an item, it created flops. Someone once thought America lusted after a variety of multicolored bicycles, and so it created them. No one bought them because they were 60 years ahead of their time. It misread the market early on for New York and European high fashion, and saw a whole line of merchandise fail because of it.

It certainly made its mistakes, but it was visionary, too.

By the time the first generation of muckrakers began slashing away at questionable business practices everywhere, Sears had already toned down the sales pitch in its catalog and opened an extensive series of laboratories to test and measure every item it sold. Patent medicines, now recognized as dangerous, addictive, or completely ineffective, were abandoned. Catalog rhetoric ever after adhered to a strict set of standards aimed at telling the customer exactly what she would be getting.

All of this primitive sales development created a tremendous legacy that rests inside of Sears to this very day. Richard Sears and his successor, Julius Rosenwald, knew intuitively that it was all about taking care of customers and whacking the competition every way they could at every opportunity. The fact that it worked so well then—and works now—sealed their places in business history.

## From Catalog Sales to Retail Stores: The Great Shift

Richard Sears was dead by the time the company decided to shift into retailing through stores in the late 1920s. (That happened when the most legendary Scarsman of them all, "the General," arrived on the scene.) Its store growth was so rapid that it became legendary in the retailing of its era. Much later, Wal-Mart's growth mimicked this pattern, making it the Sears of its day. But Wal-Mart at least had a template to look at. Sears had to invent itself as it went along.

There was no handy template for a catalog company to transform itself into a store business. No one had any world-class models to imitate, no tested marketplace data to build a business on, no army of veteran retailers who could step in and keep everything running smoothly. It amounted to a long and passionate march for thousands upon thousands of people who learned from their mistakes, constantly tested the marketplace to see what people were buying, and then built on what worked.

At mid-century, long before the institution went so far off track that its future was in jeopardy, it was viewed as such a stunning model of modern management that all of the important business gurus of the day were pointing to Sears' structure as the model to emulate. It was huge, but well organized, they said. It had power at the center, but was connected to its distant customers by stores that supplied their wants and needs. And how could anyone measure its role in the development of American culture? It is fashionable these days to look back on what it sold—its furniture, for example—and call it functional but clunky. But imagine what it meant to people who had almost nothing for comfort and convenience in their lives.

## Sears History: What to Shed and What to Keep

The challenge of helping to run a business with 300,000 individual partners (the people who worked at Sears) after I arrived was knowing what to cherish from all of this history and what to run away from as quickly as you can. You don't ever want to forget how great it was and why.

Our own first turnaround came with a rapidity that stunned nearly everyone, and I certainly don't want to diminish its importance or the role so many people played in carrying it out. But we always have to remember that Sears' history is the story of meeting the challenge of cultural change, that it has been "transformed" many times over the past century. The trouble we hit in 1998, for example, took its place in the long line of difficulties Sears had faced, and overcome, over time. The conditions that created it may have been different, but the result was the same: Sears had to move quickly to address the problem and get itself back on track with its customers again.

There is an undeniable brilliance shining through all of this Sears history, a reminder that we are standing tall today on the shoulders of the people who constructed this business from nothing but a box of watches, an idea, and a big dose of passion.

Sears history says everything that needs to be said about the primacy of customers, the impact of culture, the risks and rewards of debt and credit, people committed to a cause, and the dangers of coasting in an unpredictable, volatile marketplace. Whenever anyone at this company feels as though the institution is frozen in place, that it can't meet the challenge of change, a little glimpse into the past presents all the evidence anyone needs on the side of change.

All the magnificence and all of the mistakes are as close at hand as our own history. What it reflects as much as anything else is the importance of being able to change to anticipate, or respond to, new challenges.

That message reaches far beyond the walls of Sears and out into the world of business. It has become something of a cliché and a mantra at the same time: "Change is good." But that's wrong. The real message of Sears history is that change is constant, that you must face it or it will most likely devour you.

## A Hundred Years Ago or Now,
## It was Always About Customers

Every time someone says, "Know the lessons of history," it sounds like something a dark, brooding professor would utter at the opening of a course on fifteenth-century Europe. But it's not. It is as fresh as whatever happened yesterday, and as relevant as how we used what we learned from the revelation.

The biggest lesson is abundantly clear: Whenever Sears turned inward and started paying too much attention to itself, it always suffered consequences in the marketplace. It saw its market share and its competitive advantages dwindle. That was the conclusion that was so apparent to me when we hit trouble again in 1998. Wrestling with credit delinquencies and federal investigators, we were paying too much attention to the inside of the company and not enough attention to the marketplace and its changing demands.

There was a historical lesson right in front of us that we chose to ignore as we struggled with our internal problems: Every time Sears decided to pay close attention to its customers, to give them what they wanted at a good price, it succeeded. It is a measure of the strength of bad culture that this condition surfaced only a few years after we had turned the company around by addressing the same problem in the early 1990s.

There are some very old, stunningly renovated delivery trucks sitting in the hallways at Hoffman Estates. To people who don't know Sears, they might seem a little bit out of place amid all the glass and concrete. Thousands of people walk by them every working hour of every working day. They are more than decorations.

Back when America was still flexing its new muscles and stretching out, long before World War II turned the nation into a superpower, those old trucks were carrying the goods that transformed the dreams of an emerging middle class into realities. They are visitors from another Sears era, reminders that the roots of Sears run deep and that its experience includes changes that shook the place to its foundations, and made it stronger at the same time.

## The General Takes Over to Transform the Company

Very early on, Sears was all about transforming the dreams of its customers into realities. It takes quite a bit of alchemy to achieve that kind of transformation.

To its credit, Sears was good at attracting those alchemists of business early on. Across time, there have been a long string of Sears leaders who recognized the mission, from Sears in the beginning on to Rosenwald, who succeeded him and presided over the growth of the catalog empire in the early twentieth century, and then on to the character who casts the longest shadow of them all, the man everyone called "the General."

Robert Elkington Wood was a product of grand experience, something of a strange bird, and the character at the heart of modern Sears history.

Logistical challenge was nothing new to him, and the proof is in the canal he helped build across Panama.

In 1905, the U.S. Army turned to Wood, a West Point graduate—thirteenth in a class of 54 in 1900—a veteran of the Philippines insurgency. He went to Panama and took responsibility for all hiring and all supplies for the construction of the Panama Canal and all of the subsidiaries and developments connected to it.

A very sturdy and determined young man, he spent 10 years in Panama, ultimately rising to chief quartermaster in charge of all supplies, and then to director of the Panama railroad and steamship lines.

Imagine the logistics of that kind of job, the challenges he faced, the nature of a man who becomes supplier for the dream of building a canal that links two great oceans.

Wood hired thousands upon thousands of workers and directed the purchase and delivery of millions of tons of supplies in a part of the world that had few conveniences and offered a witches' brew of troubles that ranged from dealing with the military bureaucracy to yellow fever. He played the central, functional role in the construction of one of the world's marvels, a project that would ultimately transform everything from politics to transportation.

Wood left the army and joined E. I. du Pont de Nemours and Company as an assistant to the vice president. Then he was an assistant to the president of General Asphalt; he was in charge of operations in Trinidad and Venezuela and manufacturing and mining operations in the United States. He went back into the army in 1917 and ultimately directed all of its port, water terminal, and shipping activities in France and England.

Think of all of that as field training for what he really wanted to do.

He joined Montgomery Ward in Chicago in 1919 and immediately began pushing an idea that made that other catalog company so nervous that it decided, after a time, Wood could no longer work there. He wanted to open retail stores, and not just a few of them. Word had it that he escaped Ward's just before he was about to be axed. He knew it was coming, and before it happened he had opened conversations with Rosenwald, then the board chairman of Sears and himself one of the most remarkable characters of the first half of the century. Here was an executive who loved his company so much that he risked his personal fortune to save it after the depression of 1921. Rosenwald advanced the money that kept Sears from going under. He built a catalog colossus, became one of the world's wealthiest businessmen, then worked passionately and diligently to give $75 million away, a heroic philanthropic act, constructing schools and funding social programs, particularly for blacks in the South.

Rosenwald liked Wood because the General fit perfectly his definition of what a young executive should be: aggressive, intelligent, and, most important, not yet a wealthy man. The Sears boss had a distrust of anyone who made money too early in life. He believed that being wealthy at a young age drove all of the passion out of a man. Give me young men who want to be rich and I will present the opportunity, over many years, for them to achieve their goals.

That was Rosenwald's philosophy of advancement.

But opportunities would come only after they had worked hard for a long, long time.

Wood joined Sears in November 1924.

Nothing would ever be the same from that point onward.

During the years that I held Wood's job, I was never very far away from his ghost and from the role he played in five crucial decades of Sears' history. He was the original tall Searsman, but not at all like the tall Searsmen who came to represent the company during much of its more recent history. A lot of what he created remains the best of what Sears is today. He believed that democracy was the best method of government, and that democracy was also the best force to put into place in business. He created an atmosphere that embraced and rewarded fierce independence to the point at which it created its own merchant class.

The institution has changed so much over the years that no one could argue that Sears is still literally the place that the General built. But there is something at work at the heart of Sears that cuts directly to his vision of what a retailing empire could become.

## Wood and His Passion for Customers: Still a Strong Lesson

For Robert Wood in the 1920s and for more than 300,000 Sears employees today, it was and is all about customers: who they are, where they live, how they shop, and how to please and attract them. Because of that, you can draw a line, admittedly with a few zigzags over the course of time, that goes right back to the beginning. It is why Sears still has such a strong connection with its customers and why their loyalty has been solid even through the most troubled times.

Even when we abandoned our commitment to customers late in the century and became so confused and self-absorbed, people still wanted us to serve them. That was the kind of loyalty the General would have understood and appreciated. I had a conversation a while ago with one of my associates who told me about a letter that popped up in one of our customer attitude surveys. The man who sent the letter had given Sears terrible marks in every single category, the lowest grades the company could get. Then, at the bottom of the survey, he wrote a little note: "All I really want to do is come and shop at your stores. Why are you making it so difficult?"

That's what loyalty is, and to find out where it came from, you have to know something about the General, an imperfect and remarkable man. He was so absentedminded in his later years that he wandered the halls of headquarters loaded down with reports, leaving a trail of candy wrappers in his wake. He was so sharp about the marketplace and what it wanted that one of his favorite sources of bedtime reading was the *Statistical Abstract of the United States*. One imagines a character who went to bed with a head full of gray columns of numbers and awoke with the vague shape of an important idea.

## Going Retail: Sears Begins to Sell
## to a Nation on Wheels

Here was one of his most valuable thoughts.

He recognized early on that Sears as a catalog empire would be running into big trouble if it continued to depend on rural America for its revenues. That is what it means to know what your customers are all about. The farm economy was not sharing in President Coolidge's prosperity. Surpluses in an era before government was involved in guaranteeing farm income were driving prices down everywhere. As farm fortunes collapsed, rural communities, long the most profitable target for the Sears catalog, began to dry up. People were moving to the cities and taking factory jobs. The catalog had been the purchasing agent for the American farmer, but a whole collection of new businesses had popped up since the turn of the century that were selling directly to customers in retail stores.

Wood knew the catalog era simply couldn't last.

Its success was a function of the isolation of rural America. Automobiles were not common at the turn of the century, and neither were good highways. And there were developments before Wood's arrival that sent important messages about where America was heading. Within a few years of the point at which Richard Sears started selling watches, about a third of the nation's population was living in cities.

Two decades later, and two decades before Wood arrived at Sears, 51% of the nation's population of 105 million lived in cities and towns. Immigration had a lot to do with that growth, but at the same time, rural population was in sharp decline.

Income figures were playing an even more important role in this shift. Farm cash receipts were $14 billion in 1919, fell to $8 billion in 1921, and went all the way down to $4 billion by 1932. The farm share of national income was in precipitous decline, and businesses that had tapped it very successfully during its strong years were now in jeopardy. And complicating all of that was the development of a collection of customer-based retailers who were gobbling up catalog market shares in huge volume. The era of the chain store began at the turn of the century, with J. C. Penney, W. T. Grant, F. & W. Grand, and Neisner Brothers eventually opening thousands of stores all over the nation.

By the time Sears opened its first retail store in 1925, Penney's already had 676 stores and was showing some $90 million in annual sales.

Wood was a very clever man. He focused intently on what might have seemed irrelevant to many of the catalog merchants of his era. Automobile registrations and city populations were growing almost everywhere. Sooner or later, highways would be constructed to meet the demand. The nation would be going mobile, and that meant it could drive to convenient places along highways to shop. He wanted Sears retail stores everywhere with plenty of parking. He envisioned a company that could become purchasing agent for everyone. The land to build stores was cheap, the market was there, and all Sears needed to attract it was a solid line of merchandise, good prices, and lots of parking space.

He planted the roots of what we have today. When we look closely at our center of gravity in shopping malls all over the United States, we are looking at the General's idea as it eventually played out. It was prescience come to life. He did not invent retail store selling. That was well under way by the time he joined Sears. But he did recognize its importance. He also knew that if Sears was to thrive, it would have to move quickly into this new market-place and transform the way it operated in the process. He was looking for a way to tap the target customer of his era, to find some way to move ahead of that great wave of change that was redefining the nation and all of the businesses that were connected to it.

He had been urging Ward's executives to move aggressively into retail stores as early as 1921, pointing out that the chains were getting bigger shares of the market, but didn't have the catalog store's advantage of extensive warehousing and the economies of scale involved in purchasing huge inventories. When he shifted over to Sears, he brought along his head full of statistics and the knowledge that Ward's early experience with a few retail stores showed the idea was right, that it could produce strong profits.

He wasn't pushing for a blind march. Wood wanted to test his ideas carefully and with minimal risk. He installed his first stores in catalog plants in Chicago, then Seattle, Dallas, Kansas City, and Philadelphia. His first store that was not connected to a catalog warehouse opened in Evansville, Indiana. A year later, he moved cautiously into Atlanta. In the first two years, sales at the new stores doubled to some $23 million. The cautious expansions continued. On the eve of the Great Depression, Sears had 385 stores across the nation, everything from big "A" stores it constructed on its own plans to medium-size retail stores and then on down to small retail and catalog stores.

His idea paid off from the start.

By 1931, retail revenues, only 9% of catalog revenues in 1926, easily matched catalog revenues. It was the start of a trend that saw catalog sales playing a less and less important role in the revenue picture—something that happened right up until "the big book" was closed down in 1993.

## Lessons from the General's Ghost

I knew shortly after I arrived in 1992 that we weren't going to get anywhere trying to reconstruct the General's era and much of what followed it. The point was to learn from Wood's experience. Better than anyone else, he would have understood the message of change. There is a lesson from the beginning of the last century that applies equally well at the beginning of this one. Wood faced tremendous resistance inside of Sears because of his plan to shift the focus from catalog sales to retail stores. They are completely different businesses. Sears knew all about buying cheap for the catalog market and then selling low-priced goods.

The insiders of the day feared that the retail stores would be stealing business from the catalog side. Wood had the perfect answer for his critics: "If we don't do this, someone else will be taking the business from us." He knew that was true because he could see it happening all around him. He was connected to his customers and astute about his competition. His perspective of Sears grew from a position far outside of the company, then moved inward. (Our current shift into Internet marketing opportunities is playing a similar role. It is not a huge part of our profit picture, but we are there and growing in sophistication and market savvy, just as Wood was there with his new retail stores.)

Sears, the catalog company, knew nothing about retail selling. How do you display merchandise? What should the mix of merchandise be? What should a Sears store look like? Department stores were already crowding that business, so what was to be gained by shifting focus? Wood persisted and ultimately succeeded because he had a vision that was constructed on that awareness of where America was heading. He used both his gut and his brain in charting Sears' course.

He understood what cultural change was all about long before anyone in business school glued that label to the challenge of transforming big organizations. You don't carve a canal out of the jungle without learning all about transformation. It is the part of Sears' history that must be kept in amber and viewed and considered frequently by everyone who works here. History is only a disadvantage if you fail to learn what it has to teach. For the modern Sears employee, it puts the challenge of change into a more understandable context. What could be more relevant to what we are doing today than knowing that the people who worked for Sears in the first half of the century completely shifted the direction of the company, far away from the sale of items by mail to sales in retail stores?

Think of our shift toward providing services in the mid-1990s.

It wasn't the result of gut instinct. It was an effective plan based on the knowledge that we had to grow and that the aging of the society we live in presented a powerful collection of opportunities for us. Early in the century, people needed and wanted us for our hard lines, our tools, our houses and paint and plumbing supplies. Those are the items that help define the needs of a young and growing nation.

But if General Wood constructed his own vision from the reality that rural America was changing, we face a similar challenge: What does the America of tomorrow want and need from Sears, Roebuck and Company? For many, many years, the answer inside of Sears was "Just what we provided yesterday."

That formula stopped working somewhere in the mid-1970s, as competition and an inability to define ourselves undermined our position with our customers. We have to be as brilliant in response to the challenge of change as General Wood was in his era. That was why finding our target customer and marketing to her was so important to us. That was why we moved aggressively into the e-business marketplace. For the foreseeable future, this society will need an expanding array of dependable, quality services, and that is what we intend to supply. An aging society is eager to purchase all kinds of services. Sears has the name that translates into trust and is building the network of service providers to meet the demand.

These are all variants in our modern version of Wood's experience.

## Sears: Inventing Retailing as It Went Along

There are so many interesting lessons behind these old Sears stories that it would be impossible to list all of them here. The point to recognize is that Sears literally did not know quite what it was doing in the beginning, but that didn't stop it. The annals of this experience of radical change are fascinating. One division manager found himself pondering the kinds of questions that came up all the time. A store manager had decided to locate women's slippers near the front door. Everyone wanted everything near the front door, because that is where people did the most shopping. But why, in what was viewed at the time as a men's store, were women's slippers up front?

The store manager reported that much of his business came from a nearby bordello, and that the women who worked there bought a lot of slippers. That was primitive local market sensitivity with a twist. It left the division manager with one of those imponderables: Were the slippers in the wrong place, or was the store in the wrong place? Why was Sears so close to this bordello?

Inventing the business of retail selling inside of a company that built itself on catalogs was no simple matter. Catalogs were generally brown and white, or black and white at best. Color played almost no role in purchasing decisions, which were so two-dimensional in the beginning that the only real challenge was loading the book up with items people would buy. Selling in stores was different. It's clear from the earliest records that the stores were something of a jumble, with no clear branding of anything and presentation left to the whim of the individual store manager. Retail selling also put a new emphasis on quality. A catalog item sold to an isolated farmer exists almost in a vacuum. Simply getting the product was often enough. But when you can look at it, pick it up, feel it, smell it, check its heft, and compare its price against something at a store down the street, a completely different set of rules comes into play.

Wood was pushing everyone to recognize that the world was changing.

He saw a "softer side" to Sears very early on, and knew that women and families were playing a more and more important role in purchasing decisions, although he still clung to the notion that Sears was all about men and the equipment they collected. That piece of Sears' history stretched right into the modern era. His store managers, for the most part, didn't get it. Their approach was simple: If you spit tobacco juice on the floor at home, well, you're welcome to spit tobacco juice on the floor here at Sears, too! It's difficult not to form the vision of the hardware store from hell, full of badly arranged tools, overalls, tires (Wood recognized Sears could create a great market in selling items for automobiles), batteries, and a host of other dingy, manly items.

The standard response to this problem early in the century was to enforce some kind of central control, a bureaucracy, that would tell everyone how to behave and how to present merchandise. That was exactly what Wood did not want, and his attitude toward centralization after his years in the military was clear: less is better.

He created a network of Sears stores in which managers and salesmen were king. Eventually, there was central planning that gave Sears stores a similar look, and as America became more sophisticated, Sears stores were cleaned up and became more uniform, too.

But Wood knew those local merchants were closest to the marketplace and the best judges of what people wanted. He also recognized some of the inherent silliness involved in centralized decision making because of some early Sears experience. Sears' buyers often ended up shipping earmuffs to San Diego, tropical swimwear to Minnesota, and heavy winter galoshes to Florida. Selling all of it wasn't their problem.

One of General Wood's smartest refinements was to break the country into five selling zones, a process that kept everyone from vice presidents to store managers much more closely connected with the markets they were competing in. It had strategic value inside of the company, too. By setting up strong regions, Wood guaranteed there would never be too much power at the center of Sears, or so he thought at the time. It was a move that also fit his own philosophy—that the people at the point of contact would have the best sense of what their customers wanted. That was why he was so adamant about encouraging independence on the sales side of the company. This apparently drove bean counters in Chicago to distraction and undoubtedly provided the fuel for the wars that would break out between the field and headquarters periodically, but the success of the strategy was apparent in the numbers Sears kept building up.

## A Formula That Worked

All of the General's experiments in retailing paid off over the decades. Sears became the business model for big-store retailing. It was offering the right products in the right places at the right prices. By the end of World War II, when a nation starved of all kinds of goods and services went out shopping again, $1 of every $5 spent on retail trade was going into a cash register at Sears. Someone estimated at that point that 1 in every 20 people worked for Sears or one of its thousands of suppliers. Because it had paid such close attention to them for so many years, it had eager customers in abundance.

This was an object lesson Sears forgot much later in the century, when it tended toward vast bureaucracies in Chicago that tried to dictate what would happen out in the stores. If it could not control the individual store managers, who were legendary for their independence and freewheeling approaches to accounting and central bookkeeping, then it would try to control what everyone could sell.

People found ways around that, too.

Elaborate hidden accounting systems developed, along with huge piles of cash. Buyers cut deals with suppliers that amounted to wholesale pricing kickbacks. Items that looked on paper as though they cost $18 each would in reality cost only $12 each. The balance of the money would go into a vast central slush fund that individual stores could draw upon for off-the-record purchases and advertising. Eventually, individual stores could even use the money to offset huge losses they built up by selling off their inventories at fire-sale prices. It was one of those systems that seemed to work, a pressure relief valve to help ease the anxieties of ups and downs in the marketplace, but ultimately it worked at great cost.

# The Darker Side of Sears:
## Lost Sales, Angry Customers

By 1977, when almost all the nation's other big retailers were showing impressive gains, Sears was in the hole again. The General was gone, leaving five decades of business history and a lot of success in his considerable wake. But there was trouble everywhere. Sears seemed as though it had vast, successful sales, but they were sales that came at such huge discounts that the slush fund was completely depleted and the company's general revenues had to be stacked up against the losses. A clean-out-the-store, fire-sale mentality was at work, aimed solely at building up huge numbers. One thing that everyone at Sears knew from the General's days was that its sales staff could move merchandise with the speed and momentum of a big freight train. But the discounts were so deep it was going deeper into trouble with almost every sale.

All of that, along with the bureaucracy it created and the empires it allowed people to build, defines the evolution of what might be called "the Darker Side of Sears." The strengths that had built up over generations, all of that independence, seemed to turn on the company with a vengeance.

Individual stores would ignore dictates from Chicago about pricing and inventories. It wasn't their problem, after all. They were in business to sell, and when Sears was at its wild best in the old days, they wheeled and dealt better than anyone in business and let their sales figures set the measure of their performance.

The structure created under the General mutated into empires. The territories constructed grandiose headquarters. People who had been fired by Chicago would be pushed off to some hinterland to live in relative obscurity until there were enough changes in the hierarchy to allow them to surface again. There was constant tension between "the home office" and "the field," complete with creative sabotage aimed at undercutting one another.

There were other battles, too. Sears had come to think of itself as a "hard lines" store. The General's perception of the place was that people might just as well avoid everything above ground and head right for the basement, where he put all of the stuff aimed at men and their passion for tools. That was where the big profits were. But competition was demanding a different and better mix, and the culture was changing as women played a more and more important role in buying decisions. This was a message that the company seemed to be ignoring, even though it was recording the trend in its own sales and survey numbers.

Its old sales staff, which had built its muscle in the glory years of the mid-century, was accustomed to selling on commission and making a fortune in the process. But as the decades passed and the 1970s arrived, the old veterans moved on into retirement and were replaced by an army of part-time people, young mercenaries for the most part, who were not connected to the company's history or to its strongest values. That piece of the legend, that you could always find someone who knew how to sell and what to sell at Sears, was chipping away.

The stores became nightmarish, particularly at sales time. Everyone wrestled with inflation in the 1970s and 1980s, but Sears fared poorly in the contest. The goal was to make selling painless. The reality was a confused sales staff; long, long printouts of new prices issued almost daily; computers that were creaking at their limits; and a surly, slow, and sometimes angry atmosphere that chased people away. Thousands of sales positions had been cut to save money. The stories are legion about the old vets, salespeople who only wanted to sell, sitting in cafeterias moaning over their coffee about the lost glories of the old days.

The heads of the five territories had evolved into chieftains, the downside of the General's plan to keep the company close to its customers and avoid putting too much emphasis on the powers at the center of the company. When Sears moved to solve that problem, it centralized everything and stripped away much of the local control that had worked so well down where the sales staff actually met the customer.

Most of all, the sense that Sears was one institution aimed at the customer was eroding with each passing day.

What might be viewed as an era of extreme competition arrived at about the same time, and that is when Sears started paying the price for its lack of focus. It drifted early in the 1970s, then started going way off track, quite rapidly, in the late 1970s. While other retail businesses were healthy and growing, it was stumbling. When the nation shifted into the "Me" culture of the 1980s, Sears seemed to shift into a "Me" culture of its very own.

People are still pointing fingers and trying to assess blame for what happened. The short version of the story is that Sears went through a transformation that deeply undercut its fundamental mission of being a seller of goods. Instead, it assumed it could ride the financial wave and become something completely different, a money supermarket that would sell banking, real estate, and stocks the same way it sold merchandise.

It made some strategic sense.

The assumption at the time was that retailing was a mature industry, that its profit margins could not compete with the kind of profits made in finance (particularly during inflationary times). There were some important cultural changes under way that played into that strategy, too. People were shifting more and more money out of traditional savings instruments and into an array of new investments. Society seemed more interested in banking than in dishwashers. The old merchandising formulas didn't seem to be working very well anymore.

But in the process of that change, Sears somehow lost connection to its own history, with all of that magnificent emphasis on customers and what they wanted and needed. It acquired a collection of businesses that were supposed to help it become the great American corporation and set a new course for the future. Under Ed Telling, one of the veterans whose stunning successes in the regional empires catapulted him to the top of the company, it acquired Coldwell Banker, the real estate broker, and Dean Witter, the stockbrokerage firm. That happened in 1981. The price was about $800 million. It moved into banking with the Sears Savings Bank. It launched the Discover credit card in 1985.

For a time, it all seemed to work.

By that time, Ed Brennan was in charge of what appears in retrospect to be a diminished retailing empire. The very shape of the company had been changed to accommodate its new shift into financial services. Merchandise might have been at the heart of Sears' history, but somehow, it was no longer in its head. Sales started to move up and revenues from the shift into financial services were healthy. It seemed as though the company had been turned around.

But that was only on the surface.

Brennan, that veteran Searsman, became president and CEO of Sears in 1984, and Telling retired two years later. Just when the institution seemed to have taken on that mystical glow of success that comes with bigness and fresh revenues, the bills attached to the true price for all of those changes started coming due.

Because the profits from financial services were so robust, the company allowed its retailing empire to drift. And the shift into financial services required vast amounts of capital. Merchandising needed attention, but it couldn't get it without eating into the capital demands created by financial services. The institutional focus had shifted away from retail. Everyone seemed to forget one of the most basic rules: If people weren't coming into your stores to shop, it didn't matter what you had to offer. Financial services made strategic sense, but only if Sears paid equal attention to its primary mission—retaining its old customers and winning new ones.

The merchandise arm wasn't passive during this period. But it made some huge mistakes. "Everyday low pricing" was one of the most significant. This was a philosophy that changed the way Sears dealt with its customers, and the change was not good. There was a traditional marketplace assumption at work at the old Sears. It marked up its merchandise for a while, then conducted a series of huge sales during which everything would be sold at great prices.

The company knew how to pack the stores without selling the merchandise off. It made its money on slim margins by creating huge sales volume. Customers were so comfortable with this process that they would wait for the big sales to come along. Then they could clean the place out at a price they liked. The fact that someone at Sears could tell you a sale was coming up was part of that contract, an inside tip from a good sales friend who only wanted you to get the best product at the lowest price.

Everyday low pricing seemed like a bargain in the beginning, but it knocked the underpinnings out of the sales assumption for customer and salesperson alike. Instead of having big sales, Sears would just keep price down all the time. That way, it could compete with Kmart and Wal-Mart and a host of other retailers who were low-cost operators and keep drawing people into the stores. There were two problems: Sears was the highest-cost operator in the business and its customers were much more comfortable with the old way of doing things. They would look at the everyday low-pricing scheme, then sit back and wait for Sears to have a big sale. But it never happened.

It was a short-lived experiment and the beginning of a desperate slide. Because Sears' operating expenses were so high, its prices were, in many cases,

50% above the prices of its competitors. Retail group profits dropped by some 7.7% a year in the last half of the 1980s.

The shareholders were up in arms. Sears' stock price had dropped by 40% during Brennan's tenure. The debt load connected to financial services was huge. The price tag for financing the Discover credit card climbed from $3.8 billion in 1987 to $14.7 billion in 1991. There was great pressure to start spinning off those businesses to get the money flowing in the right direction again.

Our share in the marketplace was evaporating even as our competitors were becoming stronger. The biggest, the best, the most responsive, the smartest retailer in American business history was now being viewed as a dinosaur, and ripe pickings for any takeover artist who wanted to dismantle a century of history and sell its parts to the highest bidder.

It all brings to mind some more of that glorious catalog rhetoric from the old days: "We aim to treat our customers in a manner calculated to secure their permanent patronage." That was Richard Sears's promise a century earlier.

By the time I arrived at Sears, all of that was such a faint echo that it was amazing we had any customers left at all. But they were still out there, waiting for us to end our own confusing search for an identity. The great irony is that, at least for the past two decades or so, we had been looking in the wrong place. Our future was right where it had always been, right there between what people wanted in their lives and what we had to offer.

It would be wrong to say that I was born to run Sears, that my arrival was somehow inevitable. When I first heard of the opportunity, it seemed out of the question. The company was in bad shape, and I was already heading in another direction. Then I started thinking about it, a process that would lead people close to me to conclude I had lost my mind.

But I hadn't. There was something about the challenge that seemed very compelling, something about customers and their connection to a company that had been so central to the history of American business.

# CHAPTER 4

# Where I Came from and How I Got to Sears

CLEARLY BY 1992, Sears had become a troubled company. I was well aware of that before I took the job. Ironically, I was ready to accept another position when Ed Brennan, Sears' CEO at the time, came to visit me in Maine, where I have a summer home, to ask me about joining his company. He flew into the Bar Harbor airport in August 1992 in what was probably one of the biggest planes that had ever landed there, the Sears corporate GIII.

I had no interest in joining Sears at that point, and the speed with which the decision was made surprises me to this day. It wasn't that I didn't like the place or recognize its role in American business. It just wasn't on my scope, on the professional track I was following. I had spent a lifetime in business, from the day I walked into a Brooklyn grocery store as a teenager and got my first job stocking shelves, on through a collection of jobs in the chemical industry, then into finance at RCA, and, most happily for me, into the retail business in 1980, when I joined Saks.

Looking back, it all amounted to a continuing education full of experiences that helped prepare me for what I now recognize as the biggest challenge of my career. Academia may end when you get out of school, but learning doesn't, and that process changes your life. My curriculum vitae—Catholic schools in Brooklyn, Brooklyn Polytechnic for mechanical engineering, two years as an officer in the army in Germany, Harvard Business School—that is the record of my formal education. What it doesn't show, as impressive as it looks on paper, is that the challenge of learning didn't end when I left Harvard.

It seemed as though each job I took, from the earliest ones trying to help chemists and engineers understand the needs of their customers, to my up-to-the-eyes experiences in retailing, presented nothing but object lessons that would prove most valuable when I came to Sears.

Sears had turned to an outsider to fill a position at this level once before, and that was when General Robert Elkington Wood joined the company in 1924 and launched his remarkable transformation project that carried the place from catalog to store sales.

It was a sign of the depth of the trouble that the Sears board would be looking for an outsider now.

I didn't know much about Sears. I think the last time I had been in a Sears store was 1975, when I bought a rack for the top of my station wagon. I still have my "slim-jim" Sears credit card, the unusual little cards they issued back in the 1960s, in my desk drawer. I got it in 1965, but had not built up much of a credit record at the place. I had heard the buzz about Sears, of course. There were a lot of critical news stories. The word was not good.

I was a very reluctant candidate for Sears, but the courtship was intense and full of intriguing promises.

I was heading in a completely different direction in midsummer of 1992. I was about to join P. A. Bergner, a Swiss company, to guide its American stores—Bergner's in Milwaukee and Carson Pirie Scott in Chicago—out of bankruptcy.

That was where I was heading when Ed and his jet came to Bar Harbor. He wanted to see me because he knew where I had been and what I had done. Sears had recognized that it simply could not turn to another insider to repair itself. It needed a fresh, even perhaps distant, perspective. It had turned to a headhunter for help, and that was how my name arrived in Brennan's office.

I tried to say no to Sears many different ways, but the campaign persisted. My family thought I had lost my senses for considering this kind of a job when I was already walking toward another position. The argument from Sears was that my background made me the ideal candidate for the job. I had a feeling that this would be a make or break decision for me.

# The Perfect Candidate?

It was the kind of offer that gave pause for reflection.

I loved the business I was in, and had loved it for almost 12 years. The move into retail had been a midlife course correction for me that worked out well, another one of those lessons about the value of change. I was still saying no to Sears and planning to head to Milwaukee to bring those stores back to life, but somewhere down inside of me, a yes was starting to form.

Did my background really make me the perfect person for the job? That was the argument I was hearing.

I was at Saks at that point but ready to make a move.

Saks had been through some big changes. I had started my career in retailing there in 1980, immersing myself in the business, first from the chief financial officer's perspective, then moving on to BATUS in Louisville, Kentucky, the parent company of Saks, when it was restructuring.

Before I joined Saks, I had never given retailing much thought. I told the man who recruited me that of the 634 members of my Harvard Business School class, only 1 had moved into the retail business—and no one ever heard from him again. Still, RCA was a stumbling company and I was tiring of spending much of my life in the air, visiting its holdings all over the world.

What did I know about retailing then? Not much.

My graduate education at Harvard had given me a strong foundation in marketing and business. I had that same remarkable Theodore Levitt experience at Harvard that has injected the passion for marketing into so many graduates. He was not an easy professor. He was very demanding and exceedingly meticulous. He also knew more about marketing than anyone in America and was a spectacular teacher.

In 1960, Levitt wrote what was to become one of the most famous articles in modern business history, "Marketing Myopia." His target at that time was transportation and the decline of the railroads. His point was clear and brilliantly defended: The railroads did not decline because of a drop in the demand for passenger and freight transportation. They declined because they failed to think of themselves as transportation companies. They were railroad oriented instead of transportation oriented. Beyond that, they were product oriented instead of customer oriented. He pursued this theme relentlessly, concluding that every major industry was once a growth industry and that assumptions of decline because of market saturation were wrong.

The failure was never in the marketplace, he argued; it was always in management. Staying closely connected to the customer and recognizing a role that went beyond products was key to Levitt's philosophy. The movie industry lost out to television because it failed to recognize its primary product was not movies but entertainment. In that sense, he argued, the potential exists for all businesses to be eternal growth industries, but they must be open to change and deeply sensitive to the needs of their customers.

The lesson I carried away from that experience remained with me through all of my retail career. Myopia is fatal. Think broadly about what business you are in, think carefully about what customers you are serving now and how you will meet the needs of the customers of the next generation. This philosophy would be central to my experience at Sears.

I published a magazine at Harvard, my own small business, with a partner. He sold the ads, I wrote the editorial copy. It helped pay the bills. I had had a good experience for two years in the army before I went to Harvard. I was a lieutenant with a fresh ROTC commission, blessed with a wise and intelligent platoon sergeant, Walter Ford, who knew more about human nature than anyone I have ever met. He knew all about what motivated all kinds of people. I still think the army is the world's greatest diversity training ground. I was surrounded by soldiers of all races: whites, blacks, Hispanics, Native Americans, Asian Americans. There were straight arrows, drinkers, geniuses, fools—every description you can think of. The fact that we were all plopped together in Stuttgart in 1961 just as the East Germans were building the Berlin Wall and the world was preparing for war helped unify us. A constant state of red alert will do that.

After I graduated from Harvard, I worked for Enjay Chemical, which was to become Exxon, and had some powerful mentoring from a man named Dave Thomas. He was the first person I ran into in the marketplace who recognized that businesses should run from the outside, that they should spend a lot of time paying attention to their customers. This was Theodore Levitt's philosophy working on the ground.

Advancement at the chemical company seemed like a slow process. You got on that escalator and then waited. For a long time. I didn't want that. I also wanted to get more of a sense of what planning a business was all about, so I left Enjay Chemicals and went to work as head of planning for a new ventures division of International Paper. I did that for two years. In the process, I ran into a man named Charlie Beall, one of the greatest salesmen I have ever met. No one could beat him. I used to go on customer calls just to watch him work, to see what I could learn about the belly-to-belly sales side of the business.

Then I moved to Talley Industries to handle mergers and acquisitions and deal with Wall Street. It seemed like a good opportunity for learning at the time, but it didn't work out well at all. I arrived just as the company was being targeted by the Securities and Exchange Commission for an acquisition that had gone wrong. Its stock tanked, there was no money for mergers and acquisitions, and trying to explain to Wall Street why the company was the target of the SEC was no fun.

An important phone call (I have learned in my career to answer these calls) arrived.

A Harvard friend of mine had gone on to McKinsey & Company and then to RCA as head of planning. He told me they were looking for people to staff the planning department, and he thought I would be a good candidate. So I moved then to RCA as one of three directors of business planning. It wasn't long before I was plucked from that staff to become chief financial officer of the record company. It was a tough business. I was 32 years old and the learning curve was straight up.

The record industry was neither friendly nor clean. It was tightly tied to the marketplace, ran on big money, and was full of monumental egos. But I was prepared for that. My parents did not have an upper-middle-class income and worked hard for every penny they got. They went to church, and their universe was defined by their connections to the family.

No one ever asked me to do anything wrong. But it was clear to me that if you were seen as a person who would wink and turn the other way, someone was more than willing to do something wrong for you. My perspective was that the only thing that I had was my integrity and my reputation. That had to be a very visible value while I was at RCA. We put an internal audit function into place. I sent a lot of signals that there was only one way to do business. The payoffs to the radio guys, the promoters—we just weren't going to do it. There was going to be no cash changing hands. If we were going to pay a promoter to go out and pitch a radio station to play our records, he was going to give us an invoice and we were going to give him a check. On the artists' side, everything was going to be right there on the royalty statement.

I held that job from 1972 to 1976, then became head of the international division. It was great experience, but it was clear to me by 1979 that no one knew quite what was going to happen to RCA.

I didn't want to be a part of it anymore.

There was another timely phone call.

A recruiter I had known for some time, Peter Grimm, contacted me. He told me not to hang up until I had heard what he had to propose. Saks Fifth Avenue was looking for a CFO, he said. The company wanted an outsider. He thought it would be a good match. I talked to them, liked what I heard and saw, was impressed by the people I would be dealing with, and said yes.

# A Wonderful Christmas Frenzy

Shifting over to Saks was an attractive prospect. It would open me up to a completely different kind of experience. I wanted to sprint, not walk, into this new opportunity. And there is no sprint in the world like the sprint of a big, abundant, and successful store at Christmas. I wanted to experience the frenzy, the excitement and the tension of it, and I was not disappointed.

It was wonderful.

Christmas is a time of high drama in the retail business, and that is a feeling that stretches from Saks all the way across the industry. I was at the flagship store in New York, a gem in American retailing and one of the best stores in the world at the time. I was surrounded by people who were passionate about their work, always reaching out to the customer and always looking for better ways to meet and beat the competition. They were intelligent and comfortable about what they were doing. I liked the feeling of it immediately.

My title was senior vice president and chief financial officer, but I had made it clear that I did not want to be viewed as Saks's chief bean counter, someone who would be limited to telling them what they had done a year ago, a month ago, or a week ago. I wanted to help them plan the course for the business, and I wanted to learn all about retailing at the same time.

I was the only nonretailer in a very impressive group. Burt Tansky was the president then and went on to become CEO at Neiman Marcus. Jay Baker was the general merchandise manager. He went on to become president of Kohl's. Roger Farah was men's clothing buyer. He went on to become chairman of Woolworth. David Dworkin was in designer sportswear, and he went on to run British Home Stores. Joe Gromek was divisional merchandise manager, and later became the CEO at Brooks Brothers. Arnold Aronson was in charge.

Off we all went down the retail road.

I was learning the wheels and gears of the business and getting my first exposure to dealing with the credit side of Saks. But what intrigued me the most was the importance of personality in a store. Saks was at the high end of the market, and its customers had very high expectations that matched that status. I was learning about how the execution of personality had to be consistent across the store. It had to show itself in the merchandise, the service levels, the ambience. This was all about creating a store that matched what was in the customer's mind, something that would be extremely valuable later at Sears. You really had to try to be faithful in all respects in every part of what you were offering.

Stores that didn't have personalities, I learned very early on, didn't resonate with anybody and therefore got lost in the marketplace. Carving out that personality and making sure it was distinctive was crucial. You had to understand that philosophy, stay consistent with it, and not vacillate.

Execution was one of the most important parts of the challenge, and Arnold Aronson set a high standard. He was very good at thinking about his competition—which, at that point, was Neiman Marcus. We had developed something he called a "meet and beat" strategy. If Neiman's was coming, as it did, to White Plains, New York, how were we going to meet them and how were we going to beat them? He would demand a very insightful level of analysis about how their strategies compared to ours. How would they address customers in the marketplace? What were we going to have to do with our value proposition? Would our inventory be the same? What about levels of service? What is Neiman's going to present to them on the first day they open the doors of their new store?

I had a six-year run at it during a very exciting time for the company. My plan to expand the role of the chief financial officer worked out well. I was completely comfortable with the merchants, and they had welcomed me into the fold.

There were important economic lessons during that period. It was a time of high inflation that included a recession in 1982. Saks just sailed right along through it all. That seemed remarkable to me. The weakness of the economy did not hurt our business. Inflation did not slow us down. I concluded that inflation is actually good for the retail trade because it encourages customers to buy things now rather than face higher prices later.

There was one of those big changes at the top of the company, the kind of thing that might send shivers through the hierarchy, but it worked out well for me. Mel Jacobs, who had been vice chairman at Federated Department Stores, came in to take over at Saks when Arnold was promoted to head the BATUS retail group. He came with a reputation as an ice man, a difficult character to work with. But he had very good credentials. I hit it off with him right away. I still don't know how that happened, but it was a very valuable relationship for me. Mel rewarded me fairly quickly by expanding my responsibilities. I picked up all of the operating functions of the company—logistics, store distribution, human resources, and the like.

Between Arnold and Mel, I was educated in the importance of walking a store, something I still enjoy at Sears. Store design was one of Mel's passions, and I learned a lot from him about how to think about the look of a store, what kind of harmony you try to create with product, what kind of environment you present to the customer. He had a wonderful, holistic sense of it all. It wasn't just the merchandise that did it, he said. It was presentation and service levels, too.

## Leaving Saks for New Opportunities

By 1986, some of the parts of the BATUS empire (Saks's parent company) were starting to struggle. Gimbels was in trouble, and had been for quite some time. The store had lost its way. It had been an icon at one point, but it was losing ground and money at the same time. There were other problems in the retail part of BATUS, too. London decided to get rid of about half of the empire. In the process, Arnold lost his job.

I got a telephone call at home from Hank Frigon, who was CEO of BATUS in Louisville. He wanted me to come to Louisville to run what remained of the retail business—Saks, Marshall Field's, Ivey's Department Stores, and Breuners. My family was not enthused.

But we talked about it and I thought about it. I remembered what had happened at RCA, when I was pulled up to be CFO and later went to the international division. Those were big changes that involved big challenges, but they worked out well. We decided making the shift to Louisville would be okay.

I took the job.

All four of those businesses had different customers, so that part of the job was still more education in the marketplace and how it worked. Saks was at the high end of the chart, with Field's at the upper-middle end. Ivey's was very much a solid, mid-market department store, and Breuners was a high-end furniture retailer. The customer profiles were completely different.

But the message was the same, a variation on Ted Levitt's message, and much the same as the one we would send later at Sears: Stay connected to customers and competition. What does the Breuners furniture customer expect from us? If we are going to sell them dining room sets that cost $10,000, what are their choices? How do they think about it? How much exploration do they do before they make a purchasing decision?

We started our own mini-university surrounding these issues. Calling it a university is a bit of a stretch, of course. It was an attempt at graduate-level education in marketing, applied directly to our business.

Then there was an earthquake.

BAT Industries restructured by selling all of its retail businesses and keeping its focus on tobacco and insurance.

We sold Marshall Field's to Dayton Hudson, Ivey's to Dillard's, and Breuners to a buyout group based in California.

Saks we sold to Investcorp, a 10-year-old merchant bank with strong Arab connections. It had done very well with Tiffany & Co. and was interested in moving a little more broadly into the top end of the retail market.

We did very well. The people in London were very happy.

And I was out of work.

It wasn't long before Saks' new owners were looking for help.

Investcorp asked me to come back to be vice chairman at Saks. I thought about it and concluded, "Why not?" I knew the business, and I knew how hard it was going to be to get the returns Investcorp expected based on the price they had paid for Saks in light of my most eloquent sales job. There was a little taste of catch-22 in that offer. I would have to help meet the scenario I used to sell Saks to Investcorp. To their credit, they put a good deal on the table. If we could meet their projections, we would all do very well.

Back I went to Saks, with the New York media sniping about selling the place to the Arabs and how that undoubtedly made Adam Gimbel turn over in his grave.

It was a good experience for me because it taught me a lesson I tried to convey to the people of Sears from the day I arrived. I really had to think like an owner of the company. It wasn't having the Brits as deep-pocketed parents anymore to smooth out the bumps with infusions of cash. When you are in an LBO environment, the question literally is "Can I meet the payroll next week?" You had to really manage cash flow and expenses. There was no one to turn to. We had to do it ourselves. That was a very different cultural experience from anything the Saks team had dealt with. And Investcorp was a pretty intrusive group.

✵

We had to watch the cash. It was our business on the line. These were good messages that would serve us well. Saks did not fare well in the 1991 recession. The investors had already put up $900 million. But we needed more equity. We needed more capital. The banks would not step up. There was only one place to go—back to the original investors, to try to convince them to put another $300 million into the effort.

And so Phil Miller (the co–vice chairman at Saks) and I put together a two-and-a-half week road show through the Persian Gulf. It was right in the middle of Ramadan, the holy month. No one eats from sunup to sundown. No one does much business at all during the day. But we needed the money, and we couldn't wait. We pulled our dog and pony show together, and off we went. Kuwait. Qatar. Saudi Arabia. Bahrain.

We met with the money people.

It was a surreal but successful trip for us. People were generally only happy to do business only after dinner. We found ourselves putting on presentations about Saks and its potential at 10:30 P.M., or midnight, or 1 A.M. It was difficult but useful, because it forced us to tell our story.

That was in the spring of 1992.

I wasn't certain what was going to happen at Saks. I was already pissed off at the intrusions of Investcorp, even though I had only been on board for two years. That was where the power was sitting, with investment bankers who wanted to play store. They controlled all the levers.

I got another timely call.

Bergner's needed someone to come in and get them out of Chapter 11. The Maus family in Switzerland owned it all and they had paid a horrific price for Carson Pirie Scott. They botched the deal. As a result, the financial underpinnings just weren't there and when the recession came along, they went under. This offered a healthy pile of gold at the end of the rainbow for me. It would be a leveraged compensation opportunity. I started talking to the Maus family.

The situation was complicated. Because they were in bankruptcy court, a creditor's committee would have to approve the new CEO, along with the bankers. But I liked the Maus family. They ran very successful department stores and home improvement businesses in Switzerland. I was sort of fascinated with the prospect. We started negotiating a contract.

The word got out. *Women's Wear Daily* reported I was having conversations. There were denials all around. That went on into July 1992.

## An Unexpected Call

The phone rang again.

Herb Mines. Headhunter.

He wanted to know if I had signed with the Bergner's people yet. I told him I had not, but that we were pretty far down the road. He said he had something that might be more interesting for me, given my background and my personality. I told him to give me a break, that I was well down the road with the Bergner's people and simply couldn't walk away now. I told him I felt personally committed to them and that I had been working for more than two months to get it structured. He asked me to hear him out.

Sears?

Out of the corner of my eye, I knew they were having troubles. They were also the poster child for bad governance, and their business was falling apart. He told me Brennan and the board decided they needed a fresh look and a fresh approach to the retail business. He told me what they were trying to do, and it sounded like shifting deck chairs on the *Titanic*.

"It's a good decision on their part to look outside, but I don't know whether it is doable," I told Herb. "There are three problems. One, the business has been neglected for so long that it may have a certain negative momentum that really can't be arrested. Two, from what I know about the company, it is not committed at all to rapid change. Three, they can't possibly move fast enough for anything to happen before I have to sign my deal with Bergner's."

Timing was his problem, he said. Would I just be willing to sit down to talk with Brennan? I told him I would, but that I was heading off to Maine for a 10-day vacation before I moved into the vortex with Bergner's. He called me back and asked where the nearest airport was to my vacation home. Bar Harbor was 25 minutes away, I told him. He said Brennan wanted to fly out to meet with me.

How un-Sears-like, I thought.

It was pretty interesting that he wasn't summoning me to Chicago. That was what you would expect from a company like Sears, an imperial summons to visit that big black tower in Chicago.

Herb told me he had shared everything with Ed, then he added that he told him I was absolutely the best candidate in the entire industry.

The back-and-forth went on and sooner than anyone could have imagined, there was the Sears GIII landing at Bar Harbor. I had offered lunch on the deck at the house, but Ed wanted to meet at the airport.

We met in a little pilots' briefing room and we talked for two and a half hours. I told him about what I had done in my life, my approach to things, the issues I would want to handle. It was all very cordial. We shook hands and away he went on the GIII.

"I had a very nice meeting with Ed," I told my wife, who was convinced by this time that I had gone completely crazy. "They have got some real problems. I can assure you I will never hear from him again."

The next day, Mines called me again. He said Brennan was absolutely convinced I was the right person, that the chemistry of our talk was good.

"That's very flattering," I told Herb, "but I have about seven days, and I have to go to bankruptcy court in Milwaukee, pledge my troth to P. A. Bergner, sign my contract. This is all very nice, but let's call it off."

He told me I was making a big mistake, that Sears was presenting the opportunity of a lifetime. I said I agreed, it was a terrific opportunity, but that there just wasn't enough time. Again, he said that was his problem.

I was starting to heat up.

"I don't want this to go any further," I told him. "It is going to drive me crazy. It is going to drive my family crazy. I feel very much emotionally, and to an extent, morally, committed to the Maus family. Tell Ed no."

He did.

Then Ed called. "You owe it to yourself to see this thing through," he told me. "I need you. This company needs you."

He pressed again.

"No. I can't, Ed. I really can't. I am just too far down the road."

"I want you to meet some of the directors, the members of the nominating committee. Would you?"

"No. I can't do it."

He hung up.

The phone rang the next day.

This time, it was Donald Rumsfeld—member of the board, chair of the search committee, former presidential adviser and cabinet member, and now secretary of defense.

He made a speech.

I can only characterize it that way. I'm not trying to be critical. It was like a campaign speech. He told me it was my patriotic duty to consider this situation and to see it through. He said the nation needed Sears. Sears was crucial to the economy, crucial to the country. Sears was an American institution.

I'm thinking, This guy hasn't even met me yet and he is slinging all of this at me.

Do it for your country!

Mines told me, "Well, they already have an idea about compensation and options, the same kind of opportunities you would have at Bergner's." He faxed me the term sheets.

I talked to my attorney. Questions about sanity seemed to hover in many conversations these days. He wanted to know whether I was out of my mind. He warned me that if I screwed this one up, I was going to get sued personally and something very bad was going to happen. We went back and forth. Now I had the Rumsfeld speech on paper. I was not legally committed, he noted, I owed this to myself.

At that point, I yielded.

I told them all I would talk to the directors. Then I went to the Bar Harbor library and pulled up some stuff on Sears. It was very clear to me that a monumental change was needed. This was no place for incremental thinking. There was no evidence that Sears was at all prepared for monumental change.

Ted Levitt would have had a field day with Sears, its declining connection to customers, its confusion about products, its inability to learn from its history without being paralyzed by it. All of those wrong things in one magnificent bundle. Wasn't that what much of my career had been about to that point, trying to find better ways to forge those customer bonds and grow businesses?

I thought about it. But not for long. I didn't have long.

This would be the professional challenge of a lifetime. This would be the cap on a lifetime of preparation. It would be one thing to help a nice billion dollar mid-market department store come out of bankruptcy, but if the Sears thing could be done, forget about the money.

The psychic gratification would be extraordinary. It was really somebody dangling the brass ring right in front of me. The question was, Did I really want to reach for it?

I visited some stores. I flew to Chicago to meet with Don Rumsfeld. Sears put me on one of its planes and I flew all over the place visiting people.

I talked to all the senior directors. By God, they were serious. Whatever it was that galvanized this group into action, it was clear there was enormous pressure behind the fact that something had to happen for Sears. The company was in danger of the ultimate failure.

I told everyone of my concerns. I exercised due diligence with them: Would they have the stomach for very big change? It was clear some huge decisions would have to be made with some serious consequences. I knew from my store visits that they were desperately in need of capital. Would I have the money I needed?

Would I have the freedom to do all of this without having a little watchbird in the form of Ed Brennan sitting on my shoulder? Was he going to second-guess everything I did? Would I have the running room to do what I needed to do?

I came away from all of these conversations feeling that they meant it, that they would back the changes and provide the resources to rebuild Sears.

They had the will and the commitment. They said they would provide the resources. There was a good financial deal on the table. It would mean living in Chicago instead of Milwaukee, not an inconsiderable thought.

I told them I would do it.

It was one day before I was due in bankruptcy court to see whether I could pass colors at Bergner's. I signed the papers with Sears and then picked up the phone to call Bertrand Maus, who was at that moment on his way to the United States to meet me in Milwaukee. I reached him as he was changing planes in Boston.

I told him I had some bad news. I would not be joining Bergner's. I would be joining Sears as chairman and chief executive officer of its merchandising group. I felt sorry for the poor guy. He said, "You can't do this!" There was sputtering. He said it was impossible. I told him, "I'm sorry, it's done."

Boom. All hell broke loose. There was the anticipated lawsuit.

At the time, my lawyer said to me, "You know, if you get this done, you will be on the cover of *Time* magazine."

"I know that," I told him. "I am either going to be a bum or a hero. It will be black or it will be white. If it works, I'm a hero and if it doesn't, I am out.

"I'm willing to take the chance."

# CHAPTER 5

# One Hundred Days to
# Come Up with a Plan

Bʏ ɴᴀᴛᴜʀᴇ I am a builder. I believe that people will be remembered for
what they created, not for what they eliminated. I knew the day I first walked
into work that my reputation was at stake, that my success or failure would
be tightly linked to the success or failure of Sears, Roebuck and Company. I
knew from the company's history where it had been and how much change it
had experienced over a century.

I also knew from the day my appointment was announced, the "Ax from
Saks" word had started to spread around the company. I didn't want the people who worked with me to think of me as little more than a grand-scale cost-
cutter. I had warned everyone during my visits with board members that we
would have to make some difficult choices about how Sears conducted its
business, how many employees it would have, and what face it would be presenting to the public.

That part of my new job—the hard part I had talked about with the directors before I decided to join Sears—would have to happen quickly. It was the
only way to stop the hemorrhaging of money and set the stage for the construction of a brand-new Sears. I decided early in September 1992 that I
would have roughly 100 days to come up with my plan to get rid of the parts

of Sears that no longer worked. I had to find some way to control its spiraling operating costs and to start creating a future that would not only change the company's role in the marketplace, but change the very perceptions of the hundred of thousands of people who worked with me.

## Killing the Venerated Sears Catalog

I didn't want to go down in history as the CEO who killed the Sears catalog. But I knew early in those first 100 days that the catalog would have to go. It had 50,000 full- and part-time employees, it cost a fortune to print and circulate, and it had been on a slide almost since the earliest days of the shift into store retailing. The shift in buying preference went all the way back to the 1930s.

But killing the big book was tough, like lopping off a huge chunk of Sears history.

I knew where it fit in Sears' culture and I knew where it fit in the history of American retailing. But I also knew the marketplace battlefield was littered with the corpses of companies that failed to see what change meant to them and to their business propositions.

Check the list of famous old names—and some not-so-old names, too—that fell on hard times and you can see what I mean. Henry Ford went from number one with his cheap black Model Ts to an also-ran when Alfred Sloan realized America was getting wealthier and changing its buying patterns. In the first part of the century, General Motors won the marketplace because of that. There was a time, not so long ago, when everyone assumed IBM would always be Big Blue; then it lost its market in an increasingly competitive computer marketplace.

Back when Sears was shipping houses, no one anticipated the price it would pay to Sam Walton and a collection of other aggressive competitors. Fate has never been kind to the companies that missed the message of change. I saw that problem early on at Sears, and lived through it again when we hit hard times in the late 1990s.

It seemed to me that the Sears I found in 1992 was making one of those classic marketing mistakes that would have fit well into Ted Levitt's lectures back at Harvard. It is dangerous for a business to identify itself so closely with a single offering. If the goal was to respond to the needs and interests of the customers, and respond in a way that would draw them back into Sears stores, then the catalog would have to be viewed as something that simply didn't achieve that purpose anymore, regardless of its role in the company's history.

You have to look back to that first three months at Sears after I arrived to understand why the big book had to go. My budget had a $4 billion hole in it, and at the bottom of the hole was a catalog operation that collected billions of dollars a year in revenue, but lost an estimated $150 million a year after taxes.

Sears was lost in the marketplace, and the catalog was one reason why. It was one of the first in a series of tough decisions that had to be made if we were to turn Sears around and put it back in the black after so many years of trouble.

We knew we would have to come up with a plan to rebuild the stores and create a new vision for what Sears was to become, but none of that could happen until we found some way to turn the company around. It wasn't just a matter of smelling faint hints of smoke and trying to guess where the fire was. What were the numbers? Where were the sinkholes? What was rotten? How bad was it?

I wouldn't say there was a point at which a light went on. But the gravity of the situation began to dawn on me as I got to know Sears. It took about 30 days, and one of the great ironies of the problem was that everyone knew what and where the trouble was, they just could not bring themselves to face it. That is the downside of giving too much weight to history in a company that has been around for such a long time.

☞

I turned to people who were a little outside of that history for advice during the first 100 days.

Russ Davis was the chief financial officer when I arrived, a man in a very difficult position. The numbers were telling a story. And for Russ, it was an unfortunately familiar story. He had come to Sears only a few years earlier from Federated Department Stores, where he had been CFO.

He was a frank and honest character who knew retailing inside and out. He also knew what it felt like to have a company sinking beneath you, to watch it become a ripe takeover target and then to slip into bankruptcy. He told me early on that it was one of the most awful experiences of his life, something he would never forget. He knew as CFO that Federated had to make some tough choices, to get rid of what wasn't working and rebuild what was. But that didn't happen because no one was willing to make the hard calls.

What worried him now, he told me, was that he was seeing the same kinds of patterns playing out at Sears. People had been debating that catalog question forever. There had been many attempts to salvage the product, to transform it somehow into something its customers would actually want.

Sears had operated catalog counters in its stores for years, one example of a fix that didn't work. If the idea of catalog selling is convenience, why would a company expect people to come to a full-line store to make catalog orders, then return later (sometimes a lot later) just to pick up the merchandise? The process of selling is supposed to be as painless as possible. Here was one of those historic catalog "fixes" that just made everything more difficult for everyone.

Russ's position on the question of cuts at Sears was clear: The company had to stop losing money and it had to stop losing money right away. It is certainly true that no one will ever be able to grow a business for long just by controlling costs. But it wasn't as though Sears was healthy and we wanted to squeeze some money out of the structure just to improve the bottom line.

It was critically ill, and cost-cutting was not optional. It was mandatory. But it is part of the nature of such an insular place, so out of touch with its customers and almost out of the race with its aggressive competitors, that it simply can't make the kinds of decisions necessary to turn things around. It wasn't that the Sears people were bad. They were honest, worked hard, and treated one another with respect and some affection.

Ed Brennan was the third generation in his family to work at Sears, and he was surrounded by people whose ties to Sears were so tight and so deep that what would be obvious to an outsider was unthinkable to them. His grandfather, Luke Brennan, had worked with Richard Sears. His father and two uncles and his brother had all worked for Sears. He had been through his share of cost-cutting when the company was flopping around in the 1980s, but he had never seen anything as deep as the kinds of cuts we were anticipating.

When you grow up professionally in that kind of culture, it is not only hard to see what must be done, it is almost impossible to convince yourself to do it. Sears had already eliminated tens of thousands of jobs during the late 1980s, and it was obvious the institution was reluctant to return to that kind of challenge, no matter what the numbers were showing.

But I was an outsider with a different history and a different agenda.

I simply could not afford to take a romantic view. The numbers I was looking at, the stories I was hearing in my walk arounds, my sense of the place—it was all coming together. The picture was one of a company in peril. The problem inside was that no one could think of Sears as anything but an essential part of the fabric of American business history that would survive regardless of its performance in the marketplace.

I knew that was not true.

I felt my obligation was to shareholders, Sears employees, and customers. I was looking at a high-cost operation that was losing customers everywhere. This wasn't the kind of problem you could solve in little bits over a long period of time. Even when I had started thinking about joining the company, during that compressed period of courtship, I knew that whatever happened to Sears would have to happen quickly.

I was losing some sleep over that.

You form a vision of what a troubled company might become based on some experience, some specific knowledge about its problems and its potential, and some inspiration. But that kind of thought only carries a CEO, and a company, so far. What would happen if I actually carried out the plan I was starting to create during those first 100 days? Would the particulars be so tough, so wrenching, that I would not be able to move Sears beyond the tough part?

I didn't want that "Ax from Saks" rumble to become self-fulfilling prophecy. It would be very difficult to rebuild the company and put it back into the marketplace if I allowed myself to be defined by these hard choices early on. The longer the process of Sears' surgery took, the tougher it would be to get everyone to pay attention to the challenge at hand, which was all about creating a new company with a new mission. I had a clear sense the Sears board would support the plan. Desperate times called for desperate measures. My question was whether the patient, in the form of all of those people who had made Sears such an important part of their lives, would survive the surgery.

Morale was already in the pits. My sense was that the Sears workforce had been given something of a permission slip for indifference to just about everything over the past decade or so. Getting them to pay attention to a bright future would be a problem if all they could see was storm clouds created by another round of deep cuts dictated by Chicago.

Some bosses have constructed their reputations on their capacity for ruthlessness. Not me. I would have to make hard decisions that would change people's lives, but to me, that process never ended with deep cost-cutting.

In the first place, the challenge in this business isn't internal. It's external, out in the marketplace. The failure takes place in the offices of management, but the success takes place in the world of customers. That is where we would build Sears' future, and I wanted to get Sears back onto that battlefield on its quest for customers, as quickly as I could.

I needed an explosion. I needed to find some way to lift Sears from its past, from a culture that simply didn't work anymore, and put it into a more profitable place that was directly connected to its customers. I also knew I needed to send a clear message to Wall Street and the analysts and the media that this was serious business, that we were not going to be tinkering or delaying this transformation at all.

Russ, Jane Thompson, and I, my emerging kitchen cabinet, were on one side of this cost-cutting question. We knew the catalog had to be shut down and we knew why. We knew Sears was going to have to close a lot of its stores and spend a fortune modernizing what was left. We knew the economies we were thinking about had to happen quickly, and in a way that would make it clear that we were closing the door on one era and opening the door to another.

Jane and I had talked about the problem very early on—in fact, from my very first days at Sears. What was the role of a money-losing catalog in an institution that had stores nearly everywhere? If most of the population was just a short drive away from a Sears store, what was the role of a catalog structure that was invented back in an era where there were very few Sears stores, most of the population had not yet moved to the city, and buying by mail was an innovation?

Then there was the question of time.

It might just be that with years of work and millions upon millions of dollars in investment in technology, the Sears catalog as it existed in 1992 could be turned around. After all, there were plenty of catalogs in the market. L. L. Bean had already been legendary for years by the time I joined Sears, so successful that the Bean catalog format had been widely imitated. Here was a business that started out selling boots by mail, and now had much of urban America dressing like lumberjacks.

But Sears catalog buyers and L. L. Bean catalog buyers—indeed the catalog buyers of the many Bean imitators—are not at all the same people. We were starting to refine our idea of what a Sears target customer would be, and her profile was decidedly not young, urban, single, and eager to send money off for merchandise she had never seen.

How much energy would it have taken and how long would a revived Sears catalog work in such a heated competitive atmosphere? Ultimately, direct response marketing would play an important role in our package, but no longer in the form of a huge book sent to everyone and her brother whether they had purchased much from Sears or not.

Time was the one component in that formula I simply did not have. We had to take Sears and put it back in the marketplace where it mattered, where its center of gravity rested, in shopping malls all over America. Heading off to some other horizon that might eventually work for us just given time and money didn't seem prudent then, and it doesn't seem prudent now.

I kept all of this to myself.

"Arthur plays his cards very close" is one of the comments I frequently seem to draw. But it makes sense, particularly in an institution in which people were so accustomed to reading smoke signals from the top and then following the perceived agenda. I needed advice and counsel from every direction before I reached a decision. I reached out to the people who were strongly behind the catalog, who believed in its future, to hear their side of the argument.

I had to give the old Sears people credit. They recognized the catalog was a black hole, and they were working hard to try to change that. They were making it a lot more efficient and bringing the technology connected to it up to date. They had already closed down the catalog desks in the stores, cut some 7,000 positions, and shifted to home delivery of all but the biggest kinds of hard-line purchases. They had opened up catalog sales to outside credit cards. I brought some of them in, good people who had been working the business side of the problem, to help balance off my analysis. I wanted to hear about the process of fixing the catalog.

But I don't think they realized that the catalog was pumping red ink so far into the air. It is part of the nature of the place that it measured itself in terms of revenue, an important part of the story, but not the whole story by any means. How else could Sears be such a high-cost operator and think of itself as pursuing the right course? The old Sears people viewed the catalog as a big revenue producer and a business unit that was at the heart of institutional Sears, something that could be fixed with an investment of money, time, and attention. How could anyone think of closing down an operation that was so central to Sears' history? How could anyone want to close down an operation that carried Sears into so many homes?

But the catalog was no longer doing what it was supposed to do. One reason for this was that America was changing, but the catalog wasn't changing with it. Obviously, people had little interest in visiting the catalog desk at a store, then waiting for the merchandise to arrive so they could pick it up. That kind of process tells people that our structure is more important than their time, a formula they don't want to buy into.

The catalog was also hugely expensive to publish and distribute. And what we were finding on the outside was that the big book had become more of an advertising vehicle than a mail-order moneymaker. Many people would look at the catalog to see what was available, then go to the nearest Sears store to buy what they wanted. There were some practical questions, too. Why send people a book that carried thousands upon thousands of items when they were only going to buy a few things from some clearly defined areas? Do you need to spend the money to offer everything to someone who is only going to be buying Craftsman tools or toys?

There were deep logistical problems, too.

Catalog and retail were drawing from the same inventories, which meant one side was always going to lose. That was a nightmare that stretched all the way back to the beginning of the century. It complicated the challenge of keeping track of inventory, and that is no small matter when you measure sales in the tens of billions of dollars every year. It became a question of accountability for which no one had an adequate answer. Because of the lead time in preparing catalogs, pricing had become a headache, too. And it had become impossible to look at any point in the process and tell what the catalog's actual costs were. There was no way we could determine how much it would cost to send something to someone.

Our "satisfaction guaranteed" promise was turning on us, too.

People would order six pairs of shoes just to take a look at what they might want, then return five pairs and demand their money back. Or they would purchase something through the catalog and then return it to a store.

Richard Sears. A clerk whose career carried him into one of the backwaters of a midwestern railroad, Richard Sears soon found solace, and profits, in a scheme to sell good quality pocket watches to a rural America eager to snap up citified goods. An institution that would help define retailing in America grew from Sears's early watch-selling schemes.

Alvah Roebuck. Alvah Roebuck was Sears's original partner in the watch-making and selling business. Only six years after Sears, Roebuck and Company was founded, Roebuck retired in 1895, exhausted, troubled by the company's debts, and worried about what might happen if Sears failed.

Catalogs were Sears' connection to the buyers of America in 1893. True to the company's roots, the 1893 catalog displayed two of its favorite pieces of inventory: watches and hyperbolic sales pitching. *Sears, Roebuck and Co. catalog, Minneapolis, Minn., 1893.*

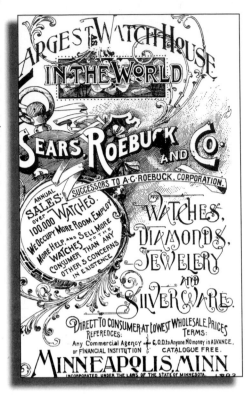

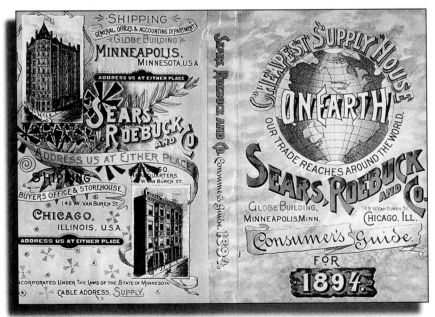

By 1894, Sears, Roebuck and Company had already settled on an early version of the theme it would carry well into the twentieth century: the "cheapest supply house on earth." This early emphasis on low prices for quality products would become the backbone of almost all subsequent Sears' sales pitches. Sears, Roebuck and Co. Consumer's Guide, *Minneapolis, Minn., and Chicago, Ill., 1894.*

Ceres, goddess of grains, stepped onto the Sears catalog cover in 1896, a volume that was the perfect reflection of the status of catalog publishing and retailing at the end of the nineteenth century. Prosperity and dependability were the subliminal messages in this classic cover. Sears, Roebuck and Co. Consumer's Guide, *Chicago Ill.*, *Spring and Summer 1896*.

Julius Rosenwald. If Richard Sears was the spirit at the heart of the early Sears operation, Rosenwald later became the brains. He was Sears's partner after Roebuck retired. By 1908, Sears was forced out of his own business and Rosenwald became chairman of the board. Rosenwald used his own fortune to bail the company out of hard times and gave millions of dollars to charities, particularly those whose mission was to educate poor southern blacks.

Gen. Robert E. Wood. There has never been, and will never be, another Searsman as legendary as "the General." He brought the skills he developed as quartermaster for the Panama Canal project first to Montgomery Ward and then to Sears in 1924, where he pushed hard on his plan to tap a mobile America by shifting from catalog sales to retail stores.

Sears Lawrence Avenue, Chicago store in 1925. The company was already on the road to its transformation from a catalog interest to a business that would plant its stores just about everywhere. The thought was to build Sears stores along highways soon to dictate migration patterns that would change America from a nation with a rural population base to a nation where most people lived in cities and suburbs.

State of the art retailing in 1925. Sears had just opened its first stores, the vanguard in a shift that would carry it in a few decades from catalog sales to dominance of the retail market. The hands-on experience proved valuable for a new generation of shoppers who had only been able to order their Sears merchandise from catalogs.

By 1948, Sears, Roebuck and Company was the dominant retailer in the United States and would grow only stronger as veterans returning from World War II went off to college and helped build the suburbs of America. The Sears store at Roseland in Chicago presented a facade that would become common across America.

Innermost chemise, $19.99.
Wrap robe, $29.99.

"I found something to help my 2 year old go to sleep."

"And something to keep my 40 year old awake."

Come see the softer side of **SEARS**

"The Softer Side." Tools in the basement and manly implements weren't doing the job for Sears at the end of the twentieth century. An intensive study of customers and their lifestyles was at the heart of the "softer side" campaign, which was aimed at the woman of the house, the new chief financial officer of the American family and Sears' new target customer.

The modern Sears store is designed to send a message about quality and comfort. The emphasis in the 1990s was put on the efficient use of space and the awareness that Sears was about reaching out to its customers, and no longer about providing convenient loading docks for truckers.

The store redesign effort banished the dark, uncomfortable sales areas and low ceilings of the old stores. "Circle of Beauty," a cosmetics display, sent a message about glamour and comfort in shopping for Sears' new target customer.

One of Sears' most effective marketing efforts tied the retailer to big public events. When Atlanta hosted the 1996 Olympics, Sears moved to quickly tap the market in its offering of sporting goods.

By 1994, the Sears multibillion-dollar store redesign campaign was well under way. Careful use of wall space, shelf display, and ambience transformed the men's section of its stores.

When he arrived at Sears in 1992, Arthur C. Martinez found a company trapped in its own history and lost in the world's most competitive marketplace. Eight years later, he retired as CEO after two turnarounds that gave one of America's most legendary companies a revived mission and bright hopes for the future.

It was one part of the institution feeding off of the other. Keeping track of costs in a system like that is simply impossible. No wonder it was losing so much money.

They seem like small, fixable problems, don't they?

But they weren't, because you have to multiply them many times to understand how serious the trouble was. The catalog was just too expensive, even factoring in its public relations and historical role. It was not only holding us in a bad place; it was dragging us down with every passing year. It had 15,000 full-time and 35,000 part-time employees.

It had to go, but it was not the only item on the list.

## Sears Had Lost Its Focus

An amazing clarity develops when you arrive on your first day at work at a company that is having the worst year in its entire history. On sales of $52 billion, just about $3 billion of the company's $3.9 billion in losses came from merchandising, from my area of responsibility. It wasn't just a onetime loss, either; it had been building for years. If you want to put a price tag on that greatest of strategic marketplace lapses, lack of focus, that's what it cost Sears.

How could the company have gotten so far off track and so out of touch with its customers?

We have one of the best track records in the history of customer service. We have been providing what people want and where and how they want it for more than a century. That meant hitting the low-price theme and selling by catalog in the beginning, then shifting into retail stores as the nation's population shifted from rural to urban and suburban America.

If Sears had stayed connected to its customers that way, it might not have been in the trouble I found when I arrived. That is what the brilliant side of the Sears story has always been about: shopkeepers who knew what people wanted and needed, and more importantly, knew how to sell it to them given the conditions of the times.

But it is a mistake to think that what worked for customers a week ago, a decade ago, a century ago, should remain in place forever. Sears' employees seemed to know that the nation was changing, that the customer was changing, that the market was changing, but they just couldn't pull themselves away from the old ways of doing things, even though they were no longer effective.

There was a high price attached to that paralysis. Sometimes it is a difficult concept to grasp, but what has been happening to change over the past few years is that the issue is no longer change itself, but the pace of change and how a company handles it. There's not a lot of time to settle in, either with a success or a mistake, anymore. This was a lesson Sears had to learn again in 1998, when its numbers were falling and trouble was coming from every direction. If the cliché about time, that it waits for no man, is true, then it is also true that markets don't wait, either.

If a competitor comes up with something that works and you respond, that's a reactive change. Sometimes you have to do that, but it's not the healthiest way to handle the challenge of change because it means you are allowing someone else to set your agenda.

The ideal is anticipatory change. Where is the marketplace heading? Where is my competition heading? Where is the world of finance heading? What about the worlds of information technology and communications? The ideal is to be able to come up with a strategy that puts you in front of the wave. If you wait for the force of change to carry you along, you are going to be part of a pack. If you anticipate and move a few paces ahead, your competition will be looking at your heels, which is exactly where you want them to be.

That was what was in my mind during those first 100 days.

I had a good idea why we were so far off track.

This company had spent much of the 1980s paying attention to everything but retailing. Insurance, financial services, the brokerage business, real estate—it seemed Sears wanted to do everything but serve its core customers.

It bought into a huge restructuring that was aimed at shifting it away from the merchandise business. The assumption was that merchandising was tapped out. But it was Sears that was tapped out at that point. It was completely dismissive of developments in the marketplace. It was as though Sam Walton did not exist. In fact, I was convinced Sears had no idea of what a core customer might even look like, even though it was facing strong clues every day in its own marketplace research. On the retailing side, we were a dingy collection of stores aimed at men, a fatally flawed target given changes in American culture. The quest for a clearly defined target customer would come later, but what was abundantly apparent to me on my arrival is that Sears simply did not know to whom it was selling.

Our competitors were not at rest.

Wal-Mart tapped a huge chunk of our market share. And it seemed that institutional Sears, that name and that reputation, was all but lost in a marketplace full of aggressive Kmarts and JCPenneys and just about any other name retailer you might want to think about. Big box places were popping up everywhere they could find space. People would walk into a Sears store in a mall and ask employees (if they could find them), "Where is Sears?" It was all around them and they didn't know it. That whole collection of much smaller retailers, some of them brilliant catalog sellers, everyone from L. L. Bean to Lands' End to Eddie Bauer, were cashing in on the culture's penchant for everything from flannel shirts to blue jeans to camping equipment.

Clearly, it wasn't that people weren't interested in buying.

We needed to narrow our focus and decide what we were going to be.

But getting the place on track would be a challenge for later.

## A Plan for the Future of Sears

Survival was the first item on the agenda, and that would have to come at great cost for the institution and for a lot of the people who had assumed that working at Sears was a lifetime guarantee, regardless of the company's performance in the marketplace.

I can't pretend that making a decision to eliminate 50,000 jobs is easy.

But what if the proposition is to lose those jobs, or watch the business continue to sink and take all 350,000 jobs with it? To my mind, I was helping to assure the future of 300,000 Sears employees, to make something vibrant out of what was left after we cleaned up the mess. If we didn't do that, there would indeed be an ax on the scene, but it wouldn't be me. It would be whatever scavenger came along to break the place into its component parts and sell it off.

At the end of that first month, it was clear to me that the catalog problem had to be faced, the stores had to be transformed, we had to get some handle on what business we were in, and we had to find some way to cut deeply into our operating costs. I had warned the board that this would be tough work, but now that I had the details in hand, I had to get the board to face reality and agree with my conclusion that all four of these components would have to change, the way night changes into day, if we were to succeed.

We had one thing on our side in those early days, a vast crisis of someone else's making that had to be repaired right away. We could no longer face the assessments of market analysts who found it quite defensible to tell the media, "Sears has been very screwed up for a long time."

I went to Ed Brennan and told him what I had found, what I believed needed to be done, and where I thought we needed to start. I wanted to deliver this message to the board of directors by mid-December. He asked whether that was enough time to deal with the questions involved, and I told him that I didn't think we had a choice.

It had to happen by the end of the year. There was no time for long-range study and, from what I now knew about Sears and its troubles, no other alternative.

I took that message to the board on a Saturday morning in December 1992.

This was another one of those defining experiences for me and for Sears. I had delivered the bad news to Ed Brennan and the others on that flight from Mexico. Now it was time to tell the board and win its support for change.

The four-hour presentation carried the board members all the way from my conclusions about what had to go to my proposals on what Sears had to become. I told them Sears was having an identity crisis, that we were very schizophrenic about where we were and who the competition was. I told them we didn't know whether we were a discounter, a specialty store, or a mass merchant. We didn't know whether we should worry about Wal-Mart or about Montgomery Ward. Should we be concerned about the specialty guys?

I presented our strategy:

- We would focus on our core business wherever we could win and grow.
- We would identify the target customer and make Sears a compelling place to shop.
- We would become market driven in what we offered to our target customers.
- We would speed up the pace of cost reductions.
- We would develop a culture that would carry the company to a greater future.

I told the board that in the course of preparing our store analyses it became apparent very quickly that there had been at least two or three decades of absolutely fabulous real estate decision making and that the company was blessed with positions in the best malls in America. I said closing failing stores would only put us in a stronger position in that sense. I told them I wanted to come back in 40 to 60 days. My belief was that we needed to rethink ourselves as a department store. Our emerging competition was not in the malls, but we were. That was our center of gravity. We had to take advantage of that and start thinking about who the target customer of that store was and what we had to create to attract that target customer into our stores. I gave them a hint. I sprung the notion that we had to start thinking about the woman and the American family.

I told them that we had to get out of the catalog and that we had to close 113 stores. My team had been crunching numbers about those stores for months. They came back with a proposal for 20 closings, and I sent them back to work. Then they doubled it, and I sent them back to work again, until we got to the 113-store level. We were looking at a situation in which 80% of our revenues were coming from 20% of our stores. That decision wasn't hard, even though Sears had never closed stores en masse before. We also planned to leave a number of product categories. We left the installed home improvement area, which we would be returning to in a different form later, and made a decision to dramatically change the profile of the automotive business. We sold a business computer division and got rid of some specialty retailing areas, such as Eye Center of America.

Then I told the board what I found when we had moved into our examination of the cost problems. We had too many people, and they were overpaid for the jobs they were doing. There were many built-in problems in middle management. We had a bonus system, but the bonuses were undercut by the fact that so many of their recipients were above the midpoint in salary. Even though an employee had earned a bonus, the amount would be cut to bring him back in line with the salary midpoint. He had to pay the price. It was an absolute, total disincentive.

The old-style Sears solution proposed to resolve that problem was even more revealing. The staff took a look at everyone who was beyond the midpoint and suggested cutting their salaries by 3% a year until everything fell back in line. I couldn't believe it. I told them simply everyone would be pissed off at that kind of proposal. My suggestion was that we find the people we wanted to piss off, then do something a little intelligent to handle the problem.

The early retirement plan, which did exactly what had been intended, was the solution for that. It was a clean offer. Associates over 50 years old with 20 years of service would be eligible. For pension purposes, we would add 5 years service time. They would receive full salary and most benefits for 12 months after leaving active employment.

We told some 4,000 people they simply wouldn't get raises until the marketplace caught up to their salary levels. We told them we would kill all that nonsense about paying back on bonuses, but that they should realize there weren't going to be any real changes in their salary levels for three, maybe five years. It was a way to take care of, in one fell swoop, all of those middle-management types who were substantially overcompensated for the jobs they were doing, and about whom I had a feeling—not a good feeling—in terms of performance. They had been on the Sears escalator for too long and just got themselves into the wrong place.

We promised our best efforts to find employment for people whose jobs were being eliminated. There would be 2 weeks pay for each year of service, up to 52 weeks of pay, for associates. Time-card associates the next step down would get a week's pay for each year of service, with a maximum of 26 weeks' pay.

The mix of early retirement, store closings, and closing the catalog would cut the Sears workforce from 350,000 to 300,000. As important, it opened up hundreds of management positions in the 800 remaining big stores, a great seedbed for the new Sears managers we wanted to develop.

I got pushed back by only one member of the board, Edgar Stern, who was Julius Rosenwald's descendant. He had his heels dug in on the catalog and just couldn't get it through his head that it was a good idea to get rid of it. He thought we ought to be able to fix it, to apply the necessary energy because it was a great business. It was the soul of Sears. I am not sure I ever really convinced him, but having said what he had to say, he went along. A lot of these proposed changes touched a deeply personal nerve in him, as one might expect they would, and the point about which he was most sensitive was the catalog.

It was 108 years old and deep in the red. You could say all you wanted about the catalog being at the heart of Sears. But if a surgeon were looking at the situation, he would reach the same conclusion we reached. It was time for a transplant. The old heart had to go and a new heart, built on what we knew about our market and our opportunities, had to be constructed for Sears.

And it had to happen very quickly.

Without it, we would be heading down a familiar path. The numbers would continue to go south as customers opted for our aggressive competitors,

Wall Street would become even more critical, and a demoralized workforce would continue to drag the place down. Maybe there would be a takeover. Maybe the new people at the top would look at all of that golden real estate and find some way to cash in.

And what would disappear in the process would be the most powerful franchise in the history of American marketing.

Sears would be gone.

I told the board I had some early beliefs about what we had to do. We needed to rethink ourselves as a department store. What did that mean? It meant new apparel lines, a big redesign effort, and an invigoration of 300,000 people, because they were all going to be playing new roles. It meant turning dark stores into inviting places of abundance and convenience. While we were at that, I said, we had to define a new target customer, and that was where I first sprung the notion that we should be thinking hard about the American woman and her role in the family.

My plan to upgrade the stores would cost $4 billion, I told them. It would be a long-range effort that played out over five years. I knew Sears had to change the look of the stores that remained. And it wasn't going to involve some fresh paint and new shrubs out front. The company had ignored that part of the business for a long time and the day for state-of-the-art thinking had arrived. If we were going to invite America back into Sears stores, people could no longer feel they had gone slumming instead of shopping.

I got what I wanted out of that meeting and planted the notion that I would be coming up with a strong plan. There was no other option. By 1993, Sears' merchandising revenues would no longer be a number lost in a collection of other numbers created by other businesses. We would be standing on our own feet, and our success or our failure would be evident to everyone from Wall Street to Main Street. I also knew how the word would be received on closing the catalog and the stores. My objective was to be remembered as the executive who revived Sears, not as the slash-and-burn expert who closed down so many stores and killed the catalog.

Getting the strategy in line to accomplish that was a huge challenge that kept everyone working day and night for weeks. I knew what we didn't want to be. We didn't want to be another JCPenney. There was a theory floating around that this would be my plan because of my background at Saks and my experience in fashion. Abandon the hard lines and go soft, get rid of that aging hardware store feeling. I considered it just long enough to reject it. We had hard lines to die for, and I wasn't about to ditch Kenmore and Craftsman so we could imitate someone else. But we were going to give all of that manly stuff a much better place to live in.

There was no margin for Sears to become another Marshall Field's or Carson Pirie Scott. I knew that business inside and out, and I knew where the room for expansion was. Sears just could not differentiate itself in that field because it was already too tightly controlled. But there was some real distinction in being a traditional full-line department store if we could execute the business extremely well. We had that golden part of our history to tap as part of that process.

We would need new people, a new theme, a new identity, a new look in the stores, and a new target customer to do all of that. We had made the hard choices we needed to save Sears and the board was behind us. Whatever Sears was going to be, it wasn't going to be walking and talking at all the way it walked and talked before that December board meeting.

Within a month, I was standing in front of a big meeting of Sears associates at Hoffman Estates delivering almost the same message. It was the beginning of 1993, our turnaround year, but that had not yet developed. I was talking to troubled people who were full of the rumors and fears and anxieties that always accompany change. I had to leave them with a sense that while some hard times were coming, they were coming as the price for a brilliant future.

"I feel positive about the things we're announcing, because I believe they're absolutely necessary to be put in place so we can become the kind of company we know we can be—strong, successful, a fierce competitor, nimble, profitable, and, most important, a great place to work," I told them.

"On the other hand, what we have to do to get there is going to take change, really meaningful change, and I can't diminish the fact that much of what we have to do is going to be personally wrenching for many of us and not easy for anyone."

I tried to find something positive to say—not to soften the blow of the announcement, but because there were a lot of positive things on the table. I had rambled all over Sears and come home with the feeling that there were terrific, creative, talented people all over the place just waiting to be unleashed.

I told them we had to take some time to find the courage to face reality and make certain we were doing the right thing. I told them they would see the wisdom of the plan as they helped me carry it out over time.

"The catalog is synonymous with Sears and it's our heritage, but we had to conclude that we could not improve our market position or achieve an acceptable return on investment fast enough, or with sufficient certainty, to support remaining in the business," I said. Then I outlined the other points: the store closings, the sell-offs, what we would emphasize.

I told them what this was all about was turning Sears into a winner.

I knew we could do it, and I knew we could do it soon.


## The First Signs of a Turnaround

With all of that behind me, I sat down with my team and started to think about how we would spend our $4 billion to bring this patient back to life. Even as I was working my way through all of this, a remarkable transformation was already under way that would help perform a modern marketplace miracle. Customers were coming back, and we were heading toward black numbers for the first time in years.

It is a cliché, but as I sat with my marketing team a few months ago, all of these huge and painful decisions seemed as though they came just yesterday. The turnaround plan worked. We started knocking the cover off the ball every quarter. There would be still more hard times ahead, but they would be landing on a company that walked away from its own deathbed and was showing some vital signs of life.

About that whole catalog question.

I suppose I will always be remembered in some circles as "the Man Who Killed the Catalog." That is probably because "the Man Who Changed the Idea of How to Reach a Varied Customer Audience More Profitably by Sending the Sears Message across Many Different Channels with a Great Degree of Efficiency" would just be too hard to remember.

But that is what happened. We are still in the catalog business; it just doesn't work the way it used to work. It no longer takes 50,000 employees. We do it with less than 100. It no longer loses a fortune. We make money. Type www.Sears.com on your computer and the Sears home page comes up.

Okay, so everyone has a home page these days. That's not the point. The General's decision to move into retailing was a response to changes happening all over America. Our place on the Internet is the same thing. We are carefully building a business on the Internet, but it is a process driven by the interests and needs of the customers. Increasing numbers of people are shopping with their home computers, and it is one of the options that drew more and more of my attention over my eight years at Sears.

We still have paper catalogs, too, but nothing like the big book. They are specialty catalogs, and they go to people who have shown us with their business that they are interested in specific products from Sears. There are no gigantic shipping and printing costs involved. They are sleek and specific and very competitive, effective little shots aimed with some precision at a marketplace the big book just couldn't hit with any efficiency.

Six years into my Sears career, I sat down at a computer to visit the cyber side of Sears because I wanted to see how that worked for Sears customers. It is not yet a simple process, but as computers become more and more sophisticated, we will become sophisticated along with them. Cars and auto shopping weren't easy in the beginning, either, but finding a way to serve that marketplace made a fortune for Sears and gave us the foundation we are building on today.

I decided to buy a Craftsman Cordless Screwdriver with a built-in work light. The price was $19.99. It arrived at my home on Lake Shore Drive in Chicago more quickly and more efficiently than anything ever could have arrived through a catalog purchase only a few years ago. It was as apparent to me then as it is now that the Internet is going to play an important role in Sears' future, but that is a role that will be dictated more by customers than by strategists at Hoffman Estates.

We developed a much stronger Internet presence toward the end of the decade, but that is a story in itself that I will tell you about later. I am happy to say that we never succumbed to the siren call of the IPO that wrecked so many other dot-com ventures after the marketplace soured and their stock prices and hopes collapsed.

Like everything else in this company's history, we found a Sears way to do it, one that kept the effort in our hands and gave us the control we needed to make it work. It has carried us a long way from my experimental purchase of a cordless screwdriver. In some ways, it feels a lot like re-creating a catalog, but making it work this time.

𝕯

But that development came far in the future. Early on, the hard work of saving Sears was the first item on the agenda.

The big book and a lot of old Sears stores had to go, along with a whole collection of other businesses that pulled our attention away from that customer who is so valuable to us. Over time, we transformed the way we reach out to our customers, but not without some missteps, more big changes, and some very troubling mistakes.

It was hard and sometimes sad work.

And it did, indeed, take an explosion before we could reconstruct the foundation of an American institution and set its eyes on the future instead of the past.

# CHAPTER 6

# Transforming the Old Sears Culture

I WAS STANDING in the conductor's spot when we held our 1997 Phoenix meeting, one in a series of annual strategy sessions that have been central to the construction of a new Sears. We chose a strongly dramatic presentation this time around and invited the Phoenix Symphony Orchestra in for some help. I had 230 of the brightest lights in Sears management with me, some of them planted with the woodwinds, some with the brass, some with percussion. Every section of the orchestra had a little Sears component attached— not to play music, of course, but to watch and listen and learn how orchestral music comes together.

We had come a very long way in five years, but I was worried that we had started to slip. The Phoenix meeting process, which I instituted in 1993, was aimed at focusing my management team on our problems and identifying solutions. This time around, my objective was to emphasize the importance of where everyone fit in the team. What better example for that than to show how an orchestra functions?

It was a passionate score: *Romeo and Juliet.*

Everyone in the room was well prepared—the musicians by their talent, training, and experience, and the Sears people by some timely lectures over a few days about the importance of "the whole" and the role that "the parts" play inside of it.

I had turned to Roger Nierenberg, conductor of the Stamford, Connecticut, and Jacksonville, Florida, orchestras for some help. He has found the symphony orchestra to be an almost perfect metaphor for business organizations. Everybody has an instrument or role to play, but the only way it works is if everybody is not only excellent at his or her own instrument, but also is aware of and linked to and connected to everyone else in the orchestra.

The point we were trying to make was relatively simple. Good orchestras could never function the way Sears had functioned. But Sears could produce its own beautiful music if it thought of itself more in orchestral terms.

Roger explained it all to the Sears executives and then went through a process aimed at showing people that sometimes you have to sublimate yourself to other parts of the orchestra to produce a good result. He showed them what happened when one part dominated, or when he simply stopped conducting and the orchestra members had to look to one another for their cues. Then he showed them what it was like when the conductor was half a beat behind the orchestra. Everything slowed to a near standstill.

It was just the most powerful demonstration of how small units and teams have to come together, how everybody has to play a role. The team really got the message. People came up to me afterward to tell me it was the most powerful thing they had ever been through, that nothing else compared.

I had some deep concerns in mind when this Phoenix meeting opened, and the need to be more orchestral in the way we conducted our business was among them.

Five years into our transformation, we were drifting back to some old behaviors. In retrospect, it was an augury of the trouble to come, but we didn't know that at the time. We would see our trumpeted transformation nearly collapse, and we gathered all the media and marketplace criticism that comes with that kind of setback. Within a year and a half of this 1997 meeting, we would be forced to take this company apart again, to examine every detail, to find out how and where we went wrong, and then to build it back up again.

It was a powerful lesson that we had forgotten as we basked in our early success. You can never let go at a company like Sears, not even for a day. Your customers won't let you, and they don't send polite warnings that the shopping atmosphere is slipping. They just go somewhere else.

# We Needed to Get Rid of the "Silo" Approach to Management

In 1997, what I call a "silo" mentality—in which different parts of a company start thinking of themselves as stand-alone entities—was creeping back in. The frightening prospect I faced was that we were moving back toward becoming administrators again and away from that crucial role as shopkeepers. I wanted to show everyone that by joining together and linking our strengths, we could become even stronger.

There were some other problems, too, that cut right to the heart of the lesson of transformation. Think of Sears as a collection of 300,000 people. I believe that after five years of hard work and more change than Sears had ever experienced, we had successfully converted only about a third of them. Another third was just going along with the new agenda, with its emphasis on the customer, the need to control costs, and the attention to Sears' mission. The final third was still out there pursuing an old agenda, somehow oblivious to the kinds of changes we had tried to encourage throughout the institution.

I fought with these issues for eight years, a struggle that never ended and probably never will, no matter who is the boss. Sears' great historical mistake was that it tended to believe it had found the perfect formula, the perfect working model. Then it stuck with it even as its numbers and its services slipped and its operating costs grew. That was the message of the 1970s, and it was the condition that put the company in such a bad place just before I had arrived.

I was watching the seeds of that old problem germinate even as we went to Phoenix for the 1997 meeting.

"I want my assets. I want my team. I want this. I want that. I don't have to worry about someone else." The natural tug at a place like Sears is to be in control of something. That is at headquarters. Beyond that, our customers experience this problem when they run into the old Sears in the marketplace, when they can't find a sales associate, when they can't find an item that they want, when they get indifference instead of passion from the people they meet.

Because of where I have been and what I have done, I understand the first problem pretty well.

That push to control your own empire, to think of yourself as a stand-alone entity within a corporation, is part of the nature of high-achievement, competitive people. If they are going to be put in charge of a business, they feel they must have all the tools and assets they think are important. They want the freedom to act, and they want to push the boundaries as far as they can. Getting people like this to reach agreement on how to share things that should be shared is difficult.

They want their own market research. They want their own authority. They want their own empires. They want complete control over their own budgets. They want to be their own CEOs. It's in the genes. The first problem with that kind of attitude within Sears is that it amounts to turning back to the old way of doing things. The company had a long and costly history of internal empire building. The second problem is that it is a very expensive institutional character flaw.

Independence and ownership were vital parts of the new message, but they stood alongside a pressing need to control how we spent our money. Of course it would have been nice for everyone to have their own market research arms, but I couldn't put my name on the bottom of a budget plan that allowed that level of duplication. We already had a strong market research division. People had to understand that and learn to use the strength that already existed.

This kind of problem plays out again and again in many businesses. I saw it personally in the various Sears budget proposals that reached my desk. For a CEO, the challenge is getting everyone to recognize the common strengths that already exist. Creating your own empire gets in the way of efficiency and allows people to build entities that keep everyone apart instead of pulling them together.

That was why the Phoenix orchestra experience was so important in the first place. Excellence and passion, even aggressiveness, don't preclude working together. In fact, they make the benefit of working together that much more apparent, and that much stronger. Who's more competitive, or more talented, than the first-chair violinist in a symphony orchestra? But that doesn't keep her from working hard with the rest of the orchestra. She shares her strength. She does not think of herself as a one-person orchestra. That was what I wanted the Phoenix team to recognize.

This level of experience represented, on the one hand, how far we had come and, on the other hand, how far we still had to go. This is not the kind of day that would have had much meaning for the people from the old Sears, those tall men in dark suits who followed the rules and took no chances for so many decades.

A vital aspect of changing a company like Sears involves getting top management on board. Experiences like the one with the Phoenix symphony help. However, you can try to effect all sorts of changes at the top of an organization without ever really touching the problems that may be at its heart. I don't want to diminish the role of strategy in the process, but it must be strategy that is aimed at everyone or it simply won't work. To have a collection of executives charging around Hoffman Estates shouting "The customer is everything" wouldn't mean much if that attitude did not spread all across the Sears organization. That kind of cultural challenge can be a little daunting, but if Sears didn't face it, I believed, the company was headed for even deeper trouble.

We would find out there was an uncomfortable prescience to that thought.

## The "Phoenix" Process: Changing Corporate Culture

I knew from the outset that Sears had to change from the ground floor up, from the sales staff right up to the executive team I would assemble to chart the company's course. The Phoenix meetings—the session with the orchestra was the fourth—were an important part of that process.

Each of them had a theme, a device really, aimed at making a central point. They weren't all as dramatic as the orchestra experience, but they were a crucial part of two Sears turnarounds. They invited everyone to become part of the company's strategic think tank.

Our culture is now over 100 years deep, as wide as the Mississippi and, in some places it sometimes seems, impenetrable. You hear talk about changing culture all of the time, as though it were as simple as making an announcement: "Here is our new culture." It doesn't happen that way. That is why, when we measured the process of transformation, we saw about a third of our people apparently missing the point. I don't believe they wanted to do that. In fact I think people wanted to do a good job.

But the culture that had evolved at Sears carried us away from our customers, our shareholders, and, in some ways, from our own employees. We had the slogans about guaranteed satisfaction and always taking care of the customer, but they had become empty over the years. It was the culture of Sears that told people they didn't have to think, didn't have to take responsibility, didn't have to become owners of their own destiny.

Changing that culture was the biggest challenge that 300,000 Sears employees faced every day, from bottom to top. I can tell you what we did, and the emphasis most certainly must rest on the "we" in the equation. These kinds of issues are usually discussed broadly, as though management can simply dictate a change and everyone falls in line. But people have simplified the concept down to the point at which it sounds something like a movie about missionaries converting native masses on some distant island. They just wave their bibles and everyone says, "Amen."

Cultural change isn't like that. It has to happen one person at a time, which makes the challenge endless. Strategic plans simply can't have a line item that says, "Cultural transformation accomplished by such and such a date."

We were not looking at a shift in direction for 300,000 people. We were looking at 300,000 individual cases, each with its own history, its own attitudes and values created over many years of working for Sears. That many people amounts to the population of a good-sized city. But at Sears, they aren't in the same place, and the simple process of reaching them can be daunting.

What was certain inside of this company, despite the complications of logistics, was the pressing need for change. Sears had become the orchestra that lived not by the talents of its musicians, but by the structure of its seating chart. It had many conductors disconnected from the music of the marketplace who were always ready to shout orders to a deaf ensemble. Not surprisingly, the audience, this time played by the disgruntled customer, was running away. It would be convenient to conclude they just didn't like the music anymore, just as one might conclude they didn't like Sears anymore.

That assumption was at work at some levels, after all.

There were those who thought in the 1970s that there was not much of a future in merchandising and that Sears should become something else. We got a taste of the same thinking at the end of the 1990s, when those who had invested fortunes in the Internet predicted, quite inaccurately as it turned out, the death of brick-and-mortar retailing.

It just wasn't the case.

How do you change the culture of 300,000 individuals?

In the beginning, I didn't have the answer.

But I know all about what cultural transformation does because I have seen it. Indeed, I saw it almost every day. Every time I visited a store, which was one of my passions, I connected with the kind of people who got the message. I was standing in the housewares section of a store outside of Detroit a few years ago, talking to one of the salespeople. She was one of those characters who had been around forever, but she was as sharp as anyone I have met inside of Sears. She knew the inventory, knew the displays, knew the sales figures, and was concerned about the mix we were offering in table settings. Expand display space and options and we could sell more, she said.

These kinds of exchanges weren't rare during my visits. It was why walking-around management was such a healthy thing. It gave me a concrete look at exactly what we were doing and erased any of the sense of abstraction that can build when you only measure your business by the numbers.

It was one of the things I loved about a lot of the veterans all over this company: They gathered experience and knowledge and put it into action every day. Those were the people at the heart of the new Sears, an important reason why it went from having nothing but a past to having an optimistic future.

## 1993: The Beginnings of Cultural Change

I didn't know how I was going to handle this cultural transformation issue in the beginning, and no one else did, either. That was when we first headed out into the desert of Arizona. It seems almost biblical in retrospect: "The Children of Sears Go in Search of a Land of Milk and Honey." It wasn't like that. Instead, it proved to be a session that taught us a most important lesson about Sears' culture and what happens when you try to change it at the wrong level.

There wasn't much to celebrate during that first Phoenix meeting in May, 1993, a condition I had the misfortune to experience later, too. We were in the process of turning this company around, but the strong numbers that would make Sears a modern business legend during the first turnaround had not yet been produced. Everyone was still a little bruised from the deep cost-cutting, the closing of the catalog and those 113 stores. We were at a very dangerous point in the process. The customers, the employees, and Wall Street would all be watching to see what we would become.

I didn't know what that would be, but I knew it would not be my exclusive creation. This company would have to be reconstructed by its own employees. That was obvious to me. I could send out all of the management edicts I wanted and never begin to touch the part of Sears that was most important, that meeting point between the institution and the customer.

I also knew we would have to find a way to create something that had some staying power, one reason why the slide at the end of the 1990s was so troubling. The annals of business are full of stories about companies that managed magnificent turnarounds and then slumped right back into their old behaviors, and their old performance, with the passage of some time. I know an awful lot about that now. Experience may not be a very kind teacher, but it is a very good one.

Durability is the central question in a turnaround: Is it going to last? Is it going to grow? Look closely at General Electric to see one that worked. Economies can do a lot to affect the bottom line, but the real challenge comes when it is time to expand the business, to take a bigger slice of market share, to build those contracts that make customers come back.

The "Sears Turnaround" story would rapidly mutate into the "Sears Faces Old Problems Again" story unless we found a way to rebuild the institution, change its focus, and start running up some solid, dependable numbers. It still surprises me that we would live through that experience, that we would slip from top dog to somewhere far down in the retailing pack so shortly after our first turnaround.

The heart of the Phoenix process was the message that change is constant and rapid and you have to be ready to meet it every day, even when it seems as though you have finally solved your problems.

There were only 60 people at the first Phoenix meeting.

I was trying to get alignment inside of my management team. We wanted to create some clarity about what we were going to do. We talked about valued behavior and what got in its way, about dysfunction inside of the organization and how we would attack it. But I think there were two important messages sent at the first session: I would be running the meeting myself, and Sears was as much their business as it was mine.

Almost all of the people who attended Phoenix I were Sears veterans because we had not had time to start bringing in people from the outside. They were unaccustomed to a chairman who would actually run his own meetings. What they expected was a visit from on high with a nice speech attached, then the chairman would retreat to the back of the room and make phone calls for 45 minutes. Then he would be gone, never to be seen again. He just wasn't there, and the notion that I was willing to work just as hard as I expected them to work to sort this all out was a very important event for these people.

This was the first time in a long time that Sears executives actually bought into the process and started believing in it. Up to that point, they just had to go along with what was dictated. Now they had to get emotionally and intellectually invested in it. It was no longer going to be Moses coming down from the mountain with the tablets. We were all going to discuss things. It was going to be a new management dynamic. "Transformation" is the word that most frequently gets attached to this kind of change. Think of it this way. The institution went into the process carrying a lot of ancient baggage that was getting in the way of its responsibilities. It would come out of it with a much clearer vision.

It would be about customers, shareholders, and employees.

I gave the first Phoenix group five new strategic themes to attack. I wanted the core business to grow. I wanted a focus on customers. I wanted cost reduction. I wanted local responsiveness. Perhaps most important of all, I wanted a cultural renewal. I set up five task forces to work on the themes. They wrestled with these assignments day and night and then carried it all back to Hoffman Estates.

In November 1993, we met again to check on our progress.

There was a problem.

The instant the Phoenix messages moved out into the field, they ran into resistance. It wasn't that people didn't want to participate. They just had no clue about what it should mean to them. It all came across to the troops as more MBA mush from Chicago. There had been plenty of that in the past, and it had created an atmosphere in which these kinds of proposals were all but doomed from the start.

Of course Sears employees wanted to have a stronger focus on the customer. They wanted to cut costs. They wanted to know how to respond in their local markets, and they wanted to take part in a cultural renewal. But what did all of that really mean to someone who was managing a department at Irving Park in Chicago? What did it have to do with selling pliers or keeping stock on the shelves or cutting the competition off at the knees?

There was one of those moments of clarity in that first Phoenix review when a particularly candid team member stood up and said, "I don't know what I am supposed to be doing differently."

That was a little scary. These were the people who were supposed to be crafting the vision of the future, and after months of talk and thought they didn't know what to do, either.

## An Old Mistake Reborn: We Forgot the Company's History

We had made the same mistake almost everyone makes.

We developed a strategy at the top, which by definition all the senior people bought into, and then we passed it along to the troops. The fact that it worked, that the company achieved a marvelous turnaround in just a year, obscured the reality that in stores spread all over God's creation, we had not yet found a way to invite 300,000 employees into the process.

It was very old Sears again, waiting for marching orders from headquarters. And that was happening from the top to the bottom of the company. It was almost as though no one wanted to recognize that the war was not fought in Phoenix or in Hoffman Estates, but at the 800 Sears big stores and 2,800 other Sears all over America, and beyond that down within the divisions and units that define all those stores.

There are no cash registers in the headquarters at Hoffman Estates. People can talk all they need to at corporate headquarters about the value of change, the brilliance of transformation, and the new realities they want to create. But if that attitude doesn't saturate the organization from the bottom on up, what meaning does it have? Months after we set up the task forces and tried to focus on the issues that would define the new Sears, we were getting no place fast.

That sense of urgency I felt during those first 100 days was still there.

We were literally surrounded by competitors who wanted to chop us into pieces and steal our business at malls all over America. They had been dining on Sears' problems for decades, and that had to stop. You don't want to let a Wal-Mart or a retailer of any other stripe set up next door just because you are there and start luring your customers away because you have forgotten how to serve them.

Customers were measuring us every minute of every day. It only takes a few seconds for a customer to decide that proper attention is not being paid. When that happens, you lose them—their money, their loyalty, and any hope that they will be coming back again and again. I could not dictate a solution to that problem from Hoffman Estates.

It had to happen out where the cash registers were.

I wanted all of our employees to recognize a crucial difference between the old and the new Sears. In the old days, they worked for Sears. Now I wanted them to know that they owned it, every bit of it, and that its success over the short and long terms would be determined by their decisions, their behavior, their dedication.

But the message simply wasn't getting through.

That was a measure of the thickness of Sears institutional culture. Changing the course of an aircraft carrier at sea comes to mind. The captain can issue all the orders he wants, but it is going to take a long time for that ship to head in another direction. And in 1993, I wasn't looking for a small course correction. I wanted to go in a completely different direction. Time was my nemesis in the marketplace and on Wall Street. And our history and the passive culture it created was my enemy inside of the company.

To understand why those problems existed, you have to leave the Phoenix process with its passion for ideas and its puzzlement about carrying them out and dive into the archives for a few minutes. You have to look at the old Sears to know why the new Sears was having such trouble reinventing itself.

The history certainly wasn't all bad.

There was Richard Sears and his purple prose aimed right at his customer's pocketbook. There was Julius Rosenwald with his big heart and his brilliant development of Sears' catalog sales. There was General Wood and his prescient decision to put Sears where people in cars were going to be. There were decades and decades of success constructed on close connections to customers and a sophisticated knowledge of their lives and needs.

There was also a healthy track record on adapting to change.

In the civil rights era, the company was up front about the need to hire and advance African American employees. It told its managers, particularly those in the South, that it would not tolerate even the hint of racism and would send them packing if they resisted. Long before that, Sears was astute about addressing the needs of its employees, paying them salaries and giving them benefits that were the envy of everyone in the industry.

It also had that stunning history of being able to take an item and sell the living daylights out of it. And it recognized early on the importance of allowing decisions to be made far from the watching eye and budgetary and inventory controls in Chicago. The assumption was that the merchants knew their customers best. Those were pieces of the old Sears I certainly didn't want to lose.

Then there was the uncomfortable part.

The old Sears had executives who thought they needed no input at all from women. I was paging through a transcript of one of our oral histories and came across an account of a shareholders' meeting from the very old days. Someone asked one of the chieftains why Sears was not paying more attention to women. His answer was quite a revelation. He said he learned everything he needed to know about the needs and interests of women from his wife and his daughters at home. That was the kind of attitude, an attitude that dominated for decades, that led the company to miss the importance of the change in women's status.

Sears was so averse to inside change that it watched its catalog division hemorrhaging money for years, but didn't have the institutional courage to close an operation that had played such a romantic role in its mythology. It bought into whole collections of strategies that only seemed to pull its focus away from the marketplace that had always been its home ground. It was making most of its money from a few of its stores, but it allowed that formula to exist long after it started to cost the company millions upon millions of dollars. It simply would not consider closing so many stores.

Institutional Sears had also constructed a bureaucracy that would puzzle even a Russian czar, along with the attitudes and behaviors that institutions like that create over the long term. That might have been why the Phoenix process was having such a difficult time moving out into the field.

## Hampered by Managing "by the Numbers"

There may be nothing more revealing than the sets of numbers Sears used to define itself and the rules it lived by for so many years, edicts and codes and values and culture that were established long before I entered the picture.

At the base level, there were the numbers. They were aimed at identifying regions, stores, products, and the like. My suspicion is that much of that evolved after World War II, when Sears had to grow rapidly and turned to the people who ran the war, the officers in particular, for its management teams. The military model was firmly embraced in corporate America, and it was a template that fit Sears like a well-tailored uniform.

Commands would be issued and people would follow orders.

Of course, even the military isn't that way anymore. It recognized a long time ago the importance of individual decision making and teamwork, along with the reality that transformation is something that happens one proud soldier at a time.

One of the legacies of the old military model in Sears was that people spoke in numbers. Don't get me wrong. I love numbers and the stories they tell. My daily dose of retailing adrenaline comes from numbers. You have to know them and embrace them and understand them in this business, because you can be sure your competitors do. But you have to translate them when you are communicating. I had seen this before on a smaller scale. You can't imagine how complicated it becomes when numbers are used to describe a company that does $34 billion in business a year.

There were class numbers for types of goods: 1, 2, or 3. There was a markup code: A, B, or C. Sporting goods, for example, were all listed under section 606. Stores that had their own auditors had a tiny "a" beside their number. The number 3 was applied to computers. Number 22 was stoves. Number 57 was televisions. Number 34 was intimate apparel. Children's wear was 629. Big stores were category 1 stores, with categories 2 and 3 affixed to smaller Sears presences. It was not the kind of structure I felt comfortable with as a language. There is much to be said for creating informality in conversation. People can say what they feel, what they mean. They can get angry. They can negotiate. But sit down with someone who talks about 1008 (1 for larger store, 008 indicating that it was one of the earliest Sears stores and was on the West Coast) and have him tell you there was a "B" markup in 629 and the whole process runs immediately off track.

Earning your stripes at the old Sears meant knowing those numbers, the secret language the institution used to describe itself. Once you had them under your control, you could talk in code all day long to other people who had ascended to the same level of knowledge. A Sears veteran could break the process right down to an item for sale in a particular store at a special sale price. The numbers would tell the listener whether it was something that had been purchased as a specialty, or whether it was an old dependable. How clubby. Once you learned the numbers, you were part of the great Sears fraternity.

One big problem. Customers don't want to join. No one walks in and asks for an item or a department by the numbers. It's a mistake to think that this kind of pattern creates problems only inside of headquarters. What the numbering process led to was an emphasis not on the *customer*, but on *products* as expressed by *codes*. It leads to abstraction in a situation that demands big doses of reality. If you think of women's apparel only in terms of a collection of numbers, it makes it easy to overlook the fact that fashion changes all the time depending on the desires of your customers. In a situation like that, it becomes almost impossible for a manager to recognize that a customer doesn't want what the store is offering. What you want a manager to imagine is a collection of real faces in real stores shopping for real items. Instead, you get numbers.

Early on, I learned those numbers and what they meant. I had to because that was how the place was describing itself. But the whole process was so disturbing, such a link to the past and such a detriment to straight talk, that I found myself telling people "Stop That!" whenever they started drifting into the mysteries of the Sears Code.

I charged offenders $1 every time they went into their numbers rap. They had to put it into a cookie jar on my desk. It still happened. During my tenure at Sears, you had to know the numbers because that's how we tracked sales, but you better not talk them and you better know what they represented beyond arithmetic.

That wasn't all.

## The Ridiculous Rule Book

Sears had rules for everyone for every circumstance. You find out all about them when you talk to the veterans. Not so long ago, the men who worked in the Seattle catalog center had to walk all the way through an attached Sears store to use the men's room. But before they did, they had to put on their coats and hats. Long after the rest of the culture moved into comfort clothing, women had to come to work at Sears in black, long-sleeved dresses.

People were expected to show up on Saturday at headquarters, and those who opted to "dress down" were called on the carpet for it. Showing up well dressed became the point, a standard that carried the institution far away from the only measure that really mattered: how well it was doing in the eyes of its customers.

"Showing up," as a matter of fact, had been one of the central measures of performance. Loyalty and trying hard were important determinants at salary and bonus time, but even that structure ran under a set of rules that made absolutely no sense.

And there was no connection to how well they performed in the marketplace, out where all that institutional history runs into its most critical judge, the customer. Bonuses, if they were paid out at all (and they had not been for many years), went to that privileged class at the top of the company. That was a terrible disincentive to the people down in the ranks and only served to divide the place into competing, resentful camps.

Performance reviews were rare and generally pro forma, particularly at the top. I had people tell me they had not been reviewed for years before I arrived. You would ask someone about one of his direct reports and he would say, "Well, he's a fine executive." And you would ask why that was and the response would come back: "Well, he's just a fine, fine executive."

Everyone was living by those old rules.

My predecessors had whittled away some of the problem, but nowhere near enough. I wanted confident people at Sears, people who felt secure enough to make their own decisions based on knowledge of their customers and their needs. What I had was a vast collection of people who were living by the rules of a game that was no longer connected to the marketplace.

✺

Of course it was all written down in the rule book.

It had 29,000 pages.

Yes, 29,000.

It was like a Britannica of dated information collected over more than a century. If it wasn't in the book, you didn't do it. That was one of the most concrete measures of the old Sears culture that I found on my arrival. How could anyone possibly know what was in there? How could it conceivably be used to run a company?

I think it was a vestige of all of that Alfred Sloan philosophy about workers as interchangeable parts, or maybe Henry Ford's experiments with production lines. You can plunk anyone you want down on an assembly line as long as you have the task broken down to its tiniest and most mindless function. Tighten a bolt. Tighten another bolt. Tighten bolts all day long. It doesn't work that way when you are face-to-face with a customer, or when you are negotiating with a supplier, or when you are trying to solve a sticky service problem. That kind of decision making is embedded in the people who translate their passion for this business into stellar performance.

But you are not going to find it in 29,000 pages of rules.

It's the kind of thing that can make you laugh when you think about it. They didn't want to be Sears, Roebuck. They wanted to be Sears, Robotic—the nonthinking automaton's place to work.

I see it now as symptomatic of the larger problem.

Even the institutional items one might expect a company like Sears to have in some depth—infrastructure, communications, computers—had been ignored for years. I thought I would be moving into a corporation that would be up to date at least at the logistical level. But it wasn't. It was a creaking old structure that had been pasted together for decades. It could not communicate with itself; it could not measure its own performance.

Given even that short assessment of Sears' history, it was small wonder that the fruit of the first Phoenix session in 1993 was not well received in the field. I knew it would be of no benefit to issue edicts from on high. The culture would just have absorbed them or found some way to glue them into the rule book.

That's just what you want your vision to be, right? Pages 29,001, 29,002, and 29,003 of the rule book.

The Sears ship would not respond to any command that carried it away from the course it had followed for so many decades. In all those pages, there was simply no category to cover the level of change I was pushing for in 1993. Like so many other things, it was all about the past. Consequently, it was useless because retailing is all about now, right now, all day long and every day.

I had little sense after that first Phoenix review that the people I was depending on had made what I viewed as the most important cultural decision of them all: They had not yet taken ownership of their company. That is the key to everything because once it happens, it becomes clear to everyone that we fly or we fall together.

## How Sears Employees Envisioned Change

I talked about this with Tony Rucci, whom I brought on board toward the end of 1993 to serve as executive vice president for administration. He left Sears in the late 1990s, and I have missed him. He probably said it best when he concluded that as far as Sears employees were concerned, I had won their hearts in that first turnaround year, but that their heads were still stuck somewhere in Sears' history.

I decided it was time to turn up the heat at the top of the company. If my eventual goal was to convince each of 300,000 people that they were the true owners of Sears, then I had to start at the top. It wasn't a matter of ignoring the question of transformation for everyone else. It was all about creating some disciples to carry the message throughout the company.

I built what amounted to a whole year of pressure on those people at the top. They knew what the concepts were because we had been talking about them a lot. We had developed the idea of a solid chain that could be used to link customers to Sears. We called it the customer-service-profit chain, and its links were welded by some abundantly simple assumptions. Good service would lead to good customers. An expanding base of good customers would lead to profits. We had talked about balanced scorecards, too. That was an attempt to shift the conversation way beyond the numbers. Balanced scorecards are aimed at getting to the real issues that drive a company. In our case, service and customer loyalty were premier components.

But those concepts would not carry us far enough. What did it mean to develop a strong customer-service-profit chain? On the surface, it all seemed so obvious. The problem was one of execution. How would we do it? And as attractive as balanced scorecards might be, they aren't setting much of a course for tomorrow. By their nature, they reflect an assessment of the past, even when you pull the process away from the numbers a business creates every day.

What these people at the top had to do was take all of those thoughts, those concepts, and those abstractions, then develop them and then use them to create a strategy.

All the time, I kept hitting that theme: This is your company to save or ruin.

Tony and I came up with a good idea to set the stage for our next Phoenix meeting—the second one. We told everyone to pretend that they were reporters for the *Wall Street Journal*. They were responsible for writing the first two paragraphs of a story describing where Sears would be in the future and how it got there.

If you could strip this process down to its essence, that is what you would find at the foundation. We asked people to come up with their own story of where Sears would be in the future, and we asked them to give us a short description of how it got there. I was asking for their vision, and I wanted it because I wanted it to become the vision of a new Sears.

They were very revealing (and, as it turned out, wildly optimistic given our performance later):

*"What a difference five years can make. Sears today released 1998 earnings which were the capstone on a five year drive to be the most profitable retailer in the world. It was a position they had enjoyed for nearly a century, but lost, and lost quickly. As recently as 1993, there were many who predicted this American business legacy might not survive to the year 2000."*

*"Sears Roebuck and Company, one of the few American companies that have been in business long enough to usher in two turns of the century, moves towards the year 2000 with strong purchasing power support from several generations of customers. The soon to be 114 year old retailer has just posted its 6th straight year of industry leading sales and profit increases."*

*"In the past 5 years, Sears has made a striking comeback when many Wall Street analysts had counted them out of the market. However, new leadership, new organization structure, new store look, but old fashion customer service has brought Sears back as a market leader in the retail business."*

And perhaps best of all from a perverse, competitive standpoint:

*"JC Penney announced today that it will take a $2 billion operating adjustment to establish a reserve for restructuring in its retail and catalog operations. Mark Migraine, Penney's chief financial officer, said that after 4 consecutive years of losing market share to competitors, J.C. Penney's will close 80 unprofitable stores, close its catalog operation, exit the jewelry and cosmetic business, lay-off 18,000 sales associates and dramatically reduce store space devoted to men's apparel. Privately, Penney officials concede that their decisions are based on Sears, Roebuck and Co.'s success in wooing shoppers away from Penney."*

And the best bow to history contestant:

*"The scuttle butt around the Sears tower ten years ago was that Richard Sears was turning over in his grave watching the decline of his beloved company. As we approach the turn of a new century, Mr. Sears would be proud to be reincarnated as a Sears store manager. Admired by its vendors, feared by its competitors and once again loved by its clients, Sears seems to have settled in a retail niche where it can play and win."*

That was where they wanted us to be. They told us even more when they moved to the second paragraph, which was aimed at explaining *why* we had succeeded:

*"A pivotal event seems to have been a regularly scheduled meeting of the top management team held in February 1994. . . . It was at that meeting that the group determined that an obsessive commitment to total customer satisfaction must drive any decisions made. Secondly, they realized that the real power of*

*their franchise lay in the ideas of their associates. Since that 1994 meeting, a relentless effort to radically change the culture of Sears to focus on customers and associates ideas about how to satisfy customers has been ongoing."*

*"Quicker decision making, financially incented managers, local market focus, relentless improvement in customer service are the reasons given by any Sears manager who is asked how they did it. . . . The underlying point of view is that Sears managers understand what customers want and they give it to them."*

*"In addition to a wildly successful television and print campaign, their strategy incorporated a combination of fresh merchandising ideas, remodeled stores and enhanced customer service that eventually attracted 'her' back to Sears."*

*"Refusing to succumb to thinking large, relentlessly driving down costs and valuing speed above all else have fueled this born again retailer's engine. And a new, keen external focus has kept them honest. As one executive remarked "around here we know our competitors numbers better than they do and I'll bet we get them first . . ."*

Set aside for a moment the awareness that there were some hard times ahead. These still were clearly not the products of people who had given up or who didn't recognize the importance of cultural change. Almost all of the mock stories emphasized the fact that Sears had tapped change to become successful again. They were telling us about their visions of what the institution could become.

## 1994: Identifying New Values and Building a New Corporate Culture

Armed with a whole bundle of those predictions, we went back to Phoenix in the spring of 1994. The first thing we did was scrap those old task forces. A new picture of what Sears had to be was starting to evolve. We were building a new culture from the ground up. Based on the analysis of mock newspaper stories, there were four new targets to think about: customers, employees, investors, and innovation.

The new task forces met for almost three days. What were Sears' organizational values? What were the barriers to change? How would we deliver value to shareholders? I told them it was a good start, but that it wasn't enough. We were going to build a new Sears on their initiatives, I said, and they needed to spend more time working on them and gathering information.

You might think, this being the second Phoenix meeting, that a lot of the institutional trouble had been tickled out of this collection of key strategists and managers. But it wasn't. Back they went to Hoffman Estates. A lot of them said the process was interesting, but they had to return to the challenge of running the company and didn't have time to do this extra work. It was those old Sears' Sirens beckoning from the beach.

Don't go changing.

A message went back to each of them: Make time.

The word dribbled in. No one came rushing into my office proclaiming "I'm confused and I'm not going to take it anymore!" It was more subtle than that, and more revealing. These were people who had grown up in the old Sears, where they were told exactly what to do and how to do it. I was hearing a clear message: "We have a problem with lack of direction here. Arthur should tell us what he wants us to do and then we will just go and do it."

At that point, the institution was waiting for lots of paper and lots of instructions. That was how it was done in the old days, like assembling a bad, complicated toy on Christmas Eve or reading the manual about how to fix operational problems on a new computer. Most managers would probably have yielded to that and dispensed a "Manual for Change"! But I knew that would not work.

I told them I had no idea what they should do, but that they had better find out. Operational strategy, I said, is your job. That was exactly what the Sears people didn't expect. You have to be careful on these matters. One wrong move—sending out rules, for example—and you make yourself not only a part of the problem but an extension of the unhappy past. If a sense of ownership was my goal, I was going to create a situation in which it simply had to happen.

On and on the process went. People wanted to know when and how to file reports. I said I didn't care, that they would have to find all of that out by themselves. What is our deadline? When the work is ready. When and where should we meet?

I told them, "It's all yours."

The Tuesday morning task force meeting evolved. It happened at 7 A.M., early enough so everyone could then put in a full-day's work. All of this was starting to shift people a long way from that 29,000-page Sears rule book. They were getting the message. It wasn't about dress codes, showing up for work, and knowing which page to turn to see how we had reacted in 1972. It wasn't about just putting in time.

It was about passion and taking responsibility.

Most of all, it was about survival.

Months into the process, people asked whether the 7 A.M. sessions would be eternal. They were all reminded that the survival of Sears was what had determined the weekly meeting schedule. There was no rule involved, other than the simple, chilling conclusion that either they did it, or it would not be done. The ship would sink with all hands.

The process started bubbling early on. Four task forces became five, with the emphasis on customers, employees, shareholders, change, and values.

What were these people doing?

The Shareholder Task Force combed the ranks of securities analysts and invented a model of what Sears would have to become to put itself in the top quarter in terms of shareholder return of the Fortune 500 companies.

The Change Task Force initiated a plan aimed at drawing all of Sears' employees into the process. They wanted a million ideas from all over the company. They also took a close look at the state of innovation and examined outside benchmarking for Sears.

The Values Task Force hit gold. They collected some 80,000 employee surveys and identified six values that were important to everyone who worked for Sears: honesty, integrity, respect for individuals, teamwork, trust, and customer focus. That was so important. It was a strong sign that the organization had outgrown its own history, that the command-and-control culture simply wasn't good enough or responsive enough. It didn't put enough value on people. Sears' own employees recognized that showing up and trying hard weren't enough, that there had to be a better measure of performance.

The Customer Task Force went on a national romp. They conducted 80 focus groups all over the country. They asked people why they shopped at Sears, what they disliked about the place, their expectations. Our customers were as smart as our employees. They liked the idea of "Satisfaction guaranteed or your money back" and "Take care of the customer." They also knew we weren't doing that anymore. We just weren't meeting their standards. Even with all of that trouble, they told us they liked us and that they wanted us to succeed.

The Employees Task Force set up employee focus groups and collected every piece of data they could find on employee attitudes over time. Once again, we were surprised. The managers at Hoffman Estates might not have realized it, but our people were quite passionate about working for Sears. It wasn't just a job to them; it was their life's work. They were proud of Sears and wanted it to succeed. They wanted to be a part of it. They valued teamwork and personal initiative.

It didn't stop with those groups. Two additions to the list turned out to be crucial. The first covered values and shared beliefs. This group was looking for a mission statement for Sears. The second, which had a much more complicated task than the others, had to find some realistic and effective way to measure what Sears was doing.

## A New Mission for Sears: To Be a Compelling Place to Work, Shop, and Invest

Mission statements are interesting devices. The goal is to reduce that most important but difficult question, "What do we do?" into a memorable and defining answer. The problem is that almost all mission statements end up sounding like a mix between Miss America addresses and the contents of Chinese fortune cookies. You just append your own company's name to the cliché of the era: better shareholder value (at Sears); making customers happy (at Sears); being kind to old dogs and children (at Sears); you will have a better day (at Sears).

Our own first shot at the process delivered something that sounded like the charter for a utopian community, or maybe the United Nations: "Make the whole darned world a better place!" We developed another vision statement that sounded like everyone else's vision statement. (In fact, it was like almost everyone else's vision statement. Ten companies had identical vision statements and 20 more had just about all of our wording, a sign of heavy duplication in the vision statement consulting business.)

Clearly, this wasn't working.

We knew what we wanted in the end. We wanted Sears to be compelling to work for, to shop at, to invest in. The three C's was what we called them. We had three P's, too: passion for customers, people add value, performance leadership.

Voilá! A mission statement is born.

Sears: A compelling place to work, shop, and invest.

No one had to say anything else. It was as simple as it could be; it didn't have to be chiseled into a wall someplace or etched on reminder cards. Anyone from the top to the bottom of Sears could remember and live by the three C's.

Making Sears a compelling place to work was obviously essential. The point of customer contact is one of the most important places in the entire company, and if we did not enliven our employees right down to the sales floor, to make it a bit of a thrill for them to show up and to make them eager do their work, we would be missing the whole point of transformation.

Making it a compelling place to shop was aimed at reconnecting with that lost customer in a very competitive marketplace. We really needed to invite people to come back and make them feel welcomed when they did. That part of the statement was aimed directly at how our stores look and feel.

We were investing $4 billion in the way they looked, after all, and we needed our employees to understand part of their challenge was making that cus-tomer feel completely comfortable and very well served.

As the third arm of the mission statement, investment carried the same weight as the other two parts and depended to a great extent on how we would carry them out. Remember the customer-service-profit chain? If Sears became a compelling place to work and to shop, that would only enhance our standing among current and potential investors.

But then, how would we know where we were in the process of meeting these goals?

We came up with the Total Performance Indicator—TPI for short. It tells us where we stand, on an ongoing basis, with our customers, our employees, and our investors. It works because it is our own creation, crafted by Sears people to measure exactly how well they are doing and where they need improvement, all tightly connected to the idea of making Sears a compelling place to work, shop, and invest.

The Total Performance Indicator also happened to be where the old Sears culture ended and the new Sears culture began.

Measuring is an interesting discipline.

There are all sorts of formulas for it, elaborate descriptions that label every part of a company: inspirational goals for employees, visions, profits, share-holder values. The problem with what was already on paper in the world of measuring was that we knew it would not fit our circumstances. A lot of what was available was intuitive or interpretive, basically too vague to be of real use.

We needed to design a measure that flowed from our mission, that would tell us whether we were a compelling place to work, shop, and invest. We needed a system that would work from the outside, from the customer, right into the center of the company. It had to be clearly presented and cleanly designed, because everyone from me to the woman who comes to fix the dishwasher to the sales associates to the investor had to understand what it was saying. Ultimately, it would be used to determine performance and raises and bonuses, so it had to be real, and it had to be right.

A lot of what we needed was already on hand.

Those Phoenix task forces had collected mountains of data. And one of the things Sears had been very good at over the years was collecting information about customers. It was just that the old Sears never knew quite what to do with it. We had to create some more information because we were moving into uncharted territories in the world of performance measurement.

We were looking for a structure that would tell us what impact strategy and behavior was having on customers and profitability. We wanted to look for causation, to use it as a tool of strategy. Most measurement systems sort of loosely assess the past. We wanted something that would be good for predicting the future. We wanted to know, for example, whether there would be practical, measurable benefits in specific kinds of management training. We wanted to know what the return would be if we invested money in improving the sales floor skills of our associates.

Beyond that, no one had ever built a metric like this that included employee attitudes. But we believed—and were proven correct—that how people felt about their work, the issues they carried with them into the workplace, had a clear, if indirect, connection to how well we were doing.

And that put us into a much different category.

We believed that if we were to create a new Sears, we would have to create a new employee at the same time. We needed everyone to buy into the customer-service-profit chain formula, and the Total Performance Indicator was one of the important tools we were going to use to do that. That was what would carry us beyond the world of gabbing about change and into the world of change itself.

Data crunching came next with the help of an outside consultant, CFI Group. CFI gathered up this mountain of information collected from tens of thousands of employees and customers, mixed it up with page after page of data Sears had already collected, and looked hard for some connections, for the explanations behind why things happen.

While I had resisted using consultants for broad, endless engagements at Sears, there were some specific situations I ran into that I believed called for some outside expertise, the kind of expertise Sears didn't already have. The data crunching presented just such an opportunity.

There were some pretty impressive results.

A couple of the components employees had cited that we thought were going to be important—personal growth and development, and empowered teams among them—didn't show much of a connection to anything. The link between the skills of a manager and the company's bottom line was quite clear.

Employee attitudes toward their jobs had a strong impact on customer service. That was obvious, but now we had the numbers to show how and why. The data also showed strong connections to questions about employee turnover and whether employees would suggest Sears products to their friends and families. From all of that, we decided a better measure for the employee part of the picture would be "employee attitudes."

Here is the kind of connection we found in the data. If you can affect a 5% improvement in employee attitudes, that leads to a 1.3% improvement in customer impression. And that translates into a half of a percent improvement in revenues.

Let me spell that out more clearly.

*That translates into $200 million in increased revenues.*

Tony's team took the consultant conclusions and worked them into a larger formula, creating a measurement that would include our compellings, all the way from shopping to working to investing, along with operating margins and returns on assets. When you put it all in one place, you have a balanced scorecard that reflects a lot more than interpretations. It has clearly described goals and constant measures that tell us where we are on the road to achieving them.

We believe we are the only company in history that has found a way to take these important measures—previously separate measures that had no apparent connection to one another—and turn them into both a mission statement and a measure of our effectiveness.

But we ran the risk of having the entire effort become yet another page in the big dark rule book (which we were on our way toward killing, anyway) unless we found a way to roll it out that would touch everyone in Sears. It took us until the middle of 1995 to construct the TPI, a full two years to transform the culture just at the top of the company.

It simply would not do to stick the instructions in the company mail to 3,500 locations and assume everyone would just sign on to this new culture we had invented. And the place did not have a good track record in field-headquarters communications. People in the field knew we were in trouble long before the temblors reached the tower.

There were a lot of assumptions at work out in the field that were damaging to the effort, too. I kept running into them whenever I visited Sears stores. People thought we were making a bundle on every dollar of revenue we created, when it reality it was just a little under 2 cents. They weren't quite certain what they were supposed to be doing, either. Some thought keeping an eye on inventory so no one stole any of it was the point. You wanted them to say, "Smile and serve the customer," but that obviously wasn't happening.

We believed it was time for everyone to start thinking, from bottom to top. Thinking was not allowed much in the old days. But we knew that it was the only way for people to understand their new mission and to buy into that crucial ownership that we knew would make all the difference if Sears was to thrive.

## 1995: A Retail Education for *All* Sears Employees

So we developed some learning maps. On the surface, they look like board games. But what they do is create thought and discussion about the world of retailing and where and how Sears fits in. There are a lot of questions attached to these maps, but no answers. That is because there are really no correct answers. "How do you meet the needs of a changing population?" is just one of the provocative questions we wanted our people to think about.

The first map went to the Phoenix team in April 1995. By this time, the

Phoenix effort had been expanded to include 60 district managers. This map was called "A New Day on Retail Street." The district managers then held town hall meetings for their store managers. Then the store managers were responsible for carrying the process down to the associates.

The old Sears popped up almost immediately. The store managers wanted to know when and how they should hold their meetings. We told them that was their decision. Then they wanted a clear deadline on when the process should be completed. We told them they should do that whenever they thought it was appropriate. Well, they asked, when should that be?

We relented. Six months, we said.

The second map, "Voices of Our Customers," went out toward the end of 1995. It moved down through the organization the same way. "The Sears Money Flow," the third map, came out early in 1996.

Toward the end of 1996, we rolled out the most recent product, "Sears Total Performance Indicators," to the 15,000 people who manage Sears. This map compressed a year and a half of work into about an hour.

I'm not going to try to mislead you about the impact of all of this work. The Total Performance Indicator and the learning maps are crucial parts of Sears' culture. We finally have a standard we can use to measure everyone every day, something they can all understand and work toward. Sears has never had that before.

Until my last days as CEO, we were still at war with our competition, and I still struggled with Sears' history and its tendency to assert itself whenever it could. There were a lot of bright points along the way. I killed the rule book, and I am still very happy about how that happened. I just rolled it all out in front of everyone at the beginning of 1995 and said it was dead. It was all replaced with two very short booklets that say everything that needs to be said about working at Sears. We called them "Freedoms" and "Obligations," and everyone got them.

We finally got real about the process of performance evaluations. Even I got one. My executive committee did a 360-degree appraisal of how well I did my job. Or not.

Salaries and bonuses are tied more directly to company performance. Job appraisal is all about how you connect with the people around you and all about what a person can do to improve.

All in all, 1995 was an important year. We took another step that was attached to my long-standing belief that education is critically important to personal growth. Wherever I have been, I have always believed that education was constant and that people who left it behind when they finished school were making a terrible mistake. We had training at Sears, but that was basically functional. We had no education about our industry. We had no way to educate people about how they could become better executives. We had no education about basic economics or about functional leadership. So we founded Sears University at Hoffman Estates.

In 1997, we had 20,000 people run through our programs, and the demand from employees since then has been unbelievable. It doesn't come without its worries, of course. You don't want something like this to be viewed as the chic management thing to do. This kind of effort isn't new to American business, but it is brand new to Sears.

I like to go down there on the closing day to spend a couple of hours with the senior leadership group, usually about 35 or 40 people. I tell them about where we have been and where we are and how we got there. Usually they are a little shy at the beginning of the course, but by the end they are just chirping away. They carry it back to work with them, and it just spreads all over the place.

There have been some interesting observations out of the Sears classes. Sometimes people go back to their jobs and find they are light-years ahead of their bosses, and it is frustrating for them. They run head-on into the old Sears.

I know how that feels.

Just when you think you have wrestled history to the floor and won the count, someone pops up and talks about a decline over time in 626 at 1008. This changing of the culture business isn't pretty, but I'm not looking at a place that is described solely by its seating chart anymore.

Still, we had a long way to go before we were ready for *Romeo and Juliet*, a lesson I would be learning, to my displeasure, during my final years as CEO.

It wasn't that we hadn't moved along, and quite successfully. The problem was keeping up the momentum, struggling against that institutional inclination to let things slide, to assume we had found the solution and would just stick with it forever.

One of the most revealing experiences in this process was our search for the target customer, the battle to transform Sears from what had been essentially a men's store full of tools and equipment into a store that reflected the changing nature of American society. This was a message Sears had missed, even as the rest of the world was becoming well aware that women had moved into an important role in the American family, that of chief financial officer.

CHAPTER 7

# Finding the True Sears Customer— and Meeting *Her* Needs

IF YOU THINK about a company that has been dominated for most of its history by men, that thought of itself as the perfect place for men to buy tools and tires, car batteries, work clothing, entertainment centers to watch football, lawn mowers, snowblowers, and every other manly thing, then it is easy to see why Sears thought of itself as a men's store.

Wasn't that mostly what it was all about in the beginning?

Addressing the problems I found in Sears' corporate culture was a battle that played out at one level, but we faced a different challenge in the marketplace. In 1993, it was clear to me, Sears still thought of itself as a men's store, which didn't much surprise me given its history. All of the important statistical signs pointed to the fact that the nation had changed. And now it was time for Sears to change again, too.

Farmers were the target market when Sears began, and it loaded its catalog with a very manly selection of stuff, everything from the latest in cream separators to a vast collection of armaments and ammunition. Even when it shifted into its retail stores in the 1920s, the assumption that men were making the buying decisions stayed in place.

The advertising, the store design, the marketing, the selection of goods—

all of it was aimed at that manly market. The fact that the company made so much money for so many years affirmed the decision. The thought that Sears was a men's store was still dominant when I walked in in 1992. Hardware and hard lines were good sources of dependable income. Why abandon a formula that had worked so well for so long?

There is a simple answer to that question: The assumption was flat wrong. What complicates the answer is that Sears was sitting on everything it needed to understand that men were no longer the right target customer, that they were indeed quite valuable to us, but not the way they were valuable to us in 1940, 1950, or 1960.

There is no end of irony in the fact that this company that had been so tightly connected to customers for so many years completely missed one of the most significant cultural changes of the twentieth century. At some point at which no one at Sears was paying much attention, women began playing a bigger and bigger role in financial decision making. When that happened, the business proposition that was driving almost everything at Sears should have changed.

Instead, the company that was always so comfortable selling pliers and wrenches failed to recognize it would now have to become comfortable selling fashion, selling perfume, selling undergarments, selling whatever it was that the American *woman* needed, and selling it to her in a setting that felt trustworthy and comfortable.

That was the problem we set out to remedy when we went searching for our real target customer. After all of the cost-cutting we did to keep the company alive, it became our most important mission. We needed to find those new customers and find a better, more effective way to invite them back into our stores.

## Recognizing that Customers Change— and Continue to Change

It wasn't something we had to do just once. Assessing the target customers and thinking about connecting and drawing them into the stores was a daily menu item during my eight years at Sears. We had our glorious successes and dismal failures, sometimes both on the same day. But what was most important was keeping the focus on those customers and what they wanted from Sears.

At almost the same time, it was clear from my earliest days that we could no longer afford to ignore how our remaining stores looked. I had a $4 billion commitment from the board of directors, and I planned to use it to construct a new public face for Sears, a transformation that would touch everything from the handles on the front door to the number of hooks we had in the dressing rooms.

We would be radically changing the mix of what we offered in the stores, too, without abandoning any of the merchandise categories that had done so well for us. The Chinese say presentation is everything in the delivery of food to the table. The same holds true in the delivery of goods to the customer, particularly to your most important customer.

The target search went deep into the company's amazing collection of data about customers and their lives, then shifted into the selection of an advertising agency to tailor the message to the new target customer. Later on, the challenge became knowing when to change again, when to revise that message when it was clear that we had tapped all we could from one strategy and needed to build another.

Beyond that, the constant assessment of the target customer was one of the most important repairs that we undertook in our first year of transformation at Sears.

In my version of Sears' history, that inability to recognize our changing customers was what went wrong in the first place. When Sears stopped paying attention, those customers abandoned us in response and took their business to a collection of competitors who would pay the closest and best attention to them. The way the stores looked—dark and old and dirty in some cases—was an open invitation to stay away. Shopping is supposed to be fun and easy.

Look at the businesses that are so strong today and think about what it is they offer. Wal-Mart is one of the most astoundingly successful retail businesses in modern history and, at least until recently, it won its stripes by paying close attention to customers who are always watching their dollars. Nordstrom is not a Sears competitor, but it is another good company to watch. Its passion for taking care of customers is legendary. Because of the vast selection of merchandise it offers, Home Depot could easily have become a nightmare, but it works hard to stay connected to the people who shop there.

Like almost everything else in the transformation of such a huge company, the search for the target customer has been a continuing challenge. But it was not enough to simply identify this new target. We had to change the mind-set of a company that had its marketplace formula running in exactly the wrong direction. It could no longer be about offering a vast collection of stuff on the assumption that people would just come into the stores to buy.

Putting the emphasis on customers involves inviting them into the process of making strategy, and that is where Sears took an important leap ahead. The new Sears is aimed very specifically at what customers want. We have sought their permission to develop our businesses. We wanted to know what they would allow us to be so that we could construct strategy built on their perceptions of Sears and its role in the marketplace.

I'm not talking about guesswork. We actually went out and asked people what kind of Sears they would accept. Should we be in health care? Should we be selling cars? Should we be selling pet food? We factored their answers into our strategy. That's one clear reason why many of the "we's" in this book reach far beyond Sears the institution and out into the marketplace. Our customers have obviously been central to our success.

All of that was a refinement that came later in the battle.

The struggle in the beginning was to shift from dealing with survival to dealing with growing our business. And we couldn't do that without finding that target customer. It wasn't as though this special character was hiding. All anyone had to do was a take a close look at the data we had collected over so many years and the answers became apparent.

Those numbers launched us on our quest.

It was a search that would transform the way the company looks and the way it behaves. In no way was it a simple mission. Like almost everything else at Sears, it did not end after the first round. In fact, it will never end. As the market changes, Sears must change with it. I'm not talking about precipitous, overnight changes aimed at trying to move some numbers. I am not going to kid you; there was tremendous pressure from every direction to make those kinds of shifts when Sears' numbers started heading south in the late 1990s.

Why couldn't we be more like Home Depot? Why couldn't we be more like Kohl's? I heard that from the board of directors and I heard that from my own staff. They didn't seem to understand at some point that we were Sears, and our role, despite the potential rewards, and our options for change were limited by that reality.

A spontaneous, short-term shift wasn't what I was looking for.

I'm talking about strategy that drives the way the place runs over the long term. It must remain a compelling place to shop, invest, and work. That, after all, is our mission. But how that happens must be closely connected to the marketplace, to the workers, and to the shareholders.

If the transformation of internal Sears is the story of changing the wings on a plane while it is traveling at 600 knots at 34,000 feet, then identifying the target customer and selling to that market is just as difficult. You don't want the company to crash during an internal transformation, and you don't want the customers you already have to flee when you change your marketing message.

How did we get from there to here?

I'll tell you about the Softer Side campaign and how it came to be later in this chapter. But it is important to know up front how well it worked.

There is one outside performance review that deserves some attention because it measured quite well the impact of our target customer decision. *USA Today*'s "Ad Track," the newspaper's weekly look at how much customers like major advertising campaigns, reported in 1997 that our Softer

Side campaign, four years old and always changing, remained a solid hit with television viewers.

The analysis included the note that Sears is an American institution and is one of the brand names people trust the most, and that its Softer Side campaign sent that message creatively and consistently since its rollout.

With an accolade like that, you might think Sears would want to keep that Softer Side theme forever. No. I watched that campaign begin to wither in its fifth year, when we decided we had to search for another theme and another advertising effort to revive our connection with customers. Softer Side had no value message, and our customers were discovering competitors whose message was value.

Still, Softer Side was a clear winner in its time, not only for the success it helped achieve, but for the transformation it reflected inside of Sears.

It was no coincidence that most of the ads in the Softer Side campaign were about women.

She had been there all along, making almost all of the important decisions in the family, taking care of the children, managing the household, and keeping close tabs on money and how it was spent. We wanted to recognize that, embrace it, and find a way to invite this crucial member of the family back into our stores.

Look at the ads from Christmas 1997. They depict a woman who is in charge of the seasonal atmosphere in the home, the one family member who will not sit back and sigh with contentment until the last course of the Christmas dinner is presented, consumed, and applauded. Women are confident, competent people who shop with a purpose. Men might wait for the last three days then come up with some gifts no one understands, but women shop thoughtfully and with family economics in mind. The ads invited a woman to Sears with an implicit promise that what she needed for herself and for her family was there (and of course, still is). They recognized her dreams about becoming beautiful. They told the story of her complicated life and worked gracefully at convincing her that Sears wanted to be one of the chapters in that unfolding family drama.

We spent $45 million a year sending that message. By 1997, some of our critics were saying the campaign was growing old, and they had a good point. But that missed the larger lesson. Sales figures go up and down all the time. I lived with them for eight years, and I know what they represented for us.

Of course we would love to win big all the time. But that is not how this competitive business works. Bad numbers are a rallying call for the troops. Part of the message of ownership is that you take these matters seriously and work hard to improve the situation.

That's where we were when we began our search for the target customer just after I arrived. We found her, and she repaid us by moving us way up in the pack. Even though advertising messages and themes might change over time, that is not the kind of connection to abandon, given the role she played in reviving Sears.

Think of it as the tip of an iceberg that started taking shape in 1992 with a collection of very depressing numbers that reflected Sears' severe, long-term decline in the retail marketplace. The need for a radical change was so apparent we literally did not have much of a choice.

The battle was taking place inside and outside of the company.

We were wrestling with divisions that were losing millions upon millions of dollars every year. That was the internal part, and we handled it with our cost-cutting plan. But over the long term, I believed, people would recognize that it was this external battle, the struggle to tap the deep loyalty to Sears and bring those customers back, that would define the company, help pull it out of its crisis, and revive its hopes for the future.

## Sears Was a "Manly" Store—but Women Were the Primary Customers

The empowering of the American woman was one of the most important cultural changes in the last half of the twentieth century. In the mind's eye of the marketplace, we were what we had always been—a boy's store full of manly tools and toys. It is not difficult to trace the source of that perception. We created it over many, many years. Inside of the company, we advanced a philosophy and culture that viewed the American man as our target.

It was almost as though the kitchens of the 1950s, with their pink-and-black tile and their homemaker moms in chiffon dresses, had never changed. Ozzie and Harriet Nelson and David and Ricky were the role models in that mythology, blissfully living in comfort on an endless supply of milk and cookies and delighting in modeling their sweater collections. We completely missed the fact that while Harriet and just about all the other TV moms were comfortable at home, real mothers were going through some huge changes.

Women were moving into the workplace at every level and playing a more and more important role in family economics. "Working mom" was becoming such a common description that women who chose to stay at home were becoming a minority. This transformed just about everything in America, from the old idea of higher education as an entrée into an exclusive men's club to notions about who is responsible for what within the family.

It transformed shopping habits, too.

Of course, there had always been stores and chains that were developed with women in mind. But Sears wasn't clearly in that group. It was in the nature of the institution to be what it had always been. That is the message behind all of the talk about the need to change culture. Culture is the force that makes people think that all they must do to succeed is what they did in the past. For years, Sears people assumed the solution to all problems was just to do what they always did, but better. The problem with that, of course, is that if the heart of a problem is cultural, then behaving the old way is only going to make things get worse.

That was the old Sears, going into the marketplace the way it had always gone into the marketplace, without recognizing that everything about that marketplace was shifting. We were sitting on the best real estate in America, but we were missing the fact that everything around us had changed: our competition, our reputation, and, most importantly, our customers.

Ignoring all of that was simply crazy from a business perspective.

This company had been collecting numbers for decades that measured social changes in great detail. It was sitting right on top of the data that was telling it what to do, but it couldn't take those numbers and translate them into an effective strategy. I knew that if Sears wanted to find a target customer to build its strategy and its future on, it could find no better candidate than the American woman. But I needed some ammunition to wage that battle.

Sears was so uncomfortable with the idea of women as target customers that some of its store managers were unable to discuss the marketing of lingerie. They thought it was not to be talked about because it was dirty. It was women's stuff. They wanted Sears to be all about wrenches and tires and all of the comfortable, beefy merchandise they had been selling to a male market forever. Of course, presentation is crucial in the display of those items, too. But selling to a woman as the target customer carries a business into a different world that demands a different look, a different smell, and a much different sense of place.

Even worse, some of the people inside of Sears didn't want the company to be about that market at all. They were driven by the assumption that retailing was a dead horse, so they dragged the company into a whole collection of misdirected adventures that only undermined our need to get better and better at the business of shopkeeping. They were paying attention to a lot of details inside of Sears—the bureaucratic side of Sears, if you will—but were not connecting with the real business at hand. They were not in touch with our customers, and not in touch with what they wanted in the form of merchandise.

I unearthed a chart shortly after I arrived, part of a confidential file called "Marketing to Women" that was prepared by the customer research people based on data collected in 1991. The title of the chart was "Female Participation in Purchase Decision." It was one of the most revealing pieces of visual information I had ever seen. It showed that *women were the key decision makers in almost every sale Sears made*. You would expect that to happen in women's apparel, for example, where they scored a 96 on the decision-making scale. But they scored a 70% in men's apparel, 92% in kid's apparel, 73% in home appliances and electronics, 87% in home fashions, 40% in home improvement, and 35% in automotive.

That is a powerful collection of numbers to ignore. This kind of data takes on an even greater significance when it is set alongside some other measures. Consider the tracking of Sears' image in the marketplace over time. It showed a potentially fatal erosion. In 1983, for example, Sears was the "store shopped most often" by about 16% of the population. That number had declined to 9% by 1992—bad enough by itself, but positively frightening when compared to the numbers put on the charts by our competitors:

- Kmart was shopped most often by 14%.
- Wal-Mart was the store shopped most often by 25%. And worse, Wal-Mart's performance was rising on a 45-degree slope tracked over a decade.
- Hapless Montgomery Ward, now being dismantled, started out down at the bottom and ended up there, too, with just 1% shopping it most often.
- JCPenney had dropped from 6% to 4% over the decade.

It is still chilling to look at the slope on those simple numbers and recognize that the people inside of Sears just had to know what was happening. All they had to do was stay the course and watch those numbers follow the trend, and it would be all over before anyone knew it. But if they were such a depressing collection of indicators about the missed opportunities of the past, they also held the key to the future.

If women were making all of those buying decisions, if they had indeed become the chief financial officers of the American family, why were we continuing to ignore their needs, their desires, and their dreams? My own suspicion was that we just didn't know how to talk to them and had not created a store that was warming or at all intriguing for them. It wasn't so much that the merchandise was all wrong. We looked closely at that and learned, much to our surprise, that we had some very strong contenders, and that the customers who found them recognized their quality.

It was just that they didn't realize the merchandise was there—it was that well hidden, that poorly promoted, and that badly displayed.

We were still a cross between a big hardware store and a department store that felt very much as though it were in decline. Empty shelves. Empty walls. The advertising messages were empty, too. They seemed to pay a lot of attention to price, and no attention to value.

Of course, the merchandise mix needed a lot of fixing. The fashion offerings were close to awful and not at all well presented. After many false starts over the years, we had no fashion brands that people were paying much attention to. It was as though Sears people didn't know how important a look was to America, whether it was a look that came through in the form of jeans and shirts and sweaters you would actually want to own, or a look that added a touch of elegance and taste.

We had trust, too. All of the survey data indicated people viewed Sears as the kind of store that was solid and worthy of their trust. But we had not found a way to tap it. Trust is the single most important component in the sale of jewelry, for example. Trust is what is behind the sale of an engagement diamond. People generally don't know what they are buying, but they trust that when their jeweler presents a half carat in a gold setting, it is not glass glued to worthless metal. Sears "the men's store" wasn't pushing jewelry, even though people trusted us enough to put their faith in that kind of purchase.

It was a natural market, but we weren't taking it seriously enough.

The research also showed there was a peculiar reality at work out in the real world that said a lot about Sears and why it was having so many problems with its customers. When we asked shoppers to measure Sears based on individual lines or departments, no one could touch us. In every category, we performed much more strongly than our competitors, including Wal-Mart, Kmart, local department stores, Penney's, Ward's, and specialty stores. But when we asked customers to rate Sears overall, it fell all the way to the bottom of the list. Once again, the culprit was lack of focus, along with the fact that we had marketed Sears over the years as a collection of nonintegrated businesses.

The price we paid for that over time was that Sears as a brand represented less and less to a bigger and bigger group of people. Think of simple word associations. Tools and Craftsman go together. Kitchens and Kenmore. Those connections had to be expanded: Tools and Craftsman *at Sears.* Kitchens and Kenmore *at Sears.* It wasn't just that we had failed to recognize and move on the message about the role of women. We had pursued a course that, by its very direction, made Sears weak even as it made the individual lines Sears offered very strong.

Once again, amid all the dark realities there was a pathway.

We had a lot of good merchandise, even though we were apparently in decline in the eyes of our customers. They were well aware of the gap between what they needed and what we were.

## A New Challenge: Reaching Our New Customers without Alienating Our Old Customers

Our new target customer had to be the American woman. She was too important to everyone to overlook for even one more month. And her connections made the target even more enticing. Think of her as the sun in the middle of the family solar system. If we were able to reconnect with her, then by extension we would be reconnecting with everyone in the family.

There were some refinements. After we crunched all the numbers, we realized we had to aim straight for the middle-American family, women aged 25 to 54 years old, with an income level of $25,000 to $60,000 a year at the time. Home ownership and the presence of children would be an important part in the formula. It was clear to us that these women were the primary purchasing agents for the family and, perhaps more important, that they set the standards for the household.

Break those numbers down and the clarity of it all becomes even more apparent. Some 65% of all American consumers over age 18 fall into the targeted group. Our numbers also showed that members of the group were already playing a significant role in Sears' current business. We had selected an income target that represented 42% of the nation.

Here is the whole picture boiled down into a little narrative. Mom has a job outside the home, so her time is precious. She doesn't have a lot of money to spend, so she is always looking to spend it wisely. She wants the best quality she can afford. Almost all of her shopping time involves the search for value so she can help meet her family's needs. And while she is about all of this business, if she finds something wonderful for herself, she is delighted with the purchase.

Then there was something we called "the Yellow Ribbon Effect." You remember the song and, more important, the symbol of the yellow ribbon during 1970s Iranian hostage crisis. That was all about letting everyone know you were waiting for someone you cherished to return. Our target shopper knew all about our decline, but she was waiting for us, and wanting for us, to come home, to become once again the Sears she had always been able to depend on. We concluded the women in our target group had imaginary yellow ribbons tied all over everything, just waiting for the sign that Sears was coming back for them.

We couldn't stop there.

In men, we had a clearly defined secondary market, even though we would no longer view the male as gatekeeper of the household. But he was too important to diminish in our strategy. In creating values attached to the new target customer, we didn't want to undermine what we already had with such a dependable group of shoppers. The male customer would become the target of a whole range of specialties, from Craftsman tools to auto equipment to men's clothing. We had to make this shift without offending him because there were simply too many other places he could shop for the things he needed in his life.

We wanted all of this constructed on the lasting trust in Sears that was apparent in all of our research. We also had an ace up our sleeve—the fact that, despite its many problems, people still wanted Sears to do well. That is the piece of Sears' history that is so essential, so valuable. It is important that people want you to do well. That is an advantage that puts you in a different league. It separates you from the newcomers and gives you an edge over the rest of the people in the field.

It was a complicated challenge.

We had to forge a strategy that would convince everyone in the company and in the marketplace that we were heading off in a new direction, and that this course change would carry us into the lives and decision-making processes of the women of America. And we had to do that without over-selling our case. Women are very smart shoppers. Let them down just once and they go somewhere else. They also know about the feel of a store, about the sense of place involved in the shopping formula. That was why our $4 billion renovation project was such an important part of the strategy.

Try to achieve this kind of change in a company as big as Sears and you get an object lesson in the depth of culture. It wouldn't do us much good to unleash a big advertising campaign if the stores were not in line with the message. That would be imperial headquarters sending dictates into a void again. I knew that if we were to make this connection, and make it work, the message had to go from the bottom of the company all the way to the top. The target customer effort would be as important inside of Sears as it was in the marketplace.

We had to find a way to do all of that honestly—first, because that is simply the right thing to do, and second, because it is bad business to do anything else. The data told us that our new target customer was just too smart to con and too sophisticated to be misled. Telling everyone "Sears has changed" would be a big mistake unless Sears had actually changed. We already knew what happened when those old promises—customers first and satisfaction guaranteed or your money back—were broken.

We had to repair those old damages and create a new future at the same time. We were going to spend $4 billion renovating our remaining stores and developing product lines and strategies. But that would take years. We needed an immediate message that told everyone what this new Sears was about. It would have to be carefully developed, tightly linked to strategy, aimed directly at our new target and built on the word that we were really changing, that this wasn't just about a collection of empty advertising promises.

I knew I would need help with that.

## A New Advertising Campaign for Our New Target Market

I started talking to John Costello about all of these issues in December 1992. He was president and chief operating officer at A. C. Nielsen U.S. and had an extensive, successful career in marketing at many different levels. I wanted him to join us at Sears. I told him that the challenge would be to identify and connect with a new target customer and to transform an icon. The conversations continued and expanded. I told him Sears needed a new image and messenger, a new advertising agency with a strong sense of what we needed to tell the women of America.

Of course he was reluctant. Who wouldn't be? Everyone knew the numbers, and the people in the business knew what they meant. Sears was in bad shape, and a big part of my job was playing evangelist and making converts who would come on board and help us turn the place around. I knew they wouldn't be staying forever, because that is not the nature of the executive career these days. Opportunities arise, and even your most favored associates move on. Business models change and skills that were valuable for one set of tasks become outdated. Visionaries don't necessarily make strong managers.

But Costello was exactly what I needed in 1993.

Costello joined on April 1, and we immediately set about the task of finding someone to create a new image for Sears, a new invitation to its new target customer. There was an advertising beauty contest. Obviously, everyone wanted to find some way to land the Sears account. Our numbers were improving quite dramatically, and that sent some powerful messages to the advertising marketplace. It was no longer just a huge account for a declining company.

By every measure, Sears was repairing itself and creating a turnaround legend in the process. This was a chance to help create an image for a winning company.

We narrowed the choice to three candidates: Young & Rubicam, Hal Riney & Partners, and Wells, Rich, Green. We were looking at ad agencies that had clearly defined strengths. Young & Rubicam and Hal Riney came forward with brilliantly designed television campaigns. Wells, Rich, Green advanced a strong print campaign. I had expanded the group of Sears people involved in the process. We had 15 strong merchandising and marketing people on board now, but I told everyone from the outset that the committee would be there for support and advice. Costello, my merchandising chief Bob Mettler, and I would make the final decision.

It was at this point that the Softer Side campaign began to emerge, along with a much closer look at the woman as target customer and some ideas about how she should be approached. Even though the advertising proposals were gorgeous and brilliantly presented, there were some key distinctions that would ultimately help us make our decision.

Hal Riney came in with a sophisticated effort that pegged Sears' image to the passage of seasons. People who have never heard the agency's name knew all about its work. It had produced a long line of winning campaigns, all of them full of texture, personality, and identity. Their concept for the new Sears was simple: Americans go through renewals every season. In spring, it is time to get the home ready for the great shift out of doors. In the summer, everything seems to move to the backyard, or out into nature. In fall, there is a sense that it is time now to return to hearth and home.

Riney's plan was to create an advertising campaign that would weld Sears' message to the consumer to these seasonal renewals. It was very intriguing because it recognized that merchandise changes with each season. It was also tightly pegged to consumer research and insight. It offered us the chance to renew ourselves every 90 days, and that is crucial in the development of long-term advertising messages. People are overwhelmed by information all of the time. These ads could reflect constant change even as they bonded the customer to Sears all year around.

But, to my way of thinking, there was a problem.

As compelling as the proposed campaign was, it did not seem to be speaking directly to our target customer. Costello and Mettler and I liked the approach, and Riney delivered that wonderful sense of America and history that is so important to Sears, a story magnificently told in his own voice. But would it fit with our long-term strategy, and would it help forge the connection with our new target customer?

Costello had argued from the beginning that one of our biggest challenges would be to pick an advertising agency that could deliver both the short-term idea and the long-term strategy. It would have to work very closely with Sears so the focus could stay on our strategy of reaching out to the American woman. Most important, we wanted to address the problem that was so apparent in the numbers we had been crunching—that the Sears brand had lost its standing.

## Finding the Softer Side of Sears

Young & Rubicam understood that from the beginning.

The Softer Side theme was their invention right at the start. Creating a strong brand amounts to a consumer promise that builds some powerful expectations. A competitor can steal your ideas, but they can't steal your brand. The Y&R Softer Side campaign came at the challenge from a completely different direction. It recognized that Sears had always had a reputation for its hard lines—its washers and dryers and electronics and tools—but that there was a softer side here, too, aimed directly at the new target customer. The Riney campaign would have given us the chance to change ourselves every quarter, but the Y&R campaign gave us the chance to develop a brand distinctiveness that Sears was missing, and to carry that message consistently over the long term.

Most important, it recognized that even as we transformed ourselves by inviting women into our stores, Sears hard lines were crucial to the success of our business. They had performed well even during downturns in the econ-

omy. We didn't want to just fluff ourselves up. We didn't want to end up looking like a lot of other shopkeepers in the marketplace, particularly in all of
those malls where our presence was so strong and the competition was so hot.
The data told us that our target customer was just as important in making
decisions about appliances and electronics as she was about buying clothing
for the baby. Y&R had to come up with a campaign that marched right
along with that strategy, and the Softer Side proposal seemed to meet that
challenge.

The message was carefully crafted, too.

It was not telling the American woman "Come and see spectacular
dresses!" because that simply would not work for a place that had a century-
long reputation for selling socks and underwear. We could not risk over-
promising. The theme was that Sears was changing to meet women's needs,
and that it was time to come back and take a look at what we had to offer. It
was merchandise based, but still emphasized that overall Sears message that
was so important to our strategy. If we had claimed we had shifted from "out
of touch" to "perfect," we would be rejected. But if we said we were working
hard to understand you better, come and take a look at us, then the target customer would respond.

We knew the American woman wanted to give us another chance. But
we also knew we had to do it exactly right this time.

Sears turned to Y&R after analyzing its presentation and conducting an
extensive ranking test that measured everything from strategic insight to
overall service. The key point was that Sears needed to make sure it was picking an advertising company, not just a campaign. We believed Y&R had a
greater strategic insight into the customer and the business challenge we
faced, along with a strong creative presence. There are agencies that have
strong creative wings or great research capabilities, but it is rare to find both
of those disciplines so closely linked.

What put Y&R up front was that the Softer Side campaign had a strategic uniqueness. It would have staying power and it could change, but it would
send the same, consistent message over time.

It wasn't an easy decision. Riney's ads were so compelling that they won many advocates. But again, we were dealing with the forging of image and strategy. I decided we would go with Y&R. As lovely as the Riney product was, I felt it was more about the past than about the future. Y&R was talking about tomorrow, and I liked that.

We sent our first big message to the new target customer in September 1993. But before we did that, we invited all of our vendors to New York for a preview of the campaign. They had to understand what this new Sears was all about, and we knew we would need their support to carry out the plan.

Then we went public in a huge way.

We invited the American woman to come see the softer side of Sears, and a little later, to visit the many sides of Sears. We had to move quickly on the campaign because, just as with our turnaround, time was a great enemy. Christmas was coming, and we had to get the word that Sears was changing into the marketplace.

The fact that it worked so well belies another reality. We were changing, of course, but had not yet changed. Softer Side was aimed at sending a message inside of Sears as well as outside of Sears. That is why we brought the 15,000 associates from our stores to Hoffman Estates to preview the campaign. We believed if we got them and the customers excited, they would forgive the fact that our store transformations were only just getting under way. The renovations were following a five-year plan, and nothing was much in place when the "Softer Side" campaign was launched.

It became a rallying point inside the company. The Sears associates knew we had better merchandise than we were getting credit for, but they were frustrated that no one was coming in to buy it. This was our chance to tell them it was going to be different, that Sears had a new leadership that had their interests and the interests of customers in mind. We wanted them to know we were going to become a customer-driven organization that focused on innovation. Honor the past, we told them, but pay close attention to this new target customer so we know how to serve her in the future.

The campaign hit faster than anything anyone had ever seen. It was an invitation in the beginning: "Come take a look at us." Then the theme became that Sears was the right place for you with the right merchandise, the right attitude, and the right message.

The whole effort was aimed on one level at telling everyone that change is a good thing, and that the changes that were happening at Sears would be welcoming to our new target customer and to everyone in her family.

It would be nice to think of that effort as the be-all and end-all of Sears' transformation, that finding the target customer was the only challenge. But it didn't stop there. I had a thought—actually a worry—that had been with me ever since the decisions were made about spinning off all of Sears' old businesses and becoming focused on retailing.

I was concerned about where our growth was going to come from. What happens when the turnaround runs out of gas? What happens when earnings start to slow down? What happens if the stock price goes sideways for five years? How do we deal with that? As it turned out, these were prescient concerns, little predictors of the trouble that was down the road.

## The Next Challenge: Maintaining Success and Growing the Business

But those questions were clearly on my agenda in 1994 because of another change that was underway. I got a call to visit with Ed Brennan in his office in the fall of the year. He told me that the board had decided it was time to spin Allstate Insurance off to the shareholders. He said he thought that was the right decision.

"The other decision that I think is right is you should step up and become chairman of Sears, Roebuck and Company and I should retire," Brennan said.

It was an emotional moment for Ed and for me.

What it meant was that the brass ring had arrived. I told myself, "This is it. This is what you prepared yourself for." To have moved through all of those jobs and all of those industries and arrived at this point, the feeling was incredible. I was the first outsider since the General to move into this job.

Ed told me he wanted to keep quiet about the change until Sears

153

announced it was spinning off Allstate. He said it was the intention of the board to elect me chairman and chief executive officer of the company, at which point I would move onto the board.

That would mean Sears, Roebuck and Company would finally be back where it belonged, in the marketplace, with no other distractions attached.

What was I going to do to grow our business?

We had our full-line stores, the 800-pound gorilla and the engine that had gotten us this far. They were always going to be there. It was a mature segment that had produced excellent profit growth, but the investment community was not going to be viewing it as a comer for the long term. That doesn't mean you discount it, ignore it, and move on to something else. Sears had made that mistake before.

But we had to find some way to freshen our mix and to reach out into the marketplace.

Wall Street always wants growth—sustainable, high growth. The higher the growth rate, the higher the multiple, the higher the stock price. What was in my mind was creating a new mix of earnings with an offering that would have clear permission from the customer. It would have to be built on Sears' traditional strengths and trust. It would have to be highly visible, and it would have to send the message that Sears was reaching out to transform the character of its earnings.

It was a matter for deep study, and I kept most of this to myself.

For the most part, I also kept quiet about the steps I was going to take to deal with my worries. Russ Davis and I had some conversations about what to do. We called in a collection of consultants for some advice on what we might do. Once again, I felt that everyone was too interested in focusing on structure and internals at Sears. They wanted to talk about core competencies, what we were good at. How would we translate all of that into programs and strategies to grow business? I didn't want to get into another engagement that would be looking at structure.

Once again, I reached out to a consultant for a limited, but important, engagement.

I wanted to look at customers, and that is where we hit gold.

Corporate Decisions Incorporated, of Boston (since merged with Mercer Management) had a completely different idea. They came in and pitched us on an outside-in approach, which agreed with my idea. CDI's argument was that Sears had to look at the decisions the customer makes when it is time to buy an item. You can't just grow businesses; you must think about how the customer thinks about you. I thought that was incredibly right on. I had been familiar with the CDI people, particularly with Adrian Slywotzky and Kevin Mundt, for years. But I wanted to know whether they were still at the top of their game.

So I called one of the three smartest people I have ever met, Ben Shapiro. He was a classmate of mine at Harvard and later a tenured professor of marketing there. I told him I had a good feeling about Slywotzky and CDI, but that it was a feeling that was now six years old and I needed to update it. Shapiro said, "Well, Slywotzky is one of the three smartest people I have ever met." So, one of the three smartest people I have ever met thought this consultant was one of the three smartest people he had ever met.

I concluded it was a pretty good bet.

I worked on this privately for almost a year, well into 1995. I began to reveal to my fellow executive committee members what I was finding out. They were a little miffed that they had not been included. I told them it was never a question of whether they were smart enough to handle the subject. I was concerned that they might have been tempted into advocating for their own businesses a little too much in the process. I wanted to avoid one of those contests where everyone becomes the editor and protector for their colleagues.

It was an unusual moment. They felt that after three years of banging the heads of our competition and forging the company, I was not really trusting them with questions about the future of Sears. They were absolutely right about that on one level, but the issue wasn't a question of trust. I needed a framework to talk about the issues, and I needed a good deal of time with CDI before I could put anything on the table.

I wanted us to get to the point where we could have an intelligent conversation about growing our businesses. People have a tendency to get obsessed with the new. I was concerned that with three years of success behind us, everyone would just want to move on to the next game in town and get off on the wrong track. By the end of 1995, I felt it was time to raise the question of growth in a more public way. The Allstate separation from Sears had been flawless. The stock price was up 70%. We delivered a 20% increase in earnings.

The future was all still about customers, I told them. But we had to look more closely at the marketplace to see which sectors were growing faster than other sectors, what parts of the marketplace were mature, how competent our competition was, and, finally, what Sears could do to make the customer believe in it.

That is a complicated set of goals that grows even thornier when Wall Street is factored in. Remember, our mission was to be a compelling place in which to shop, invest, and work. We had to develop a growth strategy that was convincing for consumers because, ultimately, that was the only way you would win credibility with Wall Street. We had a good object lesson in front of us about what not to do. Kmart had a strategy that seemed sound in the beginning. The discount store industry was fairly mature, Wal-Mart was a big, hot competitor, and Kmart needed to find something to get itself moving away from the pack. Off they went and bought Borders book stores, OfficeMax, and Builders Square. They all seemed to have potential for growth.

The problem was that Kmart did not have customer permission to do any of that. They were unable to transfer their authority to any of those places. That is exactly what I did not want to do. We had built a good business with a new target customer. I wanted to expand by developing businesses that had synergies with Sears, with the Sears brand, and had, above all, permission from Sears customers.

## Getting Customer Permission to Move into New Markets

How do you do that? Some companies try to do it instinctively. They follow their guts. Others involve themselves in sophisticated guesswork.

But at Sears, we asked the customers.

If you need a washer-dryer for your laundry room, who would you think of first in that shopping category? It is no surprise that about 40% of all Americans answer "Sears" to that question. We have permission from our customers to be in that business. On the other hand, if you ask them, "First thing tomorrow morning, you realize you need supplies for your pet, where do you go?" we don't make the list at all. We aren't in that business, never have been in that business, and, hence, shouldn't be in that business. The customers don't want us there.

What we wanted CDI to do was to ask that kind of question about all of our merchandise categories and all retail categories, and then sort that against the size of the segments available and where they fit in the marketplace. How strong are our competitors in these areas? How strong are we?

Obviously, a lot of things beyond pet supplies didn't make the cut.

It seemed to make sense, for example, to think of Sears as a natural place to become the first nationwide auto sales outlet. One of the benefits of the old thinking that put us in all of those shopping malls was that we have lots of prime parking space. You need that kind of space to sell cars. We had the heft to handle that kind of business, which amounts to about $500 billion a year, and the institutional savvy to pull it off, too.

So we asked the customers. They said no. In a way, we were paying the price for the 1992 auto service debacle. But the more important message was that our customers just didn't want us to become the national auto sales outlet.

We thought about home health care, too. The population is aging, and we have a natural entrée into the American home because of our service business. Our technicians go in there to repair washers and dryers, so should we refine that process a bit to provide some level of home health care? It seemed like it could be a good emerging business in a society that is aging and that has a varied collection of health needs. It made sense to us. But not to our customers. They didn't want us to be home health care providers.

There were some big "ahas!" that came out of this process.

We had primacy in areas like hardware, home improvement, lawn and garden, and appliances. We also learned that our apparel strategy, as far as it had gone, was not going to carry us much farther. There was no opportunity to take our apparel business into specialty stores in the malls, to move into off-price apparel retailing. Those industries were already too well organized, and our customers simply would not give us enough support to put that area into the top three contenders, which was the measure we used in the process.

The big development to come out of all of this was our new home services business. An aging population married to the idea of home ownership is a strong potential market for these kinds of services, everything from appliance repairs to new roofing to home painting and remodeling. We can even drive over and help get rid of your termites.

Home services is a $160 billion a year business in the United States. The marketplace is split into so many little collections of interests that the day we opened the doors, we collected 2% of the industry's total business and became the national leader. We believed it had the potential to be a $10 billion business for us in a few years. It tapped that same golden vein that the "Softer Side" campaign was aimed at—long-standing trust in what Sears had to offer. In the first year of the business, we were already collecting a 95% approval rating for home services customers.

But the real engine behind the move, other than the pressing need to assure everyone that Sears was looking to the future and planning to strengthen its revenues over the long term, was the fact that our customers told us they trusted us to do it.

We have their permission to be home service experts.

## Fixing the Stores

It was also pretty clear we had their permission to rebuild the look and feel of Sears stores. Once again, we didn't want a collection of decisions made in a vacuum. We wanted to spend our $4 billion giving our customers what they told us they wanted. We knew it would take a long time to transform hundreds and hundreds of Sears stores. But we knew we would pay a steep price if we ignored that part of the formula.

I turned to a Sears veteran for help with that. Fred Rosenberg joined Sears in Buffalo in 1965 as a management trainee and followed the course that had led so many Sears executives to headquarters, a long journey through a whole collection of positions. He was vice president for planning and construction and the man to see if you wanted to talk about the look and feel of Sears over so many years.

I stayed away from the process until Rosenberg had narrowed down the field of design candidates. He interviewed 28 firms, then boiled the lot down to the 5 best contenders. We asked the finalists to visit our stores in Concord, Delaware, and King of Prussia, Pennsylvania, and to critique what they saw there.

I spent 16 hours with the design team, and then settled on a company called HTI in August 1993. Then we brought in all of our merchants for a discussion on what we were going to become. Nothing happens by accident in the design business. I wanted a design that would address the needs of our customers and the needs of our business, all wrapped into one package. Sears had been through all kinds of experiments over the years aimed at coming up with a look, but the company had still not settled on a whole-house plan.

What it had in most of its stores simply didn't work. If you could look at the typical Sears store plan from 500 feet in the air, you could reach only one conclusion about the target customer: It was a trucker who needed to get his vehicle backed into an inventory storage area so he could unload his dishwasher without too much hassle.

Because of that, we had stores that were U shaped. The whole center of the U was set up to handle this delivery process and store the inventory. Shoppers were expected to scamper around the back and the legs of the U looking for merchandise. Two problems: No one likes to shop that way, and the U gave up huge amounts of space to the parts of Sears that really don't make any money. Of course you have to have inventory, but it shouldn't take up 50% of your space.

Inventory has to be out where people can see it. More important, it has to be out where people can buy it. Nothing sends a more negative message to shoppers who are looking for abundance than half-filled shelves. You have to present as much as you can comfortably present so that message—we have what you need—is unstated but well sent in every department of the store.

It was also revealing that Sears stores were still so dark. That was a product of the mid-1970s Arab oil embargo. When energy prices went up, the lights dimmed all over the world of retail sales. Then that problem eased, and a whole new collection of competitors emerged who were very astute about the look and feel of their shops. They went for brightness, but we stayed dim—as though the oil embargo had never ended.

People don't think much about those kinds of changes, but they have a great impact on the feel of a store. Accent lighting aimed at products needs to be two to three times the general lighting standard. We hit that problem hard and solved it to the point at which I would argue we are certainly the brightest stores in business today. But we didn't just toss money at it. We went to solid-state ballasts in our lighting and shifted to 32-watt instead of 40-watt bulbs, an efficiency that will help pay for the change over time.

Because of the emphasis on the woman as target customer, we wanted to increase our market share in apparel and home fashions. That was one of the keys to reaching her. And we had the square footage to do it by getting rid of that old U-shaped design. That allowed us to shift the amount of actual selling-floor space to about 65% on average, up from 50.

That change completely revised circulation patterns in the stores. Sears had missed the fact that shopping patterns were changing, and that people didn't have the time or energy to go searching for badly placed items.

Families were an important part of the target plan, and families like to shop abreast. We increased all of our 6-foot aisles by 2 feet, and added another 2 feet to the old 8-foot aisles. Parents feel more secure about their children if they are beside them on the escalator, so we expanded the size of the escalator treads, too.

We even tested assumptions about carpeting. The old Sears used carpet squares. That was one of those decisions that only makes sense on paper. The thought was that if a square was damaged, you could just pick it up and replace it. But that wasn't happening at all. On top of that, when maintenance did get around to replacing carpet squares, the new squares didn't match what was already on the floor.

Broadloom was the answer. But not just any broadloom. We added to the heft of it so that it felt more luxurious underfoot. It was cheaper than carpet squares, but looked and felt better at the same time. People notice that kind of change when they are walking through a store. They can tell when you are not paying attention, when you are being cheap. A thick carpet might just remind them of how they want things to be at home, and that adds to the comfort level inside of the store.

That was another problem we had to address. If you are selling home furnishings, you want them to seem as though they are in place in a home. Some parts of Sears stores simply had to feel more residential. You use that atmosphere for two reasons: It makes people comfortable, and it offers the customer some solutions about what goes with what and where everything might be sitting in the living room at home.

Our research told us that women like large fitting rooms. How many hooks did they want? We came up with three: one for the purse, one for the old garment, and one for the hanger. We put benches and chairs in the fitting rooms so they would be more inviting.

We had to watch the budget all the way. Four billion dollars is a lot of money, but not when you are spending it in hundred-million-dollar chunks spread over years, and that was the level of investment we were making in our stores. Everyone didn't get the same amount of money. Everyone didn't get the same amount of renovation. But we had to keep the emphasis on the fact that it was a look and a feel we were trying to present, matched to a much stronger collection of merchandise, particularly in apparel.

I talked to Bob Mettler about this part of our transformation. People reacted to three things in a store, he said—to brands, to ideas, and to specific items. If what you have doesn't fall into any of those three categories, in Mettler's dictionary, it's just a bunch of stuff. And customers don't get excited when what they face is just a bunch of stuff.

We made a very low-tech investment at that point that provides a good lesson in how you can touch a market with a simple change. We bought $4.5

million worth of tables. Sears didn't have much of anything on tables out on the selling floor, and all the research indicated our target customer liked to shop from tables. Think of tables full of sweaters and flannel shirts and sales items, right there where you can reach them.

We sold *$100 million worth of items* from that $4.5 million table investment in just *the first two months* that they were on the sales floors.

We also started to see the results of our decision to put more square footage into sales. Just cutting the size of the center of that U gave us 12 million feet of additional sales space.

All of that changed "the visuals" inside of many Sears stores. But it would take something stronger to change the buying habits of our target customer. We had a whole collection of apparel brands that didn't sell at Sears. We decided to get into the game with products people were already buying, whether it was shoes or clothing from Sperry, Russell Athletic, Starter Athletic, or Leslie Fay. That allowed us to become a merchant of goods that had solid brand names that customers would recognize.

We had terrific hard-line brands—Kenmore, Craftsman, DieHard, Weatherbeater paints—but we didn't have a single brand in apparel that meant anything to anyone. Sears had wrestled with this problem many times over the years, and not with much success. It aimed Johnny Miller sports coats at the wanna-be market, but missed the chance because they were overpriced.

We had to go about building, developing, and designing brands we could use to get some consumer equity. That business amounted to $300 million in the first year, then jumped to $900 million, and is now at the $2 billion level. Take one item, Canyon River Blues, our own line of jeans.

Everybody sells jeans, right? How much of a business could there be in jeans? The answer is surprising. Mettler told me he thought we could do $100 million in Canyon River Blues after the second full year. I thought that would be a pretty good business.

*We sold $100 million in the first six months.* In the first three weeks of December 1995 alone, when everyone was pushing to meet those Christmas expectations, we sold a million pairs of jeans *a week*.

Fieldmaster, Sears' men's sportswear brand, hit $100 million. Trader Bay was almost at that level. For our Barrington line of dress clothing, it was the same story. In women's clothing, we thought our Crossroads line could do $55 million of business a year. It did $110 million in its first full year.

It makes me wonder whether Richard Sears might have felt that same flush of success when catalog items hit with consumers more than a century ago. Transformed stores and new lines of merchandise all add up to something very old and valuable for Sears: quality goods at great prices.

When you pay attention to your customers, the track record of those first four years shows, they pay attention right back.

That is the business message that is sent by these success stories: Find your target. Know what she wants. Make it comfortable for her to shop. Tell her all about yourself and how you share her dreams. Even though she might be a little miffed at poor treatment over the years, she will come back.

The franchise is that strong.

All of it creates a good point at which to look back to how the company was before the transformation.

When I got here, we had no idea who the Sears target customer was. We were nearly $4 billion in the hole with a demoralized workforce and a lot of businesses that simply didn't work. There were serious questions about whether Sears would have a future at all.

By the time we launched our new home services businesses in 1996, we were a completely different company well into the transformation of a century-old culture, tapping its history and reputation to forge a new bond with its customers. We had put enough stunning numbers on the board to prove the turnaround wasn't a fluke, that we were back and strong in the marketplace.

## Maintaining Focus and Staying the Course

I had the brass ring and a new responsibility I decided to take on.

The price a business pays for losing connection with its customers should have been apparent to everyone by then. But I had this nagging concern that everything could slip away once again if we didn't keep our focus where it belonged. I concluded there had to be someone inside of Sears who would always keep an eye on customers, someone who would serve as their representative inside the company.

That would be me.

The more deeply I worked my way into the Sears culture, the more I recognized that part of the puzzle was missing at headquarters. It is in the nature of institutions to pay close attention only to themselves. Whenever that tendency had popped up over Sears' history, the customer got lost.

It doesn't change the "we" formula at all. But what it means is that no matter how complicated or thorny the situation might become, someone will be responsible for keeping that connection alive, the one Richard Sears recognized over a century ago.

We had come a long way, and I didn't want that focus to be diminished. We didn't look, feel, or seem at all the way we looked, felt, or seemed on the day I came on board. No one in the history of retailing had been able to manage that rapid and that successful a transformation.

The challenge became keeping it all on track, which is what our customers expected of us. But we were headed for hard times again, more quickly than anyone could have anticipated. It was a mix of the old demons, that customer disconnect, and some brand-new demons that would bring our first turnaround into question.

Before this second round of challenges was over, I would find myself treated by federal and state authorities like a retailing candidate on the 10 most wanted list. I would also watch our businesses slip while we wrestled with troubles—including a big one not at all of my making—that would cost us a half a billion dollars, and I would help my company reach deep down, grab its own bootstraps, and start pulling up hard once again.

CHAPTER 8

# The Dark Days: Legal Disasters, Customer Nightmares, Employee Complaints

THE BEST I CAN SAY about the interrogation room at the U.S. attorney's office in Boston is that it is very governmental and very sterile. There are Formica-topped tables and straight-backed chairs. There isn't a cup of water or coffee to be had. It is like going to jail, or at least like getting ready to go to jail. I didn't feel as though the feds were going to run over and clamp the cuffs on me and haul me away on that day on Ash Wednesday 1998, but I was an invader in the U.S. attorney's space, and he and the three FBI agents and assorted associates in the room were clearly in control.

The civilities that a modern CEO comes to expect—comfortable conversation, maybe some heated disagreement, but at least a sense that everyone is on the same team—were missing. I was sitting full in the face of the government, and clearly in the wrong, which made it all the more difficult.

You try to be cool and calm in a situation like that, because there is no room for bluster or blowing hard. Federal agents are masters at body language, with their stony faces, sitting with arms crossed. Maybe they practice showing nothing, which is a strategy in its own right.

They do it very well.

It makes you feel very bad.

I had absolutely no idea when I arrived at Sears in 1992 that we would become the target of a federal criminal investigation. But that is what it amounted to. In my wildest imagination, I never expected at any point in my life to be in a situation like this.

I was in Boston to plead our case, to try to convince federal authorities that although we recognized we had done wrong, there was no criminal intent and we had done everything humanly possible to remedy the situation.

What situation?

That is a complicated story that takes some telling, and it was made all the more complicated in 1997 and 1998 as Sears' fortunes, its stock price, and its reputation began to slip. About half a billion dollars in fines and restitution later, it is all over.

It presents a story full of lessons.

## The First Disaster: Mishandling Customer Bankruptcies

I kept an open door in my office at Hoffman Estates so the people I worked with could bring their business to me whenever they needed to. One morning in March 1997, Sears' chief counsel at the time, Mike Levin, stopped in to say there was a problem in a federal bankruptcy court in Massachusetts, something about reaffirmations and filing forms and a judge who was deeply angered about a case closely connected to Sears.

Big things come from small visits.

I still feel the sting of it.

We had all worked hard to develop a strong sense of ethics inside of the new Sears, but what I learned in a few brief days in March was that there was a cancer gnawing at the heart of the place, an aggressive, big problem that would cost us $475 million and leave us worrying about what other monsters might be lurking deep inside of this huge old corporation.

Trouble eventually knocks on everyone's door.

The measure of an institution—just as it is the measure of an individual—is how the problem is handled and what you learn from it. I don't want to diminish the situation by implying it all turned out to be a good learning opportunity. There are no half a billion dollar good learning opportunities. It was a disaster by any measure you want to apply. But from my own perspective, it proved the point that trouble must be confronted aggressively. The truth that hides somewhere inside of it must be identified. The pursuit must be diligent and unending, even though it carries the institution—even though it carries you—deep into a very uncomfortable place. Your responsibility is to know how it happened and what parts of the institution must change so that it doesn't happen again.

We collected a lot of bad news in 1997, so bad that it put a big dent in our performance. Our net income declined by 6.5% to $1.19 billion. That was stacked up against $1.27 billion the year before. We didn't make plan. Profits were down in the stores, where our growth was only 2.3%. It had been 5.8% in 1996. It damaged morale all over the company, and left everyone wondering how anyone could take the question of transformation seriously.

The whole institution had completely missed an egregious violation of law and allowed a breach to form in the delicate relationship we were trying to rebuild with our customers and shareholders. I am not the kind of leader who bangs on the table a lot, but what happened deep inside of Sears, inside of our company, angered me then, just as it angers me now.

Our problem with bankruptcy law was just one layer of the problem.

Before the year ended, we would see a damaging and expensive increase in credit delinquencies that would hit us hard in the marketplace, then face a collection of angry pensioners who were upset because we had decided to cut back on life insurance payments for retirees to save $60 million. The bankruptcy and credit situations, we learned after an exhaustive investigation, were almost directly connected to one another even though they seemed to involve separate issues.

The pensioners and their complaints? Well, that was something we knew would be coming back in 1993 when we first started talking about it. It was tied to our trying to keep such a tight control over our costs and still remaining competitive in the marketplace. But that situation, too, demonstrates the need to develop clarity about issues, to make certain you have examined them from every perspective. Knowing the consequences is basic because it is the only way to ascertain how much of a risk you are taking with any decision.

The bankruptcy problem was another one of those dark stories about Sears' culture and bureaucracy, a measure of the depth of the words "embedded practices." It amounts to a violation of trust so deep that it is every bit the equal of stealing money from customers. I knew the day I arrived that the cultural transformation we faced would be vast, but I had no idea that there was a part of the old Sears so poisonous that I would find myself negotiating with the U.S. Department of Justice, with attorneys general in all 50 states, with the Federal Trade Commission, and with a U.S. District Court bankruptcy judge who was deeply offended, and rightly outraged, by long-standing behavior deep inside of Sears.

What good came of the trouble we hit in 1997, which seemed to take on all the earmarks of our own annus horribilis?

We came out of the experience with a new commitment to ethical behavior, perhaps the most stringent internal frisk any corporation has ever had, and the knowledge that running straight toward trouble and tackling it is by far the best approach anyone could ever take. You fool yourself, your shareholders, and your customers when you go the other way, but no one stays fooled for very long.

It's like having an elephant in the corner of the sitting room.

No matter how hard you try, you can't ignore that it is sitting there, and you can't hide from the reality that you have to do something about it or the mess it creates is only going to get worse. Sears had a well-established track record at avoiding problems of all kinds, and I knew immediately I didn't want to let this one sit, not even for a minute.

## A Problem Rooted in History

The roots of the reaffirmation crisis—the problem that carried me to that uncomfortable meeting with the U.S. attorney—run deep into Sears' history. As with almost every other challenge we have faced since 1992, it involved a question of a business practice that developed early on and then went along for years on its own dynamic. In the wake of our own investigation of the problem, I can tell you that the comparison with cancer is not at all hyperbolic. It was undetected and grew quietly and with some determination each passing day for many years.

There is no small irony that it all centers on the question of credit, the essential role it has played inside of Sears since the Great Depression, and a culture that told all Sears employees for many, many years that the most important task of all was protecting the company's assets, even if that protection put you on the wrong side of the law.

The old Sears used to have credit centers in each of its stores. They were very local, very familiar, and very good at making decisions about customer accounts. It amounted to several hundred little lending departments spread all over a vast company that had come to view credit as the Siamese twin of merchandising. The two run so closely together over the history of Sears that you cannot image one without conjuring up the image of the other. Credit was the avenue Sears created to bring the comforts and pleasures of middle-class living to an America that was strapped for ready cash.

The birth, growth, and dependence on credit was and still is a very good thing for Sears and for its shareholders. First, it makes a lot of money for us. Second, it is like a spigot Sears has used for decades to give people more and more access to merchandise. Back when everything was so localized, when interest rates on the money Sears borrowed to finance the system were low and when people were generally deeply embarrassed about getting behind on payments for anything, the system worked well.

It was highly personalized, of course. But it was also massively inefficient. Over time, technology changed that picture. Computers allowed the centralization of credit activity. The whole process became a lot more scientific. And as that development grew, Sears began closing down all of those little credit centers, shifting the responsibility to the center. That left the company with a huge pool of institutional knowledge and memory among the people who had worked in local credit departments for so many years. The company wanted to find a way to tap that pool, and it concluded that a good way would be to use the expertise to keep a close eye on personal bankruptcies.

For many, many years, personal bankruptcy wasn't much of a problem.

Throwing your finances into court protection carried such an onus that it kept the numbers down. But Sears was able to call on its network of early and late retirees to represent Sears when those relatively rare bankruptcy proceedings did come up. Long ago, the company took the position that it held a security interest in the property it sold on credit. We believed we had the right to repossess an item if a creditor failed to make payments. When a bankruptcy case came up in court, Sears would generally have a representative onsite to reflect the company's interests in the case. It was an extension of that security role. Very few other institutional lenders had such a tight connection between credit and actual merchandise, and that gave Sears a special place in retailing.

The mortgage companies and the Ford Motor Credits of the world would usually show up in court, but as a retailing company, we were generally the only secured creditor and the only people in the business who would actually show up in court to get people to reaffirm their debts with us.

Our investigation showed that all of this became codified inside of Sears back in the early to mid-1980s, when the company still had its five territories. One of the legal executives in the field was the company's equivalent of a bankruptcy guru. He codified a lot of the procedures and protocols and put them into the business process of the credit department.

A mandatory part of seeking reaffirmation agreements with people who have filed Chapter 7 bankruptcies, which are aimed at freeing them from all debt obligations, is that any agreement to continue payments on a loan must be on file with the court. The court is there to protect this troubled debtor from creditors. That is where Sears got into so much trouble, and that is where the case becomes very complicated.

Eighty-five percent of all bankruptcies today are Chapter 7s, the move to clear the record of all debts. The other option, Chapter 13, involves getting court protection from creditors while loans are rearranged so that payments can continue. Debtors in these cases can take one of two routes: They can be represented by an attorney, or they can stand before the court pro se, representing themselves.

The Sears procedures we uncovered during our investigation suggested that it was not only proper, but sometimes appropriate, not to file reaffirmation agreements with the court. That was wrong. The belief was that debtors who had their own attorneys would be protected on this issue, that their lawyers would know what filings were necessary. The company believed those attorneys should be competent in advising their clients what to do.

But people who were not represented by attorneys were somewhat vulnerable in this situation. They didn't have an adviser to tell them that these kinds of agreements must be cleared by the court. There are some signs that the courts were not diligent, for whatever reason, in watching the reaffirmation process over the years. That problem was compounded as the number of personal bankruptcies skyrocketed.

That was what was happening in court.

There were developments inside of Sears at about the same time. As best we can tell, the people on the ground, the people who were going into court for us, were concluding that if Sears' attorneys sanctioned these processes, then there must not be anything wrong with them because they set down circumstances in which reaffirmation filings were not necessary. The conclusion somehow became that these filings were discretionary, and the people comforted themselves that a Sears attorney at some level had said it was okay not to file the documents.

That is my polite version of what happened.

Having said that, these people on the ground knew bloody well, frankly, what the rules of the road were in bankruptcy court. I also think there were some dubious conclusions made by our in-house attorneys in the old days, who either didn't know the law or weren't smart enough to know the law. They didn't provide accurate guidance to the people in the field. On the other hand, there were people in operations on the ground who had every reason to know what was going on. It is very clear from the record that they knew that we were not following the bankruptcy code despite what the lawyers were saying.

This is where I get uptight about the whole process, because they were concluding out in the field that the interest of Sears in protecting its assets comes ahead of all other considerations. It is not surprising to me given the culture of the place, given its mind-set and its sense of self-esteem, that people would conclude the corporation's interests were more important than doing what was required under law. They were not. They could never be. We were deeply in the wrong.

The practice went on and on, at least for a decade, unidentified by any internal control staff. The internal auditors didn't catch it. Deloitte & Touche didn't catch it in their external audits, either; nor should they have, because in the scheme of things, it was very small potatoes when you look at the materiality tests that apply to these matters. Even though it was well below the radar screens, this lousy little practice was alive and well. It took a federal judge to surface it.

## The Smoking Gun

A customer came before U.S. District Court Judge Carol Kenner in Boston, in March 1997, to say that he was simply unable to keep up the payments he agreed to after he filed bankruptcy. He told the judge he couldn't keep food on the table for his children and continue those payments. She asked him what arrangements he was talking about, because there was nothing in the record of the case in which she discharged his debts that said he was to continue making payments to anyone. Well, he told her, I still have this arrangement with Sears where I pay them so much a month on the amount of money I owed them.

She went ballistic.

For all these years, nothing like this had ever surfaced in court. That was the smoking gun, the big event, that got this whole thing started. She issued immediate show cause orders and accused us of outrageous, irresponsible corporate behavior. "How dare you do this?" she said. How many other cases were there in her court? In the state of Massachusetts?

That was what brought Mike Levin to my office. He said he didn't know how big the problem was, but he knew that the judge was very angry. He said he would report back as soon as he had identified the size and the nature of the problem. I told him to tell me as soon as he could. It took one day. He said it had become clear overnight that we had some very bad practices in the company around the issue of bankruptcy and reaffirmation procedures. He said it looked like it was going to be a very serious problem for us because we were clearly out of bounds.

I asked him one question: "Have we stopped this practice?" He said he didn't know. I told him that before we did anything else, I wanted to make absolutely certain that we had stopped the practice immediately and everywhere. The legal department issued an immediate directive putting a stop to everything until we had sorted out the issues. I brought in Steve Goldstein, who was running credit at the time, and Alan Lacy, then our chief financial officer. I told them the first job was to find out how big the problem was, how pervasive the practice had been. We immediately pulled together an audit team to send to Boston to find out everything we could from the court. It was already March 30, and the judge had ordered us to return to court on April 8 or 9. She wanted to know how many of these cases we were involved in and why we did it. She said she was as mad as hell. She warned us that we ran the risk of being severely sanctioned in her court and that she was considering referring the matter to the U.S. attorney for a criminal investigation.

Then we started some fact gathering. We had nine credit units around the country, and each of them had people who performed this function for their particular geography. I started thinking hard: Was this a Boston problem, a Massachusetts problem, or a national problem? It took less than a week for us to recognize that the reaffirmation crisis was indeed national in nature. It was going to be big, and it was going to be difficult to attack.

I called everyone involved to Chicago for an emergency meeting on Sunday, April 6, 1997. It was down at the Sears Tower. We had lawyers, credit people, bankruptcy specialists, and public relations people, all in the same room. We spent four and a half hours detailing every fact we knew about the problem. I wanted to know how long the practices had been in place, whether we had ever faced sanctions before, and whether we had any internal processes in place that might have identified the problem.

At the end of that meeting, I knew we had a crisis of major proportions.

We ended the meeting and Levin, Lacy, and Goldstein came to my office. I asked them how in the name of God something like this could have been happening for so long with nobody knowing about it? We had had an ethics hot line in place for three years, on which we received 15,000 calls a year, and no one ever told us they wanted to question this business practice because they didn't think it was right. I was absolutely and totally frustrated at that point. We had a national problem of major significance sitting right in front of us. We had an angry judge who was going to call the U.S. attorney to determine whether we would be indicted for a criminal offense.

Mostly what we did at that meeting was grumble. There was no one I could confront and ask, "How could you let this happen?" The people who were with me were all new to the company, and it was clear even at this point we were trying to cope with a deeply embedded practice that had been festering inside of Sears for many years.

We shifted into a full crisis mode.

What were we going to do about this?

We were only a few days away from the hearing with Judge Kenner on the issue. Were we going to ask for a delay? Fog up the issue and try to obfuscate it a little bit? No. I said there was absolutely no lack of clarity here. I told them we were absolutely out of bounds on the issue. There were no mitigating circumstances I heard from anybody that would justify what we had done as an acceptable practice. We had listened to bankruptcy experts at that session telling us it was clear the company had no business doing what it was doing.

I told them there was nothing to be gained by foot-dragging on this issue. I said we should spend the next two days finding out everything we could about the practice. Then I said we should decide to tell everyone, absolutely everyone, about what we had done and what we were going to do about it. I didn't want us to wait to hear the court tell us what to do, I wanted us to take the initiative immediately. My management team and I talked about it constantly for the next two days, even as the information came trickling in. The Boise, Idaho, credit center reported that over the past five years, there had been 1,400 of this kind of case and 1,200 of that kind of case. It was just growing and growing.

## Coming Clean

I made my decision, and no one tried to fight me on it.

I said we had to come clean. We had to tell the judge and the world that we had been doing something inappropriate, that we had stopped it, that we were going to refund all of the money that we collected from these people, and that we would pay them back with interest. I had no idea how much money that would be, but I realized we weren't talking about hundreds of thousands, or even a few million dollars. It could have been anywhere between $20 million and $200 million. I knew that it was not chopped liver.

I told everyone we would be paying prime rate on what we owed and delivering to each of those people a coupon good for a nice discount on their next purchase from Sears. Then I said we should go to the appropriate legal agencies and approach them on this issue before they approach us. I told them to agree that we know we have a serious problem, that we have stopped it, and that we would cooperate fully with any investigation.

To my mind, it was the only proper response. Even early in our investigation, before we were able to determine how muddied the whole bankruptcy code is and how reasonable people might misinterpret it, it was clear to me that we were in the wrong. There was no point in trying to fight. In fact, I decided we had to go in the other direction—to fix it and make the situation right.

I think that approach surprised all of the agencies we were dealing with. We made their lives very easy, instead of making them difficult. We could have erected defenses and obstacles at every step of the way, but we told all of the agencies we would produce all the documents they needed and present people for whatever interviews they wanted to conduct. I have to admit in retrospect that I think some of them saw us as easy pickings. There is no doubt in my mind that there has been a little piling on. But we decided to go into this with a clear conscience and a good heart. We still didn't know how big the problem was. We had hundreds, no, thousands of cases to document. We had to check court records on every one of them. There was no statute of limitations involved, so we had to go as far back into our own records and the court records as we could.

It took three months. We negotiated a settlement with the Federal Trade Commission, then with all 50 attorneys general. Judge Kenner allowed us to proceed to settle these cases. She made us tweak our restitution a little bit, but with some diligence and hard work, we were able to resolve most of the problem in 90 days.

What remained was the U.S. attorney's office, which was conducting a criminal investigation. Obviously, the outcome could be crucial to us. If we were indicted and convicted of a criminal offense, it could wreck hundreds of contracts we had with subcontractors in jurisdictions that did not allow convicted felons to hold legal agreements. I don't want to underestimate the importance of this set of negotiations, because the outcome could not only have further damaged Sears, it could have wrecked hundreds upon hundreds of small businesses that were connected to us at every level.

The negotiations were difficult. The Boston U.S. attorney's office remained resolute in its decision that a criminal offense was involved. As time passed, we hammered out an arrangement that would cost us a horrific amount of money, but would allow us to maintain those crucial relationships all over the country. We agreed to plead guilty to one count of bankruptcy fraud, but the plea would be taken by a subsidiary called Sears Bankruptcy Recovery Management Services. That had the effect of insulating other parts of the company from the fallout of the guilty plea. Our home services businesses would still be able to get state licenses, and the name of Sears itself would not be branded with a felony.

The U.S. attorney's position was clear: Go to trial and we will convict you. We will prevail. But to make all of our lives simpler, we will let you take a guilty plea and pay a fine to the government. It took until December 1998 to reach this agreement, and I cannot let the moment pass without noting that as difficult and distasteful as the process had been, we finally reached closure.

I kept the board fully apprised of the situation and warned them there was a high risk of some pretty severe media attention attached to it. It was important that everyone at Sears knew what had happened, what we were doing about it, and, perhaps most important of all, how we felt about the whole debacle.

We issued a company-wide communication in which I wanted to express my personal disappointment that we could have this kind of fundamental flaw going on deep inside of the company, undetected but apparently sanctioned. I told them the situation was completely antithetical to the values I held personally and to the values that Sears ought to have.

Ironically, none of this was hurting us much with our customers. We conducted intensive surveys throughout the incident. The vast proportion of the general public had no idea it was even happening. There was not a single sign of change in the response to one of our most important questions: whether Sears was a company they could trust. Basically, the public relations problem was limited to the business pages.

But we couldn't afford to view the situation in that context.

I told everyone I felt this was a problem that cut to the very core of our company values. This was cheating the customer in addition to violating the law. It was no different from charging the customer too much for merchandise or giving him the wrong credit when he would return an item. It was a true breach of trust with the consumer and reflected a complete breakdown in compliance inside of the company. If there is anything that Sears has represented over its 114 years, it is integrity and trust. When you put that at risk, you put the entire company at risk.

Although it was obviously not convincing, my argument to the federal investigators flowed from the realities of the situation and how we handled it. First, there was no senior management knowledge of the practice. It was buried two or three levels down. When we found out about it, we did everything right in response. We stopped it, came forward, raised our hand, and said, "Here are the facts. Here is what we want to do. We want to cooperate and we want to get this all behind us. We have presented a model of good corporate behavior."

If Sears had taken the criminal charge at the highest level, it would have been a terrible blow to the 300,000 people who worked for Sears. They would have been branded as part of a criminal organization, when there were only a couple of hundred people embedded deep inside of the corporation who were actually engaged in the practice. The dark spot would then have spread to all kinds of people who had business relationships with Sears. We licensed our name to the pest control people, the carpet cleaners, the plumbing people, and so on. In many jurisdictions, if you are convicted of a felony, those contracts could be in jeopardy. Those circumstances could have forced a whole collection of truly innocent people out of business. We believed that kind of punishment was not warranted because of the company's behavior.

All of that being the case, it was clear we weren't having a no-fault conversation inside of Sears. I wanted to get right to the bottom of this as quickly as I could. There were clearly people at fault inside of Sears, and my objective was to find out who they were. We put together an outside legal team to do that headed by Bob Fiske, a former U.S. attorney in New York. That team has now talked to 400 people and reviewed hundreds of thousands of pages of documents. Who knew what? When did they know it? Who should have known?

There was still an overwhelming worry that there might be some other monsters lurking somewhere inside of the company. The reaffirmation case centered quite clearly on a question of compliance with law. We found one rotten apple. How would we know that we didn't have three or four or five? In response to the problem, I set up a new position, chief compliance officer, who reported directly to me. This office had carte blanche access to everything at Sears. It reviewed all of our business practices, all of our contracts, all of our processes, all government regulations, all requirements for filings. You name it. Needless to say, it took a particularly close look at our credit operation.

There was a perverse upside to all of this, although it was an upside that had that half a billion dollar price tag attached. It helped us to reinforce the kind of moral tone we wanted to have inside of Sears. You have heard of burning platforms? We had a burning moral platform in terms of reaffirmation, and it gave us a great example of how not to behave.

Of course, a seminar would have been better.

I don't think we were able to completely contain the reaffirmation problem. The way we reacted to it—what we shut down, and how we flipped the switch on all kinds of credit activities to take a close look at what we were doing—played right into another batch of troubles that came knocking toward the end of 1998.

## Another New Credit Problem

Credit was getting a bad name in 1997, but I think that obscured the reality that at Sears, credit had always been a service to the brand. It had always been about access to goods and services, the key that opened the doorway to the cornucopia of Sears, Roebuck and Company. It was fundamental to the way this company got started—remember Richard Sears and his COD plan to have the watch company finance his newborn business? Credit was what helped us create and maintain our relationship with customers. And by their very nature, the Sears customers were credit-dependent customers.

It costs a lot to buy into the American dream.

Sears recognized that in the beginning, and so did Julius Rosenwald and General Wood. They created such a deeply placed relationship between merchandise and credit that the two can no longer be separated. It is not an exaggeration. There would be no merchandise business without access to credit, and there would be no credit business without access to merchandise. Everyone on the outside likes to think of them as separate entities that have independent and autonomous parts, but they are inextricably interwoven. Anybody who thinks that they aren't simply doesn't understand the special relationship between this company and its customers.

We had a problem that became apparent toward the end of 1997 that was connected to the level of credit delinquencies. It wasn't something that just popped up. Like everything else at Sears, it had a history. And the history helps to explain why it was there, what it meant, and what we were going to do about it.

That it arrived just as we were coping with the problems presented by the reaffirmation crisis was not a coincidence. They were very tightly tied to one another. Go back six or seven years, to 1990. It was a different world for Sears as far as credit was concerned. Delinquencies were running at about 3.5%. We were even lower than the credit card issuers in that sense. We were running an extraordinarily profitable operation because we were a medium- to high-priced lender with very low charge-offs. No one knew it at the time—not inside of Sears, and not anywhere else, either—but that world was starting to change quite dramatically. Over the previous seven years, consumer credit debt had been picking up and picking up. When that happens, the risk associated with extending credit increases.

Go back to 1994. Credit quality at Sears began to decline then, just as credit quality declined in the rest of the marketplace. It looked like a slight but consistent increase on the graph of credit delinquencies. That wasn't much of a problem to worry about because our numbers were tracking every-one else's numbers. We were essentially in a parallel situation.

In the third quarter of 1997, everything started to peak out for the rest of the industry. Their lines began to flatten, which meant delinquencies were no longer on the increase. But that didn't happen at Sears. Our delinquency rate actually started to increase sharply.

The reaction was "Holy mackerel. What is going on here?"

Did the world just come to an end? Did our computers break? Did we for-get to send out the bills? Did everyone stop processing the cash? We were wor-ried about this. The credit business moves very slowly over long periods of time. You simply don't expect to see these kinds of spikes in your numbers. When you have 30 million credit accounts, you just don't expect to see it. When it came time to issue third-quarter earnings, we had a big spike in our write-off experience. Worse, we had to tell Wall Street we weren't quite sure what was happening.

Wall Street hates uncertainty. It knows quite well how to deal with good news, and it even knows how to make a lot of money on bad news. But it can't handle uncertainty. What we had because of that was a flight from Sears stock. We told everyone we knew it was going to affect our fourth-quarter per-formance, but we didn't know how. And we didn't know how long the prob-lem was going to last or where it was going to carry us.

"Adios, baby" was what we heard from the stock market. We had exited 1996 at $45 a share. Then we moved up into the high 50s. When we announced the reaffirmation problem, the stock dropped back to around $50 a share. It kind of sat there for a while until we announced our settlements in the reaffirmation case, at which point it went from $50 a share to $65 a share in about 45 days. That was an outrageous price for us. It was just settling back down to where it should have been when we announced the third-quarter delinquency problem. We took a big hit. The stock dropped from $55 a share to $40 a share very quickly. People were bailing out. By the end of the year, we had worked our way back up to $45 a share, but there were some pretty wild swings during 1997.

What happened?

There are two theories, and my advice as I play them out is that you don't buy into either one just yet.

The first recalled that we had gone on a major new account acquisition program beginning in 1994. We really wanted to be aggressive about this because of the connection between credit and merchandise sales. This theory claimed that we brought in a lot of lousy credit accounts, people who didn't deserve to have Sears cards. The criticism was that their credit scores were below what they should have been and that the program brought a bunch of lousy accounts onto the books. Call this the "Paying the Piper" scenario.

Our critics say we should have known these accounts were inherently riskier.

The second theory, called "the Collateral Damage" theory, was what was in my mind. During the second quarter of 1997, we were beset by the bad news about reaffirmation. We were in the newspapers every day. And inside of the company, we were all over the place on the question of credit. We were changing the procedures our collectors had used. We were trying to be squeaky clean about everything in terms of compliance with the law. The long and short of it is that we took our foot off of the gas. We weren't encouraging people to pay as much as we should have when they fell into delinquency. We weren't as persuasive as we should have been. The cash stopped coming in at the same rate.

After a lot of examination, I can report now that both theories are true.

The scenario should have been labeled "Paying the Piper and Suffering Collateral Damage." Both of these situations were connected, and they played out in that rising delinquency rate.

But the rationales, the explanations, are a lot more complicated than the ones advanced by those two scenarios.

I admit I was out looking for new customers. In my eight years at Sears, it was a perpetual search. There is no doubt that the customers we were adding to our portfolio in 1994, 1995, and 1996 were apparently a lot more risky than our old customers. But that wasn't because we had lowered our standards in any way. It may have been because the pool we were swimming in was a lot deeper, and a lot longer and wider, than the one we had been swimming in before.

Think about the numbers for a moment. We were bringing in 6 million accounts a year during that period. Half of them signed up in response to offers they got in the mail. Another 3 million accounts came right at the cash register. We had been training our associates to handle these accounts for months. A woman would come in to make a purchase, and the associate would ask whether it should be put on her Sears account. The customer would say she had no account, and the associate would ask if she would like Sears to open an account on the spot. If the answer was yes, the application could be processed in two minutes.

But that didn't mean automatic credit. About 6 million people a year applied for credit on the spot, and about 3 million of those could not pass the score model. In the cases of the mail solicitations and the point-of-sale applications, we stuck tightly to our credit standards. The criticism has been that we relaxed our standards to bring in new accounts, but that is not what happened.

The problem was that we had shifted the distribution of people who actually formed the credit pool because of those processes. The people who decided they wanted and needed credit from us, and were willing to pay 21% interest to get it, were essentially a higher-risk group than they had been in the past. On top of that, they were getting credit offers from everyone else almost any day of the week in the mail. We were not just shoveling plastic out of the door. We were aggressive about these new accounts, but we maintained our standard in approving the applications.

What that led to was the credit version of something like a pig being digested by a python. We carried these riskier people on our books, and because they were riskier their delinquency rate was going to show an increase. It was going to go up, not flatten out, before the numbers floated back to a much more normal situation. We expected that we would eventually fall back into a roughly parallel situation with the rest of the market in time, but not until that problem moved through the system.

That is phase one of the explanation.

Phase two deals directly with what was happening inside of Sears.

Traditionally, our collectors had worked Monday through Friday from nine to five. What that meant was that they were getting a lot of answering machines whenever they made their phone calls to remind people they had missed payments on their Sears accounts.

Unfortunately, if you want to use the telephone effectively, you have to make the calls when people are at home. That means dinnertime and weekends. So as both of these problems, reaffirmation and a riskier credit portfolio, were bubbling away, we were in the process of completely changing the way we reached out to people who weren't paying their bills.

We shifted from a daytime to an evening and weekend workforce. That led to a tremendous turnover in our collection department. We had an 80% turnover because of the shift. People who had been working as collectors for 20 years said, "Nope, weekends and nights are not for me," and they left. We were in the process of retraining an entirely new workforce when the reaffirmation crisis hit.

Between the second and third quarters, we had a dramatic drop in the number of collector hours worked. We were just losing altitude on our normal hit rate on collections against this riskier portfolio.

What can you do about this double whammy?

First, you can train your collectors more effectively and more rapidly. We ramped up that workforce in response. But the problem was that they were still approaching a riskier pool of debtors, so this situation was destined to get a little worse before it got better. It was going to take time for us to work the nonperformers out of the system. It doesn't matter how many times you call them, people in this riskier group are not going to get much better about paying their bills.

The problem is now under control and being well managed, but I am afraid we are never going to be able to go back to the old days because the debt burden on the American consumer just keeps on growing. Even with high employment, with good job growth, American consumers are less creditworthy today than they were seven or eight years ago. All of us are going to have to accept that risk when we approach them to lend money.

Back then, our critics took a simplistic view of all this: Why don't we just shut off the spigot and stop lending money? Problem solved!

The answer to that one is simple: You can't.

Remember that connection between merchandise and credit. Shut off credit and you shut off the flow of merchandise. Stop the flow of merchandise, and then where are you in this business? As uncomfortable as the reality of delinquency and debt load are, they're nowhere near as uncomfortable as a scenario in which you break the bond with your customers and tell them to go someplace else where they can buy on credit.

There is a larger lesson hidden in all of this, and it applies to those two scenarios people advanced for the trouble we were having. If we had bought into either one alone, we would have failed to solve the problem. If the portfolio problem was the only one and we shut off credit to address it, we would have paid a huge price for it. If we had embraced scenario two, that it was an operational problem, then we would have missed the trouble at the heart of the delinquency question.

We had to look at them both to see how they related to one another to come up with an effective solution.

At this point, it must seem as though Sears had more than its share of trouble in 1997. Sad to say, it wasn't over. But the next problem that came along was of our own making. And maybe it wasn't really even a problem; maybe it was just a perception that there was a problem.

# A New Challenge
## —Regaining Control of Operating Costs

Back during my first 100 days on the job, Russ Davis, the CFO when I arrived, and I were looking at one of the biggest problems Sears was facing. It was non-competitive in the marketplace because it had lost control of its operating costs. We had just been through the plan for the big restructuring, with its 50,000-job cut and its store closings and its early retirement plan. But Russ and I were musing over what we could do to squeeze costs out of the company over the long term. Controlling costs is one of the most important measurements we have in establishing shareholder value. We had a responsibility to do that as aggressively as we could.

So we decided to take a close look at all of the big chunks of money we spent. One outcome of that process was the strategic sourcing initiative that we used to crack down on the spending of $12 billion on merchandise. We wanted to look at how smart we were in buying the things we turned around and sold to consumers. We wanted to know if we were getting the best value from a collection of long-term relationships with our suppliers. One of those old Sears assumptions was at work at the time. If you asked people how Sears was at the process of buying, the response was that it was great, that it had tough, aggressive buyers who were just terrific at their jobs.

Unfortunately, that assumption could live only inside of the walls of the institution. Our buyers weren't very aggressive at all. Our relationships were old and had become so entrenched that a lot of suppliers were telling Sears what it should buy and when. You don't want that to happen in this business.

We found out that if we just opened the door on this question of supply a little bit, there were millions upon millions of dollars to be saved. The first area we looked at was DieHard batteries. For 26 years, we had been buying them from the same place, Johnson Controls, up in Milwaukee. No one ever questioned whether there was a better alternative in the marketplace. We brought in A. T. Kearney to take a look at that question, with a particular emphasis on the factory operations of our suppliers. It had the expertise to look at production techniques and quality issues. It also gave our buyers the courage they needed to ask the tough questions themselves.

We took a close look at batteries and found a $46 million savings. We re-sourced the business. That made headlines. We were dumping a 26-year supplier. We put some of that $46 million in our pockets, and gave some of it back to customers in terms of lower prices. Our decision to change suppliers sent a vast wake-up call through the whole system. We found a new sense of cooperation and won lots and lots of concessions.

At the same time, we were looking at the dollar costs for company benefits. We did a little reengineering work on medical benefits. We didn't take anything away, but we expanded the options and made it very attractive for people to turn toward the lowest-cost packages. We thought we could save money if we allowed people to self-select their medical packages, and we did.

Maybe that same process could work for retirees.

A brief diversion. Pension benefits have come to be viewed as entitlements by the retired. But they are not. A lot of them are optional, and a lot of them flowed from an era in which Sears viewed itself as a paternalistic company. The problem with that process is that no matter how you feel about the reality of the situation, paternalism is dead in the modern corporation. People are expected to take more and more responsibility for their own retirement planning. But we had a structure that put us completely out of competition in the marketplace. Our very substantial retiree benefits were not even coming close to being duplicated by the other companies in retailing we were fighting with.

We had a mismatch between what we were doing and what we felt we needed to do to remain competitive with the Home Depots and the Wal-Marts of the world. We started first with those medical costs for active employees. We changed our pension plan formula. I am in the same program as everyone else, even though people believe I have a special package. I don't have an executive medical plan. I don't have an executive life insurance plan. The pension package was changed because we have both a pension plan and a profit-sharing plan, and there are only two other retailers that can say that.

What was sitting there and staring us right in the face in 1992 was an earlier decision that had moved Sears away from company-paid life insurance for our active people. We had a group universal life program they could participate in at a reduced cost, but the company was not subsidizing life insurance for its active workers.

And yet we had a life insurance benefit for 130,000 retirees that was costing us $60 million a year. It's kind of hard to see the benefit in that level of expenditure. I could put $60 million a year into marketing and get something beneficial in return. The question was what to do about it.

187

There were some hawks in the company who said we should just terminate the program immediately, send a letter and be done with it. Their argument was that we owed that savings to our shareholders. Then there was a group that said we shouldn't touch it, that we had been paying that benefit for a long time, that a lot of the retirees would be dying soon and it was manifestly unfair to get rid of it. We went round and round for a whole year on this subject. What were the benefits? What were the alternatives? What was the reaction going to be?

The benefits people said they concluded it was proper to change this benefit, but they warned that there would be an outcry like none we had ever seen. I thought about it for awhile and came up with a plan. I decided we were not going to eliminate the benefit, but that we were going to cut its size substantially. But not for everyone.

The company initiated its pension plan in 1978. We put it right on top of our profit-sharing plan. That meant that those people who retired before 1978 didn't have the benefit of a pension and received only profit sharing. My thought was that life insurance would be a much more important part of estate planning for that group, so we shouldn't touch it. They would be grandfathered in. For those who retired after 1978, I said, let's let them down slowly. We eventually agreed on a 10-year phasedown. Whatever they had would come down in increments until they had a flat $5,000 benefit.

Then I suggested we go to Met Life and negotiate a package for a group rate on a replacement policy for these people. They would not have to prove they were healthy. They could just go to Met Life and buy whatever amount of replacement insurance they wanted. There was still a lot of concern about the outcry. I prepared a videotape explaining the situation. I asked them to understand our situation and recommended they take advantage of the bargain rate we had negotiated. Along the way, I talked to the board, warning them they were going to see letters like they had never seen before.

The shift went into place in September 1998 and, as predicted, there was trouble. There was no surprise here. We anticipated it. The one development that drew my interest was the people who emerged as leaders of the group. They were mostly retired officers of the company, led by the man who used to be president of the catalog division.

They painted themselves as the newfound conscience of the company and said we were slashing away at the widows' and orphans' money. They said they were going to get us and that they were going to get this decision turned around.

I wondered about that.

Maybe I was really dealing with the revenge of the Searsmen. Maybe they were actually angry that we had been able to achieve what they were not able to achieve. There was a push for some retribution at work. A couple of my long-service people here at Hoffman Estates told me that was exactly what was going on. The retirees were angry at someone who was able to revive the company when they couldn't. They were jealous of the outcome, and they wanted to find some way to bring down the house.

Remember that old Sears culture, that embrace of insiders and that firm belief that what came about in the outside world didn't matter?

There was an ego agenda at work, and I was the target.

Okay.

I have to say that I understand the discomfort of the retirees. A lot of them sold all of their stock when they left and didn't get the advantage of that huge run-up in value we had after the first turnaround. That might have made them bitter. But I would make the same decision today if I had the choice. We were trying to prepare our current workforce to take responsibility for their own lives. We could offer them a stimulating place to work, pay for performance, and wealth accumulation through stock options that allowed them to participate in the company's success.

But after a certain point, we are all on our own.

This has been called a public relations fiasco, but I don't think it was. There was a noisy group, but it was a very small percentage of the 130,000 retirees who protested. Picketers showed up at just about every Sears event, even at the stores as we were getting ready for Christmas. Their message was simple: Sears had broken its promise, and it was unfair to pensioners because it cut deeply into one of their benefits—life insurance.

A lot of them undoubtedly were worried that we were planning some other cut, too, even though we weren't.

I'm sure you could get a collection of retired IBM executives to do the same thing to Lou Gerstner. They would say he is just riding on the coattails of all the stuff his predecessors put into place. It's all just natural sour grapes. Our retirees found a platform to express that.

What an irony.

We gave them that, too.

## Team Support Even in the Darkest Days at Sears

I don't want to leave the impression that that most difficult of periods was without its high points.

I was with my management team in Phoenix in November 1998 on the eve of my trip to meet with the U.S. attorney and the federal agents in Boston. We were having the latest in our series of meetings in the desert. The first Phoenix session had been aimed at getting some alignment in management, and that was the theme we were addressing once again.

I had to leave the session early, and I wanted to give everyone there a full explanation. I told them I was going to go to Boston to fight for this company, to try to keep it from being branded a felon. I told them I thought that an indictment and a criminal charge in connection with the reaffirmation problem would be unjust and unfair to all of those people at Sears who had nothing to do with the problem.

The explanation didn't take long. I said good-bye.

There was a brief hesitation. Then everyone stood up and clapped and cheered. Say what you want about trouble. But in the face of this latest challenge, they were sending me into battle with a head full of applause and their best wishes as I prepared to face the federal government.

In that instant, with the applause echoing around the auditorium, I felt deeply connected to everything that was so good about the place for so many years.

I would need every ounce of that good feeling as the year played out, with its expensive settlement and the early signs that we were headed for trouble in the marketplace once again. Within another 12 months, Sears would be battling for its reputation yet again, its vaunted turnaround now the target of a hostile and skeptical business press. As the decade was heading toward its close, and as my tenure as CEO was moving way past midpoint, it seemed as though we had slipped back into the world of the also-rans.

It was another one of those chastening experiences, and before long, it had all of us reaching down to find our own bootstraps, to confront that old Sears arrogance again and to start rebuilding.

We had some tough decisions to make in a retailing world that can turn a winner into a loser in the blink of an eye.

CHAPTER 9

# Leadership Is Never "Done": Confronting New Problems and Management Challenges

Iᴛ ᴍɪɢʜᴛ sᴇᴇᴍ that after a company the size of Sears goes through the deba- cle we faced with the federal authorities and the reaffirmation crisis, every- one would just be able to sit back, take some time to reflect, and rest after the long and wearying battle.

The problem with that approach is that the rest of the world doesn't stop in its tracks and wait for you to catch up. Retailing is a daily battle, and when you and your troops are distracted, for whatever reason, you lose ground, and lose ground quickly.

We were out of trouble with the authorities, but in trouble in the mar- ketplace. We did not perform well in 1998, a year that raised serious questions about the Sears turnaround and its staying power, about my strategies, and about our place in the market and whether we had lost a cherished and valu- able leadership position.

At the same time, it was a year in which the awareness of our problems led to another transformation, a new commitment to our business, a strong and very cautious development of our Internet presence, and the birth and development of a new message, and a new connection, to our shoppers.

It was also the year that set the stage for the traction we regained in 1999 and the performance that pushed us back up in the field of intense retail competition. If we had problems aplenty, we found ways to address and solve them one at a time in a process that was as simple, and as complex, as going back once again to the basics.

Despite our problems in 1997, the business seemed to be doing well. We knew we were going to have difficulties with the credit card debt as it moved through the system, but we also knew that with time, that picture would improve. What we didn't realize was that 1998 would see a return of a new version of Sears' old problem, it's tendency to focus on *itself* instead of on the *customer*.

## 1998: New Problems, New Challenges

It was clear to me early in 1998 that our apparel business was starting to slump. But by the middle of the year, we had a commensurate kind of slowdown in our hard-lines business. The sales went from a very respectable 4 to 5% range to a flat line, and then into the negative, with a predictable effect on profitability.

It was a very challenging year.

There were problems inside, and the perceptions outside were not good. All of those uncomfortable old media critiques started flooding back: "The struggling Sears." "It wasn't a real turnaround, it was just fiction, built on the back of all of these credit cards." "The Martinez Strategy had stopped working."

I was grinding my teeth over all of this.

Had I gone out to look for more customers, and was credit one of the ways I did it?

Guilty.

We were losing customers at a furious rate when I arrived in 1992. We worked hard to get them back by offering them good products at great values.

We used our credit offerings the way Sears had always used its credit offerings, as a doorway to the comforts of life for the great American middle class. That was the key to our success. It wasn't as though we were selling our customers schlock at 28% interest rates.

There was another element at work in the media and among the analysts, too. Increasingly, the world of retail was being bifurcated into perceived winners and perceived losers. The gist of the message to investors was clear: There are a handful of companies in the retail business who are going to be long-term winners and the rest will be a bunch of also-rans who are going to struggle. Maybe they will survive, but they will never develop and execute the kind of credible growth strategy that will attract investors and drive their stock prices up.

Because of our operating difficulties, in 1998 we were being cast among the also-rans, the places that are seen as increasingly irrelevant in a world of big box success stories.

I was thinking at the time that I wasn't surprised by this development, in one sense, because I always believed we would hit a pothole along the way. We enjoyed amazing success in 1993, 1994, 1995, 1996, and into 1997, but nothing lasts forever, particularly in a business as fragile as retailing.

My only question was when we would hit that pothole and what we would do about it when it happened. Would we have the ability and resilience to flex, in our strategies, our programs, and our response, so that we could make that depression a shallow one as opposed to a deep one?

Did we have the will and the resources and the creativity to minimize this business problem?

We found in our apparel business that our people, when confronted with this dilemma, kept trying the same tricks. Their idea was to do what they did before, but to work harder at it.

## More Competition, New Competitors

We were watching our competition during this dark part of 1998. Kohl's became a meaningful force in the apparel business. They were opening stores at a furious rate, and they were very successful against us wherever they opened their doors. We were not borrowing from their playbook to adjust our strategies. We saw Target coming on strong, too, and the first evidence that Wal-Mart could be a powerful force in the apparel business. They had upgraded the quality of their products while keeping their price points low.

The old Sears mantra, "Be the Value Leader in the Mall," was no longer sufficient to ensure success, because the customer was beginning to find more value off the mall than on the mall. Our strategies were not reacting and responding the way they should have.

## The Loss of Key Managers

Adding to those problems, the Sears management team was shifting. It is difficult to keep talented people on board when so much of their compensation sits in stock options. Sears was having trouble, its stock was having trouble, and its managers were responding to invitations from greener pastures. Internet businesses, with their siren calls of huge stock options and the promise (a false promise, as it turned out in most cases) of rapid fortune, had become a strong magnet.

There was also a general, intense competition for experienced executives among traditional businesses. One thing Sears had in the wake of its first turnaround was a rich field of experienced executives, and the headhunters knew who they were, what they had done, and where they were.

John Costello, who had been a flag carrier for a lot of branding and repositioning, and one of the architects behind the "Softer Side" campaign, left. Bob Mettler, the apparel chief, left. Steve Goldstein, the credit guy, left. Tony Rucci, as close as we had to a chief cultural minister, left. Gary Crittenden, chief financial officer, who had the intellect and retail savvy to be a legitimate contender for my job, left. Later, Jane Thompson, who had played such a big role in developing strategy after my arrival, also left.

We had a management flight issue, which is destabilizing on the inside of a company and is perceived from the outside as a crisis. The cumulative effect of all of those departures was a conclusion that the business situation had become so difficult that people were abandoning ship.

But there were other realities at work.

In some cases, it was time for people to go because the demands of the business were changing, and they had the wrong skill sets to cope with that reality.

## The Failure of New Ventures

It was also time, I believed, to look at every point on the Sears star to find out what was working and what was not, make the personnel changes to address the problem, and work on ways to grow the business.

We had stumbled on some of our "off-the-mall" concepts.

For example, the auto parts business was going nowhere. We had a clear issue to decide. We either had to invest dramatically more money to become the number two player in that market, or we were going to be marginalized as the number five player and go nowhere.

The returns were not going to be compelling enough to justify spending hundreds of millions of dollars of capital to make us the number two player behind Autozone, so we sold that business. This was not viewed as a confident move from the outside and was seen as a sign that my vision for the company was starting to unravel.

But it was the right thing to do for the shareholders because we were concerned about our ability to execute successfully even if we put the capital behind the auto parts business. We sold that business to a Virginia-based company called Advance. We took a little bit of cash and held on to 40% of the combined company. It is a story yet to be written, but if it takes off, our shareholders will benefit.

I didn't feel badly about it because the auto parts business was not my idea. It was something of a prehensile appendage from an acquisition in the 1980s, and we kept trying to find a way to make it work. I felt like I was cleaning up behind someone else's elephant.

But there was another problem on my desk that was my creation: Sears HomeLife. I believed I had permission from our customers to be in that business. They trusted us and we should have been able to make money, but we were never able to get the economics to an acceptable level. We put too many stores in too many markets, and not a sufficient number of stores in a given market where we could achieve saturation density and leverage all the fixed costs.

We closed a number of HomeLife stores, but it was still going to be a negative value-added problem for us for as long as we could see. Once again, we were sending good money after bad, and can you keep investing on the chance that something might eventually develop? No.

We wound up selling 80% of the business to Citicorp Venture Capital.

## The Crux of Our Problems: Complacency

Through all of these problems—the management departures, the exhaustion connected to dealing with months and months of federal investigation, and, of course, the business problems—I knew that Sears had fallen back into one of its old traps again.

It wasn't that we thought we were invincible. It was just that we all kind of assumed that we had everything figured out at Sears and that our problems would just pass. We thought we could handle it all by just doing more of the same and working harder.

But the problems were starting to create pressure from all directions. The board, which had been immensely supportive during the federal investigations and the resolution of that problem, was becoming very concerned about the business. It was a lot easier for the Sears board to understand the reaffirmation crisis and how we were handling it than the problem we faced in the marketplace.

We were having a hard time solving those problems and an equally hard time communicating them in an understandable way to the board. We got into a series of conversations about whether our strategy was right. Behind those talks was an assumption that there was some strategic alternative we could seize that would turn our difficulties around, make them go away, and transform us into a very successful company again.

One of the frustrations was my inability to communicate to the board that we actually had very few degrees of freedom to change our strategy. If apparel is a problem, you can't just get rid of it, for example. It is a $9 billion business with a gross profit margin in the high 30s. You can't exit that business because there is nothing else to fill the space. We could never expect our hard-line businesses to occupy the same space and create the same returns.

We were working hard to come up with some strategies to solve our problems. How do we fix the full-line stores? Should we lower our prices to compete with Target and Wal-Mart? Do that and you destroy your margins. We can't go upmarket because we have no credibility, and we can't move downmarket because it would destroy the economics of the business.

Amid the thought there was a simple fix, I concluded it was best to tell everyone that I believed the answer to our problems lay in grabbing ourselves by the bootstraps and pulling ourselves up again by working on the fundamentals of the business.

My message was simple: We are always going to be a general merchant. That is Sears. What is it that we are all about? We are always going to sell a mix of hard lines and soft lines to the Middle American consumer. We have to continue to try to focus on making those businesses as good as our competition, whether it was on the mall or off the mall.

We put the unhappiness of 1998 behind us and began working hard on that theme with the arrival of the New Year. It all began with a big question: Are we still comfortable with being a mall-based department store?

In 1992, we said that was a space we would occupy with distinction. Was that still true, or had something so fundamental changed about the competition that our real estate positioning was less desirable and a less-valuable asset for the company?

The answer to that question was that it was still a great place to do business, but an increasingly difficult place to do business successfully because of what was happening among our hard-line competitors. Home Depot was opening 150 stores a year. Lowe's Home Centers was opening 75 stores a year. Circuit City and Best Buy were opening maybe 60 stores a year each.

We were being pummeled in terms of share of outlet, which measures the numbers of outlets we had relative to the outlets our competition had.

We did not and could not have any sort of meaningful shopping center growth, just because there weren't any more of them being built. Our competition was advancing despite that because they didn't locate themselves in shopping centers. The gap was widening.

## One Solution: Giving Customers More Options by Broadening the Merchandise Mix

But did losing share of outlet mean we had to lose share of market?

We knew that if Sears was going to remain a force in the home improvement area over the next decade, we couldn't do that by operating exclusively out of regional shopping centers. We had to have that freestanding presence in the home improvement business to fight against stores like Home Depot and Lowe's.

Our vehicle of choice was the freestanding hardware store, the neighborhood convenience hardware store. We didn't want to go head-to-head with Home Depot. We didn't want to be the place where the contractor loaded up with everything he needed to refurbish a four-flat. We didn't want to try to draw the gear heads.

But we also knew that our hardware offerings would not be competing well if we stuck exclusively to Craftsman tools. Craftsman is as American as apple pie and guaranteed for life and a great line for Sears. But our research indicated the tool-and-hardware shopper wanted the same kind of plentiful options that other shoppers looked for.

Sometimes you want to play with a tool from DeWalt or Black & Decker. Early in the year, we created something we called Tool Territory, where the tool shopper could find just about anything. There was a lot of concern inside the company that offering other product lines might damage Craftsman, and no one wanted to do that. But there was also an awareness that the abundance offered by our competitors could become an advantage for us if we looked at it the right way.

Think of it this way. You could go to Home Depot and buy a Milwaukee drill. But you could not go to Home Depot and buy a Craftsman socket set and a Milwaukee drill. We created Sears Tool Territories where the shopper could get both of those, and lots more.

We tested the idea in 22 stores in Connecticut. We put a couple of stores right across the street from Home Depot in Virginia. This new approach, we found, led to a 22% improvement in sales, none of it at the expense of Craftsman. Virtually all of the increase came in expanded sales of national brands. It was a clear sign that the customer would respond to the Sears offering.

There was nothing about Sears that disqualified us from being a success in the mind of the consumer if we got all of the parts of our offering in proper alignment. It was a great way to win the war against the onrush of competition without having the advantage of creating a lot of new real estate. We tested it for six months and then said, "Let's go."

I thought the experience presented us with another object lesson in what happens when you get inwardly focused. We were paying lots of attention to Craftsman tools, but we weren't listening to the customer who also wanted to handle, and maybe buy, a big DeWALT tool.

When we listened to the customer and responded, we learned there was nothing about shopping in a mall that made it an unpleasant place to do business.

During that same early 1999 examination, we searched for a way to attack the problem of loss of hard-line sales to our competitors. We didn't want to be permanently handicapped by the inability to match them wherever they opened new stores. We had some strong ideas on the table.

Kenmore Elite, an upscaling of the Kenmore brand to a new price point and new feature and quality levels, became a huge home run. Just out of the box, Kenmore Elite became a $500 million brand in its first year. We were also able to convince Maytag, which had been a long-term holdout, to sell us appliances. That meant our product line became a lot more robust.

The objective was to convince our customer that she didn't have to go anywhere else. We had the product. We had the infrastructure. We had the delivery. We had the service. She wasn't going to face some guy named Bob in a rusty old pickup truck when it came time to deliver and install the product.

People love options. Kenmore is still the biggest player in the game, but Sears shoppers now have Whirlpool and General Electric and Amana and Frigidaire and Maytag, too.

## New Disasters with the Softer Side of Sears: The Benetton Debacle

There were different problems, and different solutions, on the soft-line side of Sears.

It was clear to me that the only way we could hope to separate ourselves from our competitors in the apparel business was through product differentiation. We couldn't achieve it through price differentiation, because we couldn't go upmarket or down-market. We were not going to have access to the upmarket, nationally branded product available to a Marshall Field's. We had to find a way to focus intensively on aligning ourselves, building private brands that had some equity in the mind of the customer, or creating what we call alliance brands—exclusive relationships with nationally branded houses that would produce a brand just for us.

This turned out to be very interesting territory, and not without some embarrassments attached.

I had a thought that we could change the apparel picture overnight at Sears if we had the right kinds of partnerships. We tried something different.

We reached out to L. L. Bean, Lands' End, and J. Crew, individually. The idea was to partner with one and become an exclusive distribution point.

That thought marched in lockstep with another idea that I was developing at the time. It was clear that retailing was becoming a multichannel world, and that if you weren't playing on all of the channels, you were not going to be successful for the long term. Those companies, it seemed to me, faced a void on this question. They were playing in a single channel. If we could find a way to make that partnership valuable to our customers, it would be beneficial to everyone.

For different reasons at each place, it just didn't work out. But we were not rejected anywhere as an inappropriate suitor or some kind of damaged retailing giant that was desperate for resurrection. We were seen as a credible partner, but for their own reasons, they weren't interested in making the move.

There are those who argue that the partnership we did achieve, with Benetton, blew up in our face.

But that is hindsight.

Benetton, a very successful Italian sportswear manufacturer, had been around for a long time. They had all but withdrawn from the United States, and we got word that they were interested in getting back into the market with rapid, and relatively broad, distribution.

But they didn't want to start building stores. It was always a very contemporary sportswear company. They were modern and high fashion, but not Armani high fashion. They were in a leadership position and their target was street-smart young kids.

We saw it as an opportunity to bring something really fresh to the Sears customer: Benetton by Sears. We went through a series of conversations with them, which included Luciano Benetton, the patriarch of the family, a striking and magnetic personality with a lion's mane of gray hair.

We pitched them on creating Benetton USA, a brand exclusively available at Sears. It would have a kid's component, a young men's component, and a junior's component for young women. They agreed. It was immediately exciting for Sears because we knew it would make everyone sit up and say, "These guys are doing something very interesting and very different."

There was one concern.

Benetton had a reputation for being a little difficult to deal with, along with a reputation for being beyond the cutting edge in its advertising with nuns kissing priests, dying AIDS victims, and the like. We understood the "social cause" nature of the effort, but we wanted to make it clear that Sears is very traditional, very American.

I recall in one meeting telling Luciano that we loved the products and loved the styling, but that the advertising just wasn't going to work in the United States. It's too edgy, too sophisticated, too over the top, too in your face, too confrontational on a social and cultural level, which can make it kind of awkward.

I told him that this effort was about product, about the right prices for the big, modern, Middle American market. We got all kinds of agreements that this was the right thing to do. We created the line. Our merchants traveled back and forth to Italy. We would pick the items we were interested in, and they would be built just for us.

We had a great launch party in New York. The trade press was writing that this was simply transformational for Sears, that it showed spark and energy and imagination. We were all basking in the glory of what we thought was going to be a fabulous launch.

We launched the product and the next thing we knew, Benetton's holding company, its parent company, opened a death row advertising campaign. They sent their mercenaries out to interview people on death row in America about the injustices that had transpired in their arriving at this state in life.

Cop killers. Child abusers. Child murderers. All of these people were being presented as victims of the oppressive culture of the United States.

We went absolutely crazy. The product was in the stores. We had bought the fixtures. We had the special rotating signs that showed the many faces of Benetton. We had spent $7 million. We had the product out there, and we were happy with it—and then, this death penalty ad campaign came along.

I'm not going to tell you exactly what I had to say to them about all of this. There were expletives. Passionate, angry expletives. The art director claimed he had carte blanche to do whatever he wanted, directly from Mr. Benetton himself.

I told them they were crazy. "We're trying to sell product to middle Americans. To kids whose parents are cops."

The furor built.

We wrote demand orders that told them to discontinue the advertising right away. But it was like punching a pillow. We were getting no response. We couldn't get anybody on the phone. Finally, I reached the CEO, who was squirming like he had been impaled on a spear. He said he was in business to make money, too, but I had to understand Mr. Benetton.

I told him it was unacceptable, that we would terminate the contract with him and that I would never allow another Benetton product on the floor at Sears. He said that would be a disaster for Benetton. I said he was creating a disaster for us with the commercials.

Then I made a decision. I said we have got to stop it. I told the Sears people I was pulling the line. I wanted anything in our advertising relating to Benetton to disappear. I wanted the fixtures off the floor. I wanted an announcement saying that we had withdrawn the line from sale because of our disagreement with the language, tone, and substance of the ad campaign.

So we got rid of it. We took a $20 million bath because of this stupid advertising campaign. That was the right thing to do. Our customers sent a strong message: "Thank goodness for people like Sears." It was so frustrating for us, because we thought we had landed on at least a partial solution to the apparel problem. They pulled the carpet right out from under us.

It took us about 10 days to erase Benetton's presence.

We had a second strategy in our pocket to address the problems in apparel. We decided to make a major commitment to product development and begin to build the organizational capability to create brands that would only be available at Sears. That is a long-term, pick-and-shovel approach that will take five years to come to fruition, but that is the track we decided on.

## The Need for a New Ad Campaign to Focus on *Value*

"The Softer Side of Sears." For a long time, a lot longer than most advertising campaigns, the idea, the jingle it created, the sense that a new Sears was beckoning to women, the chief financial officers of the American family, had worked for us. It was the right message at the right time.

But as the end of the 1990s approached, we were beginning to see the first signs that it was wearing out. No matter how good a campaign is, you can't keep coming up with puns and slogans forever. Beyond that, everything was changing all around us, and our strongest competitors were collecting gold with a single-word message: value.

We weren't sending that message—not because we didn't offer great value for money, but because of our image, because of where our stores sat, and how America felt about that. The very idea of higher-than-average prices is firmly attached to the idea of regional shopping centers, where Sears had so many of its stores. We picked up a sense that people thought Sears simply couldn't be a great value place if it was in a shopping center.

Our own price surveys were telling us we were absolutely price competitive on comparable products, but the customer just wasn't getting the message. That reality was the backdrop for the conversation about the Softer Side campaign: what it had done well for Sears, and what it wasn't doing well as competition increased.

It was clear we were not telling anyone anything about price or value with those messages, as lovely as they were, and price and value had become magnets to the customers of our competitors. Kohl's, Target, and Wal-Mart were sending very powerful messages about value, but we were sending messages that were literally soft, no pun intended.

We decided we had to punch up our promotional message and get across to the consumer in a much more overt way the great values we had at Sears. The competitive campaign had changed since the unveiling of the Softer Side, and the news attached to the Softer Side wasn't news anymore. John

Costello, who had been present at the creation of Softer Side, was gone, so I turned to Mark Cohen late in 1998 to fill that position.

In the best way possible, Cohen was down and dirty, an accomplished, promotionally driven merchant who believed passionately that we were just not sending the value message as clearly and as strongly as we needed to. He provided the architecture for the new campaign and also introduced some crucial disciplines into Sears' promotional marketing campaign.

Cohen, a man who loves a good fight, implemented a tool we had borrowed from the supermarket industry, a process that measures the effectiveness of promotional advertising. Sears was sending promotional advertising messages all of the time, but wasn't very good at measuring their success. They had almost become legacies for our individual merchants. If merchant X had the front page of a newspaper promotion on back-to-school jeans, for example, he wanted that spot every year, regardless of the effectiveness of the campaign.

We spent two years building the database to make this tool work for us. It allowed us to take a look at what happened, for example, when we put an Arrow men's shirt on the front page of a Sunday newspaper insert. We could actually measure the incremental sales and margins associated with doing that against the cost of giving the product that space.

Mark's thought was that if, in the month of August, you got three of the four Sunday newspaper covers for Levi's jeans because that is what the back-to-school market wants, and you lost money for two out of the three campaigns, then you just aren't going to get all three of them. We are going to put something else there.

There were near food fights over this. The retail voodoo would tell the merchant he had to protect last year's promotion and repeat it this year, or else he was going to put a lot of volume at risk. These kinds of fights used to be expressed in simple terms: Are we going to spend money on branding, or are we going to spend money on promotion? The answer, actually, was both. The questions were how much to spend on each and how much ineffective spending could be cut without hurting the business.

It's like the old advertising joke: half of the advertising money is wasted, but nobody knows which half. What we were trying to do with our model was to make progress on identifying which half was wasted and just take it out. But that flew right in the face of the ethos of merchants, because they are driven by volume, and anything that puts that dollar of sales at risk was just not acceptable.

What came out of that was a promotional effort based on what works. Who wants the cover of a promotion? The question becomes: "What can you do with it if you get it? What evidence is there that our sales trend would support this kind of a lift in sales? What evidence is there that this will make our target shopper drop her newspaper and rush to the nearest Sears store to purchase that item, and maybe a few other things?"

We built contention into a process that had once been all about entitlement. These were great management meetings, and Mark was the character to take on that challenge. It is one of the reasons, I believe, that we were doing so much better in 1999. Our promotional message was stronger, more coherent.

But promotional reforms alone would not have changed the picture. We were still faced with the challenge of shifting from the Softer Side advertising message. We decided we wanted to stick with the advertising agencies that had helped us so much the first time around. Young & Rubicam had been receptive during the Softer Side effort. Y&R mourned the passing of Softer Side just as we did, but they realized we had to move on, too.

They gave us "The Good Life at a Great Price," and I added the word "Guaranteed". There were debates, of course. Should it be "A great life at a good price" or "A good life at a great price"? How do we test every word in that slogan and make certain it is not just a wish, but a real, deliverable promise? We had everything we needed to back it up.

## Expanding the Business for the Future: The Great Indoors

Sears is an institution that always operates on a variety of levels. Even though we were severely distracted from the business with the troubles of customer credit and bankruptcy and our slide in the business place, in the background we were working on what I believe is a terrific idea that has the potential of becoming a $10 billion opportunity for Sears.

We put a small team together in 1996–1997 to look at the concept. Back then, I didn't know how much potential it had. We called in Kevin Mundt, then of CDI, for some consulting on retail growth strategies. We wanted him to help us find some white space in the marketplace where the customer simply wasn't being presented with the right kind of solutions.

One of the smartest things I did was to disconnect the team from the Sears apparatus. You are out there, I told its members; you are going to create this. You don't have to go to character X for approval; you don't have to go through a formal process. You are a swat team, but your job is to create a product, a store, concept test it with the consumer, and bring it to the point where we can decide whether we should start building.

The Great Indoors is the result. We opened our first store in February 1998 in Lone Tree, Colorado. It has been a huge, smashing success. The Great Indoors is something the customers have never seen before. We turned to our research about that all-important chief financial officer of the American family, the woman of the house, to build the concept.

She told us that when she wanted to redo her home, she had to go to one store for wallpaper, another store for rugs, another store for bath towels, another store for appliances, until the whole prospect of renovation became more of a transportation challenge than it ever should have been.

If someone could just put this all together in one place, that is where I would shop, she said.

And that's what we did.

There was an incredibly powerful emotional response from our customers, matched by an incredibly powerful financial response. We found people were making long visits to The Great Indoors, and multiple visits over the course of a month. Most important, some 85% of the customers at The Great Indoors were new to Sears.

We made a deliberate decision about The Great Indoors. We didn't want the Sears name on the door. Our research told us that if we offered this option as "Sears Presents the Great Indoors," the customer would say, "Oh, I know what Sears is about, and I don't think I need to try them today." It was a hard concept for us at first, because what it said was that the Sears brand, so valuable in the mind of Sears shoppers everywhere, would be a negative in this new concept.

We were trying to reach a market that might visit Sears from time to time in isolated product categories, but it was not made up of general Sears shoppers. The numbers tell the story. The median income of the average Sears customer is $40,000. The median income of the The Great Indoors customer is $75,000. Clearly, we traded up.

After we opened the first store, we thought, "This is too good to be true." We soon had another one in Scottsdale, Arizona. There were advocates inside the company who were arguing, "This is a home run, an incredible winner. Let's go as fast as we can!"

I loved the place. But I had a concern. Were these results sustainable? Each one of these new stores represents a $25 million to $35 million bite of capital. So if you put up 100 of them, you are spending between $2 billion and $3 billion. I wanted to watch for a while, just to see what was going to happen.

There aren't any hotter markets in the United States of America than suburban Denver and Scottsdale, so my thought was that there was a rising tide at work that was lifting these stores. But I wanted to get ready, line up real estate, and figure out how the plan would be executed.

In retrospect, I think my contribution was to keep my hands off and protect the team from the rest of the institution. Five years from now, when everyone in retailing is looking at The Great Indoors and wondering exactly how we did it, that will be my claim to fame: "Well, I left them alone."

The team had to do an amazing amount of very difficult work. It had to line up agreements with vendors who would not have sold to Sears stores in the past. These are the Sub-Zeros, the Waverlys, the companies that would not have viewed mainstream Sears stores as markets. I believe the team's effort in building The Great Indoors was heroic.

It remains one of the brightest spots in a difficult stretch.

## The Internet and the New Economy . . . Not!

Remember the world before the collapse of NASDAQ?

It seemed as though everyone had a plan that was going to make a fortune overnight, transform the world, collapse the world of brick-and-mortar retailing with the power of a big earthquake, and lay waste to just about all of the old rules about shareholder value and marketplace performance and customer relationships.

These were the rallying cries of the "new" economy.

There was no new economy.

It is now an obsolete term. The artificial distinction that was created between old economy companies and new economy companies was the confection of the moment. I don't think it was ever real, although there is no doubt that a powerful, transforming technology has presented itself.

The question had more to do with harnessing that particular technology to run a business more effectively, as opposed to becoming a new business entirely distinct and separate from an old business. I have gone through a learning curve on this subject. I started out as a skeptic.

I shifted from thinking that the Internet was the domain of the ultimate twinky-type nerd to really wondering if there was a business model that could, in fact, disintermediate the existing business proposition. Then I moved to another level, the thought that while this technology is not a business model that will create a new relationship with the customer, it could become an enormous facilitator of the business proposition we already had.

It is a way not to just sell more things. It is not just another distribution channel. It is an enormous resource to help the customer prepare for and make decisions about major product acquisitions, which is a big part of our business.

For someone who wants to take the time to do the research, the availability of information and the ease of access to that information makes it possible for consumers to become much better and much more informed purchasers of our merchandise.

These thoughts were developing even as Sears was moving through the dark months of 1997 and 1998. Our Internet presence developed and evolved over that time frame. Now we have an understanding about the influence the Internet has on our sales performance, as opposed to how many Sears sales can go through the Internet.

But we didn't go down that road with our eyes closed hoping for the best.

We were seen by many of the potential investors in the Internet as the ultimate dot-com, an old-line brand with great assets, enormous customer relationships, brands, products, and infrastructures. Everybody and his brother wanted to invest in our Internet business.

They wanted to create Sears.com as a separate subsidiary of Sears. They wanted 25% of the action and promised they would eventually take the whole operation public. We could structure option packages that would attract the kind of people you need to build a strong presence. We could get the business capitalized with an incredibly exaggerated multiple, which would create great value for Sears' shareholders.

There wasn't a venture capital firm, there wasn't a deal maker, there wasn't an investment banker, who didn't want a piece of Sears. Of course, what they were lusting for was that IPO part, that transaction, that would create an instant fortune.

I never took the bait.

Sears is a rich company—rich in terms of cash, rich in terms of information, data, resources. My thought was that we didn't need anybody else's money. And we really didn't need anybody else's legitimization, or what they could try to convince us was legitimization. And why should I give up 20 to 25% of whatever this was going to be to some other shareholder, as opposed to our own shareholders?

The potential investors were obviously in it for themselves. One must respect that. It's business. But it seemed to me that we could accomplish what I thought we needed without sharing this largesse with anybody.

So instead of yielding to the sirens, we created an internal Sears.com division in 1998.

Inside Sears, everyone wanted us to do everything. Every division wanted to have its own website, its own Internet presence, its own Internet relationship with its customers. I was convinced what we had to do was discipline ourselves in terms of priorities.

There were two sides to that thought; the first: Where can we create the greatest value? The second: Where is the greatest value destruction risk if we fail to pay attention to this new medium? We turned to our hard-line businesses—in many ways, the essence of the Sears brand. I believed that was where we would get our strongest market position, and that was where we faced the greatest risk if these perceived new business models actually had legitimacy to them.

Our greatest fear of failure centered on our hard lines. What if General Electric decided to go direct to customers? What if Whirlpool went direct? What if Value America (now bankrupt and out of business) was successful with its Internet only business strategy? All of those potential challengers would be going after our strengths. I am sure the loss would not have been catastrophic, but it would have been considerable in terms of the perceived loss of leadership.

As it played out, we watched our competitors and saw the idea of going direct on the Internet collapse. We knew Value America was a very narrow, one-product, one-price-point, one-off kind of offering. The concern was that it might develop into a full-range, full-service appliance purveyor. They kept hammering away at the same theme: "We've got this Hotpoint range and this Whirlpool dishwasher, this one-off item." I felt it was not sustainable at that point. They didn't have an assortment point of view. They had an item point of view.

You can't build a business and sustain it with a key item focus. You have to have a comprehensive assortment to be successful in any category and to leverage all the investments that are required to execute the plan.

Value America came to us and asked if we would like to handle fulfillment for them, which was an absolute laugher in my book. That would have been like handing the enemy the last of your ammunition in a firefight and saying, "Sure, I will help you out."

We also had some field guys come in and pitch us on the idea of taking our logistics operation, spinning it off, and setting it up as a fully integrated e-commerce operation.

Fulfillment, it struck me at the time, is a strategic barrier that keeps competitors out of the marketplace. Why make one of the most important things you need to be successful available to your competitors, even though you might create some value in it?

I never had any stomach for giving any of our strengths away. I had spent a lot of time with Gus Pagonis (the key logistics general in Operation Desert Storm and, after his army retirement, the key logistics general at Sears, too) building a world-class logistics operation, and I wasn't going to hand it over to someone coming right at our sweet spot.

The question became one of deciding how to use the Internet to advance our cause, recognizing that the traditional store business has been and will continue to be our most important source of relationships with our customers.

I had gone from a skeptic to a not wild-eyed believer to a believer that there was something happening that we had to understand better.

And we wouldn't do that by going to conferences. We would only do that by investing in it. In 2000, we spent $90 million on Internet infrastructure, technology, support, marketing, consultants, and outsource software development. That led to about $70 million in sales of stuff through that direct channel, so we have a loss. In 1999, we spent nearly $30 million, and in the year we started, 1998, we spent $5 million.

We have an objective. We want the distribution channel to break even by 2002, and we are willing to take losses until that point.

I don't think we would benefit much by going from $90 million to $250 million in annual Internet spending. The key has been to place our bets behind the right merchandise categories. We are presenting what consumers respond to. Hard lines is on that list. Apparel (which I believe is always going to be a hard sell on the Internet) isn't. That is why our revenues have ramped up faster than the revenues of a lot of other companies trying to find the right formula on the Net.

There is another benefit, too, that I did not anticipate.

We have conducted a lot of survey work to measure this. It appears that about $500 million of Sears' annual sales are influenced by what we present on the Web. Consumers go to their computers, look up Sears.com, research the various possibilities that are available, then go to the nearest Sears store to complete their transactions.

That sounds a lot to me like one of the important roles the old catalog played in its heyday.

I am aware of the ironies involved in this development. The Ax from Saks kills the catalog and then helps reinvent it, except we don't have to print it this time and the operation is a lot more efficient.

There is a broader message.

What this foreshadows is having a direct relationship with the customer if that is what the customer wants. Accept the premise that the Sears brand is pervasive, well fixed in many homes and in many minds. The idea that a customer can only approach us through one channel is pretty limiting.

One of the ideas that came out of our Phoenix process in 1998 was a new slogan: "Anytime. Anywhere. Any way." If the customer wants to have an Internet relationship with us, she can. The notion of having only a store base was such a limiting definition given the pervasiveness of the brand that it amounted to tremendous untapped potential. So the Internet was a very natural way for Sears to demonstrate the idea of being available anytime, anywhere, any way.

## Next in Line: Finding a Successor to Run Sears

Our revived commitment to the basics—and especially to the customer, as shown by our new message—had gotten us back on track just in time for the end of the twentieth century. But even as we were struggling with the challenges of 1998, it became clear that it was time for me to think about a successor.

I told the board that I was concerned, and that they should be concerned, too, that we did not have a particularly large pool of candidates inside of the company. I was getting close to 60, and it was time to start focusing on succession in a serious way. But I believed that even though we had some great candidates on board, we needed more choices.

I decided to go outside and begin to look for someone to come in to run the retail business at Sears. If we brought that person in, we would have time to look at the candidate and measure him or her against the internal competition, which at that time included Paul Walters in Canada and Alan Lacy at headquarters.

We worked with Bob Kerson, who runs a retail search company, between December 1998 and the summer of 1999 looking for the right person. We ran into a problem.

We found that the only way we could attract a candidate who could replace me was to give the person a guarantee of succession: "Come in here and you are anointed as Arthur's successor, and if you don't mess up, you've got the job." Basically, it was a guaranteed path to succession, but with all kinds of punitive payments if we didn't give the job to the candidate at the end of the day. Any agreement of that type would have been disclosed in our contractual filings with our Securities and Exchange Commission documents.

That might have precipitated another management outflow as those insiders who thought they had a chance learned the company already had someone in mind. At that point, the board and I agreed we should stop, and that I should stay focused on the business.

Ultimately, Sears decided to select Lacy to succeed me.

For me, my remaining time at Sears would be devoted to doing business and trying to implement the plans we came up with in 1999 to address our problems. I had a new management team, with Mary Conway, who started at Sears as a secretary at age 17, running the stores. Mark Cohen moved into Bob Mettler's job.

Toward the end of 1999, we began to get some good traction, particularly over the summer. *We ended up with the best fourth quarter in Sears' history*, a performance that continued into 2000.

It hit me once we had constructed some breathing room with good performance that I had come into Sears facing a crisis we all had to work hard to solve, and I would be leaving Sears in just about the same position, with the performance challenges of 1998 slipping ever more distant in the rearview mirror.

What I had learned at every point along my retailing career was indeed as true at the modern Sears as it was at the Sears of old, when retailing legends were being constructed, and collapsing, every year. Turn away from the customer, and the customer soon turns away from you.

The frustrations and challenges are endless.

At the end of the day, the merchant who stays sharply focused on the customer and what she wants and needs wins only the right, and the obligation, to stay focused on her for yet another day.

# CHAPTER 10

# Sears:
# Rising Like the Phoenix

I NEED TO GO back now, to our Phoenix meeting in February 1998, to share a moment during which I rallied the Sears troops with an unpleasant picture of what might happen if we continued drifting away from our customers. The signs of trouble were abundant, and we knew that we were losing time. We had already become media punching bags. Our first turnaround was in question, along with our prospects for the future.

I opened with two shockers. The first involved an almost Dickensian "Ghost of the Future" touch that was aimed at getting people to think. The second was the sharing of a secret of sorts, my self-appraisal as delivered to the Sears Board of Directors. I wanted them to know I felt I had not performed well and had set strong goals for the coming year.

First, the vision of what the future might hold:

I want to let you know about some decisions that your management team and board of directors have been working on quietly for some time. These involve a very important series of transactions. The first one is with General Electric. We have sold our credit business to General Electric and we are merging our full-line stores with Montgomery Ward. [What an irony! A competitor in 1998, Montgomery Ward is now just an historical footnote.] They will be renamed S&W Stores. We sold our automotive business to Pep Boys. We sold our hardware stores to Home Depot. We merged our direct response business with Signature [an industry leader at the time] and we're going to spin it off. We sold our service business to Service Masters. We sold Hoffman Estates to McDonald's for a new corporate headquarters. All of this is very good news for our shareholders. The total value of this package is $95 a share. We expect to complete the program by the end of the year. We will then liquidate any remaining assets.

Unfortunately, the Sears, Roebuck and Company that we have known will cease to exist.

Was I kidding?

My point went beyond the mock drama of the situation. If Sears ceased to exist, what would be lost? Would these executives care? They would all be a lot richer. Would the customer care? Would anyone care? I was presenting a serious scenario, a little troubling this far into what we all wanted to be a new era for this old company. That, I told them, is what happens to companies that drift too far off track. They are chopped up like old steam locomotives and sold as scrap iron, sometimes at a very healthy profit for everyone.

The big downside is that when it's all over, your locomotive is gone.

Does anyone want Sears, Roebuck and Company to disappear?

Everybody knows we have come a long way since 1992, and not without our share of trouble. But I was certainly not at the top of the mountain at the opening of 1998, and neither were any of the 200 or so executives who were sitting in the room with me. I was just far enough up the side that I could see we had a long, hard climb ahead of us. One of the presenters at the meeting was a rock climber. He had a good analogy. He said that Sears had reached the Everest base camp, and what was in front of everyone was a big, scary mountain.

I wanted to give these leaders some measure of where I believed I was in the process.

"I wanted to share something with you that I haven't done before," I said. "But to give it a little bit of context, our board of directors and I have a conversation each year about my performance and my personal performance priorities.

"I gave my self-assessment this year as below expectations. As I look at the range of things that happened inside of our company, our failure to meet operating plans, some of the things that chipped away at the values of the company, I told them I felt I performed below expectations."

## My Goals for the Future of Sears

Then I shared my goals with them. I told them one must be careful in the process, because it shouldn't involve a recitation of what everyone who works under you has planned. It had to be honest and personal, I said. I told them I was sharing these goals because I would be talking to people about them a lot as 1998 moved along.

My first target, I said, was *to restore momentum to shareholder value*. I asked for their help in meeting our operating plans. I pledged to remediate our problems with credit delinquencies. I warned them that 1998 would be a year of important decision making.

"We need to come to some strategic conclusions about businesses that are not adding value to the company," I said. "There is a point in time when we either have to hold those cards or fold those cards."

My second priority was aimed directly at *our problems with the bankruptcy reaffirmation question*. I told them compliance and control issues would take important priorities in 1998. We had to be absolutely certain that we were within the boundaries of the law in all of our business practices. "Nothing we could do could be more destructive to our strategic net worth than to find ourselves out of compliance again."

My third priority was to *keep a tight focus on expense management*. Controlling costs had been one important element in the company's vast improvement in performance, and I didn't want us to lose sight of that fact in 1998.

Fourth on the list was *a continuing emphasis on innovation*. I told them I wanted to spend 1998 looking at acquisitions, strategic alliances, and new business concepts. That was how we could expand our franchise rapidly. I certainly didn't want to diminish our emphasis on the stores, but everyone had to recognize that we must grow if we are to thrive.

I saved perhaps the most important goal of all for last.

"I put these thoughts up here the way I wrote them," I said. "Because of that, my last priority in fact might actually be the most important, the first. *I want to accelerate our efforts to improve customer and associate satisfaction scores. . . .* It is perhaps the most important source of the enduring success of our company. If we are doing that, we have a much higher chance of exceeding our operational plan."

I didn't do this because I felt the need to confess. I shared these private goals with the Phoenix team because I wanted the team members to embrace them, too, as we moved through the New Year. I believed they addressed the causes of the trouble we faced in 1997, and that they also kept the focus on that critical need for constant change and cultural transformation.


## Sears Is Blessed with Great Employees

I was in a room full of very good people. Make no mistake about that. Everyone certainly didn't agree with all of the directions we were taking, but I believed these were honest, professional disagreements. I am not surprised by tensions or disagreements. I encourage them. You simply can't expect uniform, unquestioning behavior from a whole room of creative people. Your job is to get them to produce their best work in pursuit of a common goal and to respect the fact that they have their own thoughts, their own perspectives, about how to get there.

I didn't have much doubt about their passion. They are the kind of characters who flew in to the session early on a bright Sunday morning and were hard at work by 1 P.M., hours before their baggage was checked and their room keys were passed out. Even though the goal was to take them away from the daily routine, none of them completely disconnected from the mission. We posted our performance numbers on a bulletin board in a lobby every morning. They were very well read and considered by the end of the day.

If you had been with me at Phoenix and spent some time with them, their stories would have told you all about the passionate side of Sears. Pat Recktenwald remembered a huge Denver snowstorm. She was running hardware. She called up Chicago and had every snowblower she could find shipped to Denver. Then the police said no one could be on the roads, so the truckers would not leave the distribution center. They were afraid of getting tickets.

"I'll pay the tickets," she said. The trucks plowed through the snow and parked in the Sears lot. The customers needed us and we were there for them. That is what it is all about.

She did a million dollars worth of business from the backs of those trucks in the Sears parking lot over a couple of days.

Mary Conway talked about getting her first prom dress from Sears in Philadelphia. It was her father's decision. Everyone who has ever awakened on Christmas morning to find a shiny new Sears JC Higgins bicycle sitting beside the tree understands the romantic connection to Sears. Mary hated the dress, but Sears was where her family shopped. It didn't take long for her to return the gown. It didn't take long for her to get a job at Sears in Philadelphia, either. She went to work in the catalog center, went back to college and then to graduate school, and moved up through the organization. She runs our stores now and has 175,000 people looking to her for guidance.

Steve Kirn, the psychologist who runs Sears University, was there, too.

He talked about tackling a particularly thorny problem by getting managers to use Tinkertoys to construct a model, first, of how a troubled business unit actually worked, then another model of how it should be. The troubled version was a real Rube Goldberg project, wildly complicated and the perfect construct of what had gone wrong. The "how it should be" model was sleek and direct and efficient. It was the play therapy of child psychology applied to grown-ups. If it seems trite, recognize that it proved that the people involved knew exactly what the problem was and exactly how to repair it.

Almost everyone at that meeting had a story to tell about the best salesperson they had ever met. These are legendary characters inside of Sears. They came to work dressed for battle right up to their eyes, armed with an array of breath mints, a big smile, and a deep knowledge of the products they sold. They had an absolute drive to measure themselves by the amount of merchandise they moved out of the store. Their whole objective was to connect with the customer and have them walk away satisfied and happy. They knew that whenever that happened, those people would be coming back.

Only about 25% of the people attending the 1998 session were there for the first Phoenix meeting in 1993. That was how much we changed at the top in five short years. There was more to come in 1998.

These are smart, aggressive people who strive to do well. The problem is focus.

## Sears' Biggest Problem Remains: Defining Its Essence

It was quite clear to me as we moved into 1998 that the people at Sears were still confused about their purpose. I'm not talking about mission statements or goals or any of those other devices companies use to help define themselves. I am talking about the essence of Sears.

A purpose is a company's fundamental reason for existence beyond making money. All good companies, all institutions, even nations, have purposes.

A lot of them have taken the time to discover what they are and have written them down:

The nation of Israel: "To Provide a secure place on earth for Jewish people."

Mary Kay, the cosmetics company: "To give unlimited opportunity to women."

Sony: "To experience the sheer joy of advancing and applying technology for the benefit of the public."

Walt Disney: "To make people happy."

Patagonia: "To be a role model and tool for social change."

Nike: "To experience the emotion of competition, winning and crushing competitors."

Teaching Company: "To ignite in all people the passion for learning."

3M: "To solve unsolved problems innovatively."

Sears: ?

At its heart, what is this company all about?

It was perhaps the most important piece of unfinished business that confronted us. Now that I have retired, it remains Sears' biggest challenge. It will always be Sears' biggest challenge. Everybody needs a guiding light, and the bigger the institution is, the brighter that light has to be. For Sears, it has to reach into dark corners all over the United States and Canada and help set the course for some 320,000 people.

In a way, the themes of the 1998 Phoenix meeting showed that we had come full circle. I walked into a Sears that was nearly on the ropes and clearly had lost much of its vision. After six years on the job, we were certainly not on the ropes, but many of the issues that confronted me when I walked in the door were as pressing and in need of solutions as they were in 1992.

I believe I could say the same of Sears today. I could have said the same of Sears a century ago, or 50 years ago, or 20 years ago.

What is this company going to be?

It wasn't just my gut that told me this was the critical question.

## What the Company's Top Managers
## Think Is Important to Sears

By the time that three-day meeting was concluded, I had in my hands the proof of how difficult it is to change a company so deeply enmeshed in its own culture. Look at the results and you will see—as clearly as I have been able to see, and my management team has been able to see—where we were on this course. In a sense, it is proof that transformation is eternal, that Sears, a unique company, will always have a long way to go.

We took some polls of these executives and then shared the results with everyone so they could understand the challenges we faced. Generally, polling is a murky science because of the difficulty of establishing a clear picture of the people who are participating. But we knew every one of these people quite well. They were at the top of Sears, and you might think that because of their positions, they were the keepers of the flame of cultural change.

But as the responses in these polls clearly indicated, we were not yet united. We were not yet aligned. We were not all on the same page, in fact. They remain quite revealing because of what they said about the difficulties of change. It is important to view these results in a positive light—they are all about what we needed to do, what we will always need to do, not about what we have failed to do. They did not reflect a budding civil war. They were a sign that these creative, ambitious people were thinking hard and honestly about what we were doing.

It is one of the realities of change at the speed of light—everyone in an organization the size of Sears can't move that quickly. You can talk until you are blue about transformation and mission, but a lot of people still view their responsibilities from the ground level. They want to know what they can do right here and right now to make things better immediately. As a leader, you want them to think of building magnificent castles in the sky. But the realities of the business pin them to the ground, where it is all about finding a better, more efficient way to get home service people out to bring a clogged toilet back to life.

You have to keep that dichotomy in mind all the time when you run a company the size of Sears, because it helps explain why cultural transformations are so difficult. You must respect the fact that people are tightly connected to their work, even as you ask them to let go a little bit and have some blue-sky thoughts about the future.

The questions we asked at Phoenix were intentionally provocative, because I wanted these people to start thinking at that higher level again.

We had been pushing the importance of the customer as hard as we could. Hardly a week passed that we didn't try to send that message as clearly as possible: The customer is everything to us.

On all the questions we asked over three days, the team members were given the chance to respond five ways. They could:

- strongly disagree
- disagree
- neither agree nor disagree
- agree
- strongly agree

## "WE PUT THE CUSTOMER AT THE CENTER OF ALL WE DO"

One hundred of the people in the room either strongly disagreed or disagreed with that statement. Another 52 sat on the fence. Only about a quarter agreed or agreed strongly that the customer was our central focus at Sears. You might be asking, "How could that be?" given the emphasis we had placed on customers. The responses to a few of the other questions I asked, along with some questions asked by three speakers who attended the conference, might help explain that.

One of the factors we identified early on as being most valuable for Sears was the investment we make in our associates. We learned that making a commitment to the people who worked at Sears was one of the most important components in the bid to draw customers back into the store and make them feel appreciated and welcomed. Remember the customer-service-profit chain? We firmly believe that productive, connected employees translate into satisfied customers and stronger profits.

*"WE CONSISTENTLY DEMONSTRATE OUR COMMITMENT TO IMPROVING PERFORMANCE BY INVESTING IN AND VALUING OUR ASSOCIATES"*

Forty percent of the executives in the room either strongly disagreed or disagreed with that statement. They clearly thought we had not done enough for the people we depended on at the most important point of customer contact. Twenty-nine percent couldn't say. Only 30% of the people at the top of the company agreed or agreed strongly with the statement. Clearly, the conclusion at the top of the company was that we weren't paying enough attention to that first element in the formula.

People at Sears should be going to sleep these days with our mission statement burned into their brains: A compelling place to work, shop, and invest. We loved it for its directness and its simplicity. It was a big business strategy all gathered into one little statement. Everything we needed was wrapped up in that brief sentence, which was aimed at driving everyone toward a clearly defined goal.

*"SEARS HAS A CLEARLY DEFINED BUSINESS STRATEGY"*

Twenty-nine percent of the people in the room disagreed strongly or disagreed with that statement. About a quarter wouldn't go in either direction. Forty percent agreed, and just 8% agreed strongly.

The response to another strategy question was just as revealing. Alignment at the top on business strategy is crucial in any transformation effort.

*"THE PEOPLE IN THIS ROOM ARE ALIGNED AROUND OUR CURRENT STRATEGY BEING THE CORRECT COURSE TO FOLLOW"*

Forty-two percent of the executives disagreed strongly or disagreed with that statement. A quarter had no opinion. Only 34% felt they and their own peers were on board on the strategy question. The message in those two responses was clear: We needed to work even harder on alignment at the top of the company.

These kinds of perplexing results played out time and time again as we polled our own executives during the strategy meeting at Phoenix.

## "If I Woke Up Tomorrow as a Very Wealthy Person, I Would Want to Continue Working at Sears"

It takes some interpretation to understand the response, but fully half of the people in the room said they would quit Sears tomorrow if they woke up as very wealthy people. Only 40% said they would continue working, and 11% couldn't decide. Was it still all about picking up a paycheck for the 100 or so people who said they would quit if they suddenly got rich? Maybe Julius Rosenwald was right back in the 1920s when he said he didn't want anyone up top who had already made his fortune.

## "We Do Not Tolerate People, at Any Level, Who Do Not Demonstrate Our Core Values"

Eighty-four percent of the executives could not buy into that statement. Only 6% agreed that we were as tough as we should be in demanding a commitment to Sears' core values. This was one of the most revealing responses of them all. It was why I wanted people to think seriously about whether they wanted to be at Sears.

## "There Are People in This Room Who Do Not Exemplify the Core Values Essential to Sears' Transformation"

Sixty-seven percent of the executives agreed or agreed strongly with that statement. Only 16% strongly disagreed or disagreed, about as many as the number of executives who didn't have a position on the statement. Again, this was a clear measure of the difficulties of cultural transformation.

*"Sears' Policies, Processes, and Structure Consistently Enhance, Rather Than Hinder, Our Progress"*

Sixty-six percent strongly disagreed or disagreed with that statement. Very few people in the room, 13%, agreed or strongly agreed with it.

I suppose I should have felt warmed by the response to the next statement, but I wasn't, because of what it said about taking responsibility for your own destiny.

*"I Feel Confident That Sears' Transformation Would Continue Unabated by Decades, Not Dependent on Any Particular Executive—Including Arthur Martinez"*

Eighty-four percent of the people in the room disagreed strongly or disagreed with that one. Only 6% thought the transformation effort had enough steam to run of its own accord. And they were not strongly in agreement with the statement.

Even this partial look at the results of the management survey presents a measure of what had been achieved and what challenges remained. My own managers were not in unison on our mission. They didn't believe we were doing enough to strengthen our associates. They didn't believe the customer was at the center of everything we did. They didn't believe our policies and practices enhanced our progress. And a lot of them still thought it was all about me, or all about whatever other executive ended up in the CEO's office.

What better measures on the difficulty of transformation could anyone ever present?

I didn't sit quietly with those results. The lesson in this kind of examination is that it cuts directly to the issues. It would have taken days, if not weeks, to establish this kind of clarity in a group of more than 200 executives. I can say all that I want to say about the need for transformation and the personal choices that are involved. But an audience only hears what it wants to hear. This way, we allowed the Phoenix team to identify its own problems. People started talking about the results the very first day, and I extended this conversation through the difficult year of 1998.

The goal was apparent.

Everyone in the room knew how far we had come, the kinds of problems we faced, and, more important, the amount of work we had to do to keep transformation alive. It was a freshened-up version of the message I had been sending since day one: This is your company to save or wreck. Your decisions will set the course for the future. Your execution will determine how the policies play out. Your diligence will determine whether we succeed.

My question in the wake of all of these responses was very much the same as the question I had been asking since the first Phoenix meeting: Okay, so what are you going to do about it?

I wanted those decisions to be individual.

We left that Phoenix meeting with our own set of marching orders that stretched beyond that important search for purpose.

It was clear from the survey results and the deep discussions that surrounded them that there was still a significant lack of trust among the people at the top of this company. There was a perception that we still didn't have the customer as our central focus. There was continuing resentment in the field about missives from Hoffman Estates, which sounded very much like the old Sears to me. There was a perception that the people at the top of this company, the senior managers—me and the people around me—weren't "walking the talk." We still faced huge barriers to innovation. We had still not created a culture that ejected people, or encouraged them to eject themselves, if they couldn't be a part of the program.

The enemy, then and now, was still us, just as it was in 1992.

## The Enormous Difficulty of Changing an Entrenched Corporate Culture

Culture runs so deep in Sears that even after an extended five-year push, only about a third of the management team, and probably by extension a third of the workforce, was actually behind the transformation effort. Another third was going along with the program, but only passively. The rest decided, for whatever reason, that it was all more mush from headquarters.

It worked well enough to shake us out of trouble and change our course. But it would have been fatal to sit back and rest then. I said in the beginning that the transformation of the Sears culture would be tough and unending, and now you can see why.

Was I upset? Of course.

Was I resigned to the fact that the place could not change as rapidly and as completely as it must to ensure its future? Absolutely not. I believed—in fact, I knew—that we could do this. Look at all of these responses in a different context. We had been through hell and high water, near collapse, and more change than any company had successfully embraced in modern history. A lot of people were firmly on board.

And a lot of other people had the confidence to say they weren't. That simply didn't happen at the old Sears. We had tapped an honesty the place hadn't had in years. To solve a problem, the first step is knowing exactly what it is. Just as we created our own method of measurement, just as we have pushed the message of transformation and thought to every level, we enabled our own people to define their problems.

That is good, because their challenge in 1998, just as it is today, was to solve them. That was one of my central messages in my eight years at Sears. Identify and solve your problems. We had burned the 29,000 page "how-to" manual and replaced it with some slim volumes and a hall pass to use your own brain to fix what troubles you.

In the beginning and now, there was an important assumption at work behind all of this that cuts to the heart of my philosophy as a manager.

I believe that people want to do a good job. I don't think they get up in the morning and decide to come in to work to see what they can screw up, to see how they can survive without thriving, to see how they can get away with simply punching the clock.

If I thought those things were true, the entire Phoenix process would be a waste. That applied not only to the 1998 session—our search for purpose—but to the experience we had with the orchestra, our experiments with writing news stories about where Sears would be at the end of the century, our struggle to come up with our three "compellings," and the construction of the Total Performance Indicator we use to measure our progress on so many critical fronts, too.

I held my last Phoenix meeting in the year 2000, but it wasn't at Phoenix. It was at Hoffman Estates. I didn't think a trip to the desert would be appropriate in light of our performance problems. The goal was still the same: get people on board, get them aligned, get them to think, get them to solve their own problems.

But I knew long ago that everyone doesn't have the same talents.

⅌

There is a distribution around the question of good intentions. Some people do their jobs very well, and some people need some help with the process. That range of ability astounds me, and I saw it during my visits to the Sears stores all over America. I remember one trip east during the dark days of 1998 when I ran into one manager who was completely connected to her store and the people who worked there. I also visited with a store manager who was "old Sears" in the most difficult sense, a man so uncomfortable with the mantle of leadership that he simply could not relax for a moment.

A manager's job is to recognize those differences in people and work hard to help those who need it. Teamwork involves a melding of those differences. Properly done, what evolves is strength and depth.

It would be foolish to think that the process of cultural transformation begins and ends at the top of the company. I pushed that agenda downward for eight years, and my guess is that even after my departure, even after we had been showing a strong performance that put us back in a much brighter light, I only was able to penetrate deeply on rare occasions. I got a sense of it during my many visits to the stores, one of the most rewarding of my responsibilities. I would run into someone who had clearly gotten the message, who was thinking on her own, who was reaching out to that crucial target customer.

I loved to listen to her ideas about everything from competition to customer service. I would write them down in my notebook and collect them and implement them where I could. Sears lives in that mysterious space between its sales associates and the customer, and watching that process when it worked well was nothing short of magnificent. I had the honor of getting good advice from great people everywhere, advice that was stripped of abstraction, stripped of numbers, and presented in terms of what we could do to make the place more compelling, more attractive, for its customers.

I cannot say enough about education in this process. People must understand that they are swimming in an increasingly complicated economy that changes from location to location. The people who run our stores have to understand that the local economy, the needs of the local customer, are paramount. What is it that separates Sears' business in communities with high proportions of retirees from Sears' business in communities that are full of young families? That is not the kind of sophistication you can package and ship out from Hoffman Estates. It must be grown locally.

We initiated a "goal-sharing" program to help with that.

From top to bottom, the people who work in the stores must vote on whether to participate in that program. If the decision is "yes," employees from management on down form committees that create plans for education, participation, how to measure success, and how to share in the financial rewards. Everyone who participates gets access to the numbers that define daily business. Then they talk about how to improve them. The emphasis is on helping one another reach specific goals. It is a door-opening process for everyone. Full- and part-time associates get to share information about the company's profit margins and its business strategies.

The aim is to get people who had traditionally been separated from the decision-making process to join in. They became managers in their own right, no matter what level they worked at in the store.

This experiment had practical benefits at many different levels. Remember those executive polling results that showed how many people thought we were not making enough of an investment in our associates? This kind of effort brings them right into the center of the process. It gives a salesperson on the floor a clear reason why she should think her job involves a lot more than ringing up the sale. In her case, it might mean suggesting the perfect sweater to go with a new pair of jeans—not because she has suddenly become a fashion consultant, but because she recognizes what that kind of connection means to the customer and to the target customer strategy she has helped plan for her store.

## Successfully Meeting Customers' Changing Needs

On the business side, I think The Great Indoors is target customer strategy come to life.

Have you ever thought about what it would be like if all of that stuff piled up in a Home Depot started to fall off the shelves? Have you ever wondered what might happen if one of those forklift trucks that are always scurrying around went a tad out of control and ran over your foot?

I haven't. But then, I'm a man.

Men don't seem to worry much about those kinds of possibilities. But women do. Home Depot is very successful, very vertical, and very manly. Our research indicated it was not a comfortable place for women to shop. No one can say that about The Great Indoors. If General Wood was prescient in locating stores where cars were going to be, we think Sears is prescient in recognizing what women want when they begin the trek to redecorate their homes.

Almost all of the other home improvement retailers pay great attention to what the outside of a home might look like. That is man-dominated thinking. In that world, homes are all about siding and hinges and hardware and paint. That is all important, of course, but aimed at only one level of the market. Great Indoors pays attention to what is inside, and then makes shopping for it comfortable. It puts hard lines and soft lines in the same place. Top-of-the-line kitchen appliances, a strong variety of them, sit right across the wide aisle from tableware and houseware displays. Your tableware is not 400 yards from your kitchen in your home, so it shouldn't be that far away in a store, either. Great Indoors is a meticulously researched effort aimed at making the business of renovation and home decoration much more comfortable for the person who takes the most responsibility for how her home feels.

Women are thoughtful shoppers.

This store has a library and a full-service European coffee bar, where you can sip cappuccino while you ponder what you have seen. I suspect you could take your own cappuccino and some biscotti to a Home Depot, but sipping it somewhere between the nails and gigantic racks of air-conditioning ductwork won't be very comfortable, particularly if it is a busy day for the forklifts.

Conversations with insiders about the Great Indoors yield some interesting perspectives. Some people see this as the modern equivalent of General Wood's decision to move into retail stores. Some think a better measure is to compare it to Sears' decision to expand the brands it offered in its stores. But I think its greatest significance is that it is a bow toward that most important part of the customer-service-profit chain, the American woman. We are telling her we know what she wants and how she wants to buy it.

Once again, we weren't just waiting for people to come and buy; we were reaching out to them with a new product—a whole new place, in fact—that showed them how their homes could be.

What does that sound like to you?

Go back to the very beginning, when Sears was inventing itself for the first time. Remember Richard Sears and his hot catalog rhetoric? It was all about finding some way to insert a company between vast collections of inventory and the thought that life could somehow be a lot better than it was.

That is where I got to sit for eight years, between what Sears had to offer and what the American consumer wanted. My job was to continue developing a deep understanding of the parts at either end of that formula, and manage the 320,000 people in the middle who carry it out.

That was as much a function of philosophy as it was of management.

## Managing and Educating People So They Can Do Their Best

It is hard to make a distinction between business philosophy and management philosophy because in this particular business, I believe, they are inseparable. You cannot have a business philosophy in retailing—or in any other business, I would submit—without a philosophy about people and how you manage them to get the most out of them.

The problem is getting people with the right attitudes and skills. I sat at the top of a company that valued order, discipline, control, and conformity. But we were living in a world in which a little bit of disorder, nonconformity, a little bit of personality, and higher levels of energy were the things that we valued. The trick at Sears was that you couldn't just move everybody around, but that you had to get people to move from that old side of the ledger to the new side.

No one can do it without a passion for the business. You can teach people about merchandising, you can teach them about apparel, you can teach them how to do performance appraisals—but passion for the business, that is something you cannot grow. That was a problem at Sears. There were still a lot of people inside of the company who had the best of intentions, and wanted to change, but simply couldn't make a go of it.

But that was the price we paid for dealing with a culture this old and this deeply embedded. We had worked hard to open all of the windows to let in fresh air, and have opened doorways to a much healthier, productive future. But at the end of the day, each individual has to make a decision about whether he or she is going to walk through that door.

It is an amazingly complicated decision to make in what is essentially a simple business.

We are nothing as a retailer but a collection of buyers and sellers. We seldom have proprietary products. We don't have patents. We don't have technology, and we certainly don't have monopolies that are granted by regulators. This is a simple business made complicated by simple people. But it is fundamentally a simple business that gets its work done through and with people.

That is at the heart of what I tried to do at Sears since 1992. I tried to allow our people to give as much as they could to their jobs. The message was that whatever the size of your world is, you can take control of it, you can take ownership of it.

Everyone in that world had to understand that the customer is the sun at the center of our solar system. The only real experience at Sears is the experience the customer has in the store. Everything else is a construct, and something of an abstraction. This business has to be built, thought about, and executed from the outside inward, with that constant emphasis on customers as the guiding force.

I do, indeed, have my own private, long-term worries about Sears.

One of them stretches beyond the front doors of the place and moves into every home in the United States. Sears offers a brilliant future for anyone who can meet its standards and wants to work. But where is Sears going to get the people it needs?

How can you demand a sense of ownership from employees who simply cannot understand the concept because they have not been well educated? This is a problem at every level. High school graduates can't add. College graduates can't write. People with master's degrees have trouble expressing themselves clearly.

Social skills are crucial in this business. The success of Sears depends to a great extent on how well its salespeople present themselves to customers. What does it say about a nation when you have to explain to its young people that smiling and being cordial and friendly are important job skills? What does it say about a country when you find yourself turning down whole bundles of applications because people can't pass a drug-screening test?

I am proud of Sears University, but I am uncomfortable with the thought that Sears must now also be an educational institution. We are not alone in this. Why must corporations spend a fortune remediating people who should have learned their basic economics in public school, or at college? It has to happen, because your business cannot thrive unless its employees are well educated. But the day is gone when a manager could assume that anyone who walked in the front door with a high school diploma was equipped with the basic skills necessary to do the job.

McDonald's can handle math deficiencies by putting pictures of hamburgers and soft drinks on its cash registers. We can't do that—and don't want to—because it is demeaning. At some level, someone has to recognize that making change is still important, that a high school diploma should be an indication that you know how much to give back if the bill is $17.34 and the customer hands you $20.00.

One of the fundamental obligations of government is to provide a sound public education for its citizens. The corporate world becoming the surrogate in this area is anathema to me, but it may be a fact of life. When I was at Saks, I was active in the Fifth Avenue Association. Basically, it picked up responsibilities the City of New York was no longer able to fulfill. We cleaned the sidewalks, took out the trash, and provided security because the city had basically abrogated that responsibility.

If you think these problems are disconnected from the realities of what we tried to do at Sears, remember that there are 320,000 people at the foundation of our company. We lost and added thousands upon thousands of people every day. As Sears expands and begins new businesses, it will be reaching out for new employees. But they have to be smart, they have to know how to learn, and they have to know the value of education, because if they come on board, I can guarantee each one of them that the process is never going to end.

We should not be sitting quietly while this problem gets worse. If cultural transformation was the challenge of my eight years at Sears, we should be working toward a mammoth cultural transformation outside of the company, too.

It must be attacked on a personal and corporate level.

I love Ted Turner. I think he is nuts, of course, but I love the fact he is giving away hundreds of millions of dollars. Bill Gates has now anted up, too. But it's time for a lot of other successful people to step up to the plate. I send some of my own money to Brooklyn Polytechnic. Giving money away is a great joy when you have it. You get to see what happens to it.

What good is it to wait until you die?

Polytechnic was the first step on the ladder for me. It was then and is now largely a university for first-generation college students from largely immigrant populations. When I went there, it was Irish and Italian and Polish and Jewish. Today it is a third Asian, probably another third eastern European, and probably 20% black, students whose families were from Haiti and Senegal. The people there don't look like me, but I am happy to give them money because of what the place still does. It is their first step into the professional world.

I like to support small community service organizations, too. There are some here in Chicago that help welfare mothers pull themselves together and organize their lives. It isn't just sending contributions to institutions; you can really have an impact with your contributions.

I'm not trying to buff my image. I believe people who are successful have an obligation to do whatever they can to help those who are struggling. There are some practical reasons for this, too. It is my suspicion that as a big part of America continues its shift from welfare dependency into independence, there will be pressure for corporations to take on more responsibility for education and remediation. I don't think that is where the responsibility should be. But that doesn't excuse us from doing what we can as individuals.

Corporations and wealthy people have power and an obligation to use it to achieve common good. I think we should all be taking a much more activist role in reforming education. I think we have the authority and the clout to help address all of the issues that surround education, everything from the skill sets of graduates to the performance of teachers. If we don't, we face the prospect of becoming the educators of last resort.

None of this is at all separate from Sears and its interests, or indeed from my own. Sears has been harvesting success from the growth of the nation for more than a century. It moved from supplier to rural America to merchandiser of the American dream, and along the way it picked up a historic responsibility that it is obliged to carry into the future.

Richard Sears knew it when he promised to put the customer first. Julius Rosenwald knew it when he risked so much of his own fortune to save the company, and when he sent millions upon millions of dollars south to improve the lives of the poor.

There are not many companies that can say they helped to define the American experience. Sears' connection to this nation of customers has been its greatest strength in the past. If the company honors and nurtures it, it will carry Sears far into the future.

My eight years at Sears took me into a world I could never have imagined when I walked in the door in 1992. I never in my life anticipated being the target of a federal investigation, and I must tell you that it pains me to this day that Sears, the company I was running, faced so much trouble as a result of the reaffirmation crisis.

I don't believe that my ethical values were challenged by the experience, but I must tell you that at some points, I wondered whether I should just do the expedient thing and make the problem go away. Every time I thought about that, or every time I heard someone say it, I really realized that the short-term answer would most likely lead to catastrophe, because nothing ever stays quiet for long.

People might wonder, too, whether taking the job was worth the difficulties it presented. I was able to bask in the glory of the first Sears turnaround, with all of the affirmation and recognition that it offered. But I also know what it was like to face the lion, to recognize that if the company's prospects didn't improve, my time in the CEO's office would be cut short. No one ever told me that directly, but I knew the company's history intimately, and I knew that it could not afford to drift for very long in such a competitive world.

I wasn't kidding back in 1998 when I presented the dark possibility of Sears' demise to my management team at the Phoenix meeting. If it could not make its way successfully in one of the most difficult businesses on earth, Sears would have been chopped into pieces and sold off to the highest bidder. It remains safe as long as it holds to the brightest parts of its history and thrives in the marketplace. It can never again allow itself to float along as though its mere presence would guarantee profits and success.

## Watch, Learn, and Know Your Business

There was never a concrete answer to the question "How is Sears?"

It always keeps changing, and that is part of the agony and ecstasy of this business. There are no carved-in-stone solutions you can write down on a laminated card that will provide an adequate guidepost for the next decade. The best advice I could give would be to watch your business, learn your business, know your business and its customers, and then write memos to your own managers. Maybe write them every day, because that is how quickly the atmosphere changes in business.

The rate of change is faster than it has ever been, and the race is still won by those who keep ahead. It is a constant journey of transformation. That is what Sears' first great leaders did. That is what Julius Rosenwald did. That is what General Wood did. They could never view themselves as custodians of this business. They had to be the explorers, the transformers, constantly.

Someone once said that genuine strengths are also genuine weaknesses, and I believe that my own strength and my own weakness is that I was too emotionally invested in the business. I was always genuinely interested in what would enhance Sears' long-term prospects.

Everyone who has ever run this company leaves a legacy. Some of them are legacies of brilliance, and some of them reflect nothing but big blunders.

I would be arrogant to rank myself alongside General Wood. He was such an original item that nothing, and no one, could compare. How do you follow the legacy of a man whose curriculum vitae includes logistics for the Panama Canal, even before he entered the world of retailing, which he also helped transform?

You don't.

But I can tell you about a particularly warm moment for me, my farewell dinner with Sears executives and the Sears Board of Directors. Alan J. Lacy, the candidate the board chose to succeed me, said there was something no one should ever forget when they look back on the Sears of the 1990s.

He said I saved the company, and gave its people the chance to win, to be successful, and to thrive—not just to survive. I did that, he said, in a way that respected their abilities and allowed them to create and innovate.

That was a great, head-swelling tribute for me, but a little misplaced.

I feel enormous connection and affection for the company and the people who really tried every day to do a good job. Sears lives in its stores, where its brand is and where its relationships with customers are strongest.

These people in the field work very hard and are often unappreciated. They are at the receiving end of an awful lot of stuff from corporate offices, but they still come to work every day and try to do their best for the customers.

Despite the difficulties of transformation and the impossible, crucial challenge of getting 300,000 people moving in the same direction, that awareness has never failed for me.

It renews me and renews my faith in this business.

I will miss them.

I didn't save Sears. *They* saved Sears.

# Acknowledgments

We stand on the shoulders both of the people who preceded us and of those who assisted us along the way, the wise friends, mentors, and loved ones who helped us create our milestones, who celebrated with us when we succeeded, and who listened in patience to our fears and calmed us when we struggled with our failures.

I owe an immense debt to my parents, Agnes and Arthur, who raised me with the values I have tried to use as a moral compass as I moved through my professional and personal life. Walter Ford, my platoon sergeant in the Army, deserves recognition for what he taught me about life and the complexities of working with people. I also want to thank Dave Thomas, an important mentor in my early career, for teaching me to think creatively and constructively about business. Arnold Aronson and Mel Jacobs (now deceased) taught me about the joys and frustrations of retailing.

I want to thank Ed Brennan, a veteran and the best of the Searsmen to his very core, for giving me, very much the outsider in 1992, the chance to lead Sears. My administrative assistant, Susan Gonzalez, kept me organized and productive for eight years, and that was no small task considering the nature of a company that had enough employees spread all over the nation to populate a good-sized city.

I thank Charlie Madigan, my collaborator, whose persistence, good humor, and skills made this project a delight. My editors at Crown Publishers, John Mahaney and Ruth Mills, provided a universe of good advice and guidance over the long course of preparation of this manuscript.

And I would be remiss if I did not thank the men and women of Sears, who gave me the privilege of leading an institution that, after more than a century, remains at the heart of American business history.

**ARTHUR C. MARTINEZ** was chairman and CEO of Sears, Roebuck and Company from 1995 to 2000 and chairman and CEO of Sears Merchandise Group from 1992 to 1995. Prior to Sears, he was vice chairman at Saks Fifth Avenue, where he worked in various senior positions for 12 years. He has a B.S. degree from Polytechnic University, where he also served as chairman of the board of trustees from 1994 to 1999. He has an M.B.A. from Harvard Business School and was the 1999 recipient of Harvard's Alumni Achievement Award, the school's highest honor. Notre Dame granted him an honorary doctorate of laws in 1997. He is a member of the boards of directors of PepsiCo, International Flavors and Fragrances, Liz Claiborne, and Martha Stewart Living Omnimedia, and he was a director of Ameritech and Amoco. He is also chairman of the board of the Federal Reserve Bank of Chicago. He was named CEO of the Year in 1996 by *Financial World* magazine and Business Statesman of the Year in 1997 by the Harvard Business School Club of Chicago, and he received the National Retail Federation's Gold Medal for Excelling in Retailing in 1998.

**CHARLES MADIGAN** is the Sunday perspective editor of the *Chicago Tribune* and a *Tribune* senior writer. A veteran journalist and foreign correspondent, he is also coauthor of the business bestseller *Dangerous Company*, and he collaborated on *Lessons from the Heart of American Business* by Gerald Greenwald, former chairman and CEO of United Airlines.